Shakespeare's London 1613

Manchester University Press

Figures

Shakespeare's London
1613

David M. Bergeron

Manchester University Press

Preface

As I use the term 'London', I mean the inclusive sense of the City of London, its surroundings, and the Jacobean court in Whitehall. My sanction comes from John Stow who, in the various editions of *The Survey of London*, included Westminster in his compilation. I make the point regularly in this book about the interconnection and interdependence of city and court, what I call in Chapter 6 the 'two great stars in conjunction', taking my cue from Arthur Wilson's observation in the 1650s. Richard Dutton, *Shakespeare, Court Dramatist*, has recently argued convincingly for the impact of the court on the shaping and revising of the dramatist's plays. Performances at court, Dutton suggests, invariably were longer in performance time than those in the public theatres; and this necessity forced Shakespeare to prepare his texts accordingly.

Shakespeare's plays certainly figured prominently in the entertainments at the Jacobean court in 1613. Two new plays by Shakespeare and Fletcher, *Henry VIII* and *Two Noble Kinsmen*, probably had their first performance in this year; *Henry VIII* was in fact on stage when the Globe Theatre burned on 29 June. About Shakespeare the man in 1613 we remain less certain, but he can be documented as buying the Blackfriars gatehouse in March of that year and by assisting with the Whitehall Accession Day tilt in Whitehall Palace, also in March – city and court intertwined. When I refer to Shakespeare, I thus generally mean the plays. I am fascinated with the 'Address to the Great Variety of Readers', a paratext of the Folio. John Heminge and Henry Condell urge readers to buy the book, and they discuss Shakespeare's writing habits. We are in 'manifest danger', they claim, if we do not like him, clearly implying the exercise of reading the plays. Heminge and Condell close by writing, 'And such Readers we wish him'. In 1623, 'him' cannot refer to Shakespeare the person, now dead for some seven years. Rather, Heminge and Condell mean the body of his works, what the two actors refer to in the Epistle Dedicatory to the Herbert brothers as his 'remaines'. Thus, 'Shakespeare's London' means not only the city which he knew in 1613 but also the city and court that welcomed performances of his plays, his cultural context, in other words.

I have been fascinated for a long time with the Stuart royal family and their possible connection to Shakespeare; the current project grows out of that interest. In this book I attempt a kind of 'biography' of the crucial year of 1613: what happened but also what was written and published that year. Thus, I will examine major events at court, such as the untimely death of Prince Henry and its aftermath, the extravagant wedding of Princess Elizabeth to Frederick of Germany and her journey to the Continent, and the wedding that closed the year, that of Robert Carr and Frances Howard. The city flourished with scores of publications on a vast array of topics, including poetry, travel narratives, music, and, of course, plays. I offer summaries and analyses of most of these texts, knowing that some of them may not be well-known to all readers. Many of these publications had a kind of link to the court. The year ends in the city with the opening of the New River, a major new source of water for London, and Thomas Middleton's magnificent *Triumphs of Truth*, the Lord Mayor's Show that honoured the new mayor.

Gathering material for this project has sent me to various libraries, and I single out for special recognition the British Library, the Folger Shakespeare Library, and the libraries of the University of Kansas, notably the Spencer Research Library. The latter has not only provided wonderful resources but also has graciously extended to me the privilege of having access to a study where I could work. I am grateful to all these libraries that help make the pursuit of scholarship a pleasure. To the National Portrait Gallery, London, the Folger Library, the Huntington Library, and the Spencer Library I am indebted for providing illustrations for this book, which they did efficiently and kindly. I thank these institutions for graciously granting permission to reproduce their images.

Numerous friends have offered all kinds of help, including reading portions of the book, providing specific references that I should check, offering advice and suggestions, and listening patiently while I discoursed about the particulars and importance of the year 1613. I name them here: John Pierce, Jonathan Lamb, Timothy Crowley, Gaywyn Moore, John Watkins, Lucia Orth, John Head, and James Shapiro, the master of the 'year' book. Such friends have lessened my burdens and enhanced the pleasure of working on this book. Other family and friends, who know little or nothing about my topic, have nevertheless enriched my life immeasurably. Ian Donaldson, whom I've not met but whose work I admire, has been a gracious and helpful long-distance correspondent.

I thank Gordon McMullan not only for his ongoing rich friendship but also for his invitation to speak to the 'London Shakespeare Seminar' at the University of London in October 2015 at which I broached my subject by speaking about the 'Stuart Brothers', Ludovic (Duke of Lennox) and Esmé, and their connection to the theatre. The annual meetings of the international Mediterranean Studies Association have also provided a forum for a few excursions into parts of my topic. I owe an enormous debt to Pam LeRow, College Media Digital Services, University of Kansas, who has worked her usual magic with all things regarding computers and has saved me countless hours of effort. She does these things with characteristic grace and efficiency.

I happily include in my extensive list of gratitude Geraldo de Sousa, who has helped in ways beyond measure, offering intelligent questions and knowledge, timely support, comfort, and love – and now marriage. Without him this book would not have been possible, nor would it have been as much fun.

Note on the Shakespeare text

I have throughout relied on *The Complete Pelican Shakespeare*, gen. eds Stephen Orgel and A. R. Braunmuller (New York: Viking, 2002) for quotations, with the exception of the text of *Two Noble Kinsmen*.

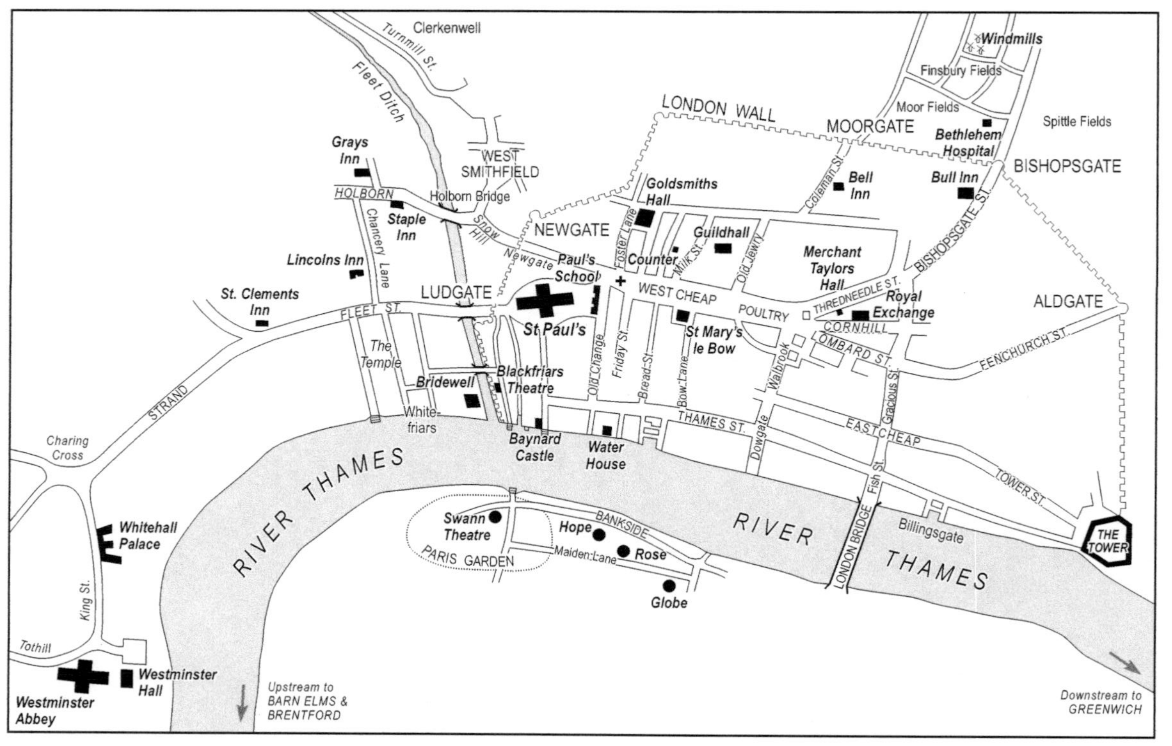

Shakespeare's London 1613 (not to scale)

Prologue

In 1599 William Shakespeare stood at a professional crossroads,[1] which led to his participation in the financing and construction of the Globe Theatre; in 1613, with the burning of this theatre, Shakespeare stood at the end of his active professional involvement in playwriting and the theatre. In 1613, King James I of England, Shakespeare's contemporary, and his court also stood at political and cultural crossroads. James had just finished his first ten years of English rule, and the events of 1613 changed the political and personal dynamic in the royal family and court forever. Further, no subsequent year in the Jacobean period equalled the moments of cultural brilliance of this year.

The burning of the Globe on 29 June marked an ending and a beginning for Shakespeare. This year likewise contained a series of such disjunctions and disruptions for the king and his family. The old Shepherd in Shakespeare's *The Winter's Tale*, which James's court saw performed at Whitehall in early 1613, comments on what has happened in Bohemia. He tells his son: 'Thou met'st with things dying, I with things new-born' (3.3.109–10). This assessment comes as the result of encountering the remains of Antigonus, who had famously exited 'pursued by a bear', and the infant Perdita, abandoned with only a bundle to accompany her now. Her life counters Antigonus's gruesome death. Such a tension between life and death also dominated the royal family's life in 1613.

A marker of Shakespeare's withdrawal appears in his apparent unwillingness to participate in the financing and rebuilding of the Globe that took place in 1614.[2] Shakespeare also sold his shares in the theatre building and in the company. His plays continued to be performed, of course, making 'Shakespeare' very much present. But Shakespeare personally no longer remained at the centre of the

King's Men. He also ceded the position as the company's principal playwright to his collaborator John Fletcher. He did not, however, immediately abandon spending time in London. In fact, in March 1613, Shakespeare purchased the Blackfriars gatehouse, the only property that he ever owned in London. In all likelihood, he resided there during parts of 1613, enjoying proximity to the Blackfriars Theatre, which the King's Men owned, and also easy access across the Thames to the Globe.

If Shakespeare resided in the Blackfriars gatehouse, westward a couple of miles away, Ludovic Stuart, Duke of Lennox, occupied the Holbein Gatehouse in Whitehall Palace, the seat of government and residence of the royal family. When King James moved south from Scotland in 1603 to become King of England, he eventually brought with him his family: Queen Anne, Prince Henry, Princess Elizabeth, and Prince Charles. At his urging, his cousin and principal confidant the Duke of Lennox, who had served him since 1583, also came to England. James gave him the Holbein Gatehouse lodgings on the western side of the rambling Whitehall Palace; here the Duke might always be nearby. Whatever the lodgings lacked in comfort, they made up for in prestige.

In terms of what they represent, the Holbein Gatehouse and the Blackfriars one help construct the narrative arc that defines 1613. These structures serve as the synecdoche for a perspective on Whitehall and Guildhall. The movement along this geographical and metaphorical axis underscores the interaction and interrelationship between court and city. Lennox and all that he represents in terms of aristocratic power defines a major centre of cultural and political authority, focused on the workings and activities of the Jacobean court. At the same time, Shakespeare in Blackfriars underscores the exceptional cultural power of the City of London with its thriving theatres and productive printers and publishers who produced scores of texts in 1613. Shakespeare's property lay but a stone's throw from theatres and the numerous book stalls near St Paul's; it required but a short walk to the Guildhall, the seat of government for the city. Although the Holbein Gatehouse and the Blackfriars gatehouse rather resembled fortresses in appearance, the cultures that they represented were permeable, flowing readily from one place to another. Lennox, for example, had accompanied Frederick, Elector Palatine (and future husband of Princess Elizabeth), to Thomas Dekker's 1612 Lord Mayor's Show held in

London's streets. Certainly when Lennox led the celebratory procession in honour of the Carr–Howard wedding from Whitehall to the Merchant Taylors' Hall in early 1614, he had to pass near Blackfriars. Shakespeare clearly travelled the other direction toward Whitehall where his troupe performed regularly. From his vantage point, Lennox looked down on the tiltyard and all the expanse of the palace, just as Shakespeare peered out on to the rough and tumble world of a bustling and thriving city. Each intersected the other's complex cultural world.

An anonymous engraving from 1621 depicts a rather youthful-looking, bareheaded King James on horseback with sceptre in hand, all quite vigorous (see Figure 1). A medallion of the Order of the Garter resides in the upper left hand of the picture. The king looks very much in command. Through the horse's legs, however, a surprisingly different image emerges: the south bank of the river Thames, including St Saviour's, now Southwark Cathedral; London Bridge, and the City of London, including St Paul's. It takes only a little imagination to see the Globe Theatre as well. While King James dominates the engraving, the landscape cannot be ignored. Taken altogether, the picture illustrates the interconnection between ruler (and court) and London. The engraver might have put James in some obvious courtly setting, as was common; instead, he has placed the king in the rivalling and completing cultural context of London. For centuries London had been known as the '*camera regia*', the king's chamber; much during James's reign underscored the interconnections between court and city. Even in economic terms they could not be separated as an increasingly financially strapped court went to the city to ask for loans. In 1603, for example, seventeen of the twenty-eight Aldermen of the City of London, who constituted the principal governing body, served as moneylenders to court circles.[3]

Thomas Campion unexpectedly linked these worlds in his *The Somerset Masque*, performed on the evening of 26 December 1613, following and honouring the wedding of Frances Howard to Robert Carr, Earl of Somerset. The year thus ends with this wedding of great political interest, which James supported, including financing the ceremony and festivities. Campion offers the usual sort of mythical, symbolic, and allegorical world, full of enchanters. He constructs an initial set of sea, woods, and a garden from which emerge several Squires, who help embody the theme of transformation, which runs

1 Engraving of King James on horseback with the City of London and the south bank in the background (1621), linking court and city

through the masque, culminating in the Tree of Gold. This imaginative approach typifies court masques, such as Campion's own *Lords' Masque*, performed on the evening of Princess Elizabeth's wedding on 14 February 1613. And yet, Campion introduces a radically different element by depicting London: '*London with the Thames is very arteficially presented in their place*'.[4] From the Thames four barges appear occupied by 'skippers', who come ashore and sing and dance. Campion may be recalling the actual movement from London's streets and the river Thames that began two of the royal wedding masques in February. Thus, in Campion's masque, a quintessential *court* entertainment, London joins Whitehall; Blackfriars connects with the Holbein Gate. Indeed, a few days later, Lennox moved from Whitehall to London in the procession that formed part of the extended celebration.

Drama permeated both the court and London in 1613 in exceptional quantity, measured by both performance and publication. On the basis of the listings in the Harbage *Annals* and the Kawachi *Calendar*, the year 1613 registered roughly twice as many dramatic entries as 1612, and three times as many as 1614.[5] Examining evidence of court performances leads to a similar conclusion about the importance of 1613. More recently, Martin Wiggins has created a catalogue of drama written during the period.[6] In volume 6, he surveys the composition of drama from 1609 to 1616. During this eight-year period, Wiggins finds forty-two plays composed in 1613; 1612 produced thirty, and 1614 twenty-six. The next highest number came in 1611 with thirty-three plays. Thus, in this time period, surveyed by Wiggins, the year 1613 stands out. Harbage, Kawachi, and now Wiggins, using different approaches, nevertheless reach the same conclusion, namely, the exceptional productivity of 1613. Throughout the Jacobean period (1603–25), the court averaged about twenty dramatic performances a year (sometimes more and sometimes fewer); these dramatic events included regular plays, most of which had also been performed in London's public theatres, and masques. But 1613 reveals some forty-three performances; no other year in this period matches this number.[7] Also, perhaps acknowledging the significance of this year, the Master of the Revels lists for the beginning of 1613 the actual titles of the nearly twenty plays performed at court, such as *The Winter's Tale*, *The Tempest*, *Othello*, and Jonson's *The Alchemist*. No other comparable list exists in the Jacobean period. These performances, principally by the King's Men, began after Christmas and extended into 1613, leading up to Princess Elizabeth's wedding in February; the remaining number of court plays occurred throughout the year. By the measure of performances alone, 1613 stands out. Shakespeare's spirit, along with that of other dramatists, hovered over the court. He had found his way from the Blackfriars gatehouse.[8]

In 1613, King James could look back over the previous ten years with unequal measures of satisfaction and disappointment, having first brought stability to the English throne and assurance about the future. He had succeeded in signing a peace treaty with Spain in 1604, but then had to face the threat of the Gunpowder Plot in 1605, leading to more stringent restrictions on Catholics. At the Hampton Court conference in 1604, the king attempted to reconcile the opposing factions in the Church of England. At the least, this conference led to the new English translation of the Bible, culminating with the publication in 1611 of the new 'Authorised Bible', or the 'King James Bible'. James set in motion this remarkable achievement, although it had not originally been his idea; ironically, it came from the Puritan wing of the Church. His dealings with Parliament can be characterised as vexed and unsuccessful. His number one policy goal of sealing the union between Scotland and England with a legal agreement failed; such official union did not take place for another century. In 1610, under the leadership of Robert Cecil, James convened Parliament with the hope of establishing a rational plan of financing the government, what Cecil called the 'Great Contract'. This, too, failed, the victim of unfettered bickering between the legislators and James. At the end of the year while the parliamentarians were away, James simply dissolved Parliament. He did not convene another session until 1614. Meanwhile, he continued to spend profligately, generously rewarding his friends. James never developed a serious understanding of economics and finances; he persisted in believing that he presided over a country of exceptional and inexhaustible wealth.

In an optimistic and self-aggrandising address to James's first Parliament in 1604, the king enumerated the many benefits that he had brought to England, such as his family and the de facto union with Scotland. The translators of the 1611 Bible dedicated it to James and praised the gift of 'your hopeful seed'. Indeed, for the first time since the reign of Henry VIII, England had a monarch with children eligible to succeed him. The value of this can hardly be overstated. The issue of succession had been secured for the foreseeable future; the royal children confirmed an orderly progression of rule. This family also encouraged and sponsored art of various kinds, such as the court masque, which Queen Anne in particular supported, and other kinds of entertainments in which the children danced and performed. Prince Henry began to collect art, which passed on to his brother Charles. The royal family also served as patrons of London's acting companies, starting with King James, who early in his reign surprisingly brought Shakespeare's group under his patronage and renamed them as the 'King's Men'. This royal protection of actors helped stave off the regular attacks on the theatre. Other writers, such as Samuel Daniel and Ben Jonson, benefited from royal patronage, as well. Whitehall, including the occupant of the Holbein Gatehouse, stood as a centre of artistic endeavours and support, complemented by the achievements of the Guildhall world.

In order to understand the context of the year 1613, this book actually begins in October 1612 with Prince Henry's illness and death in November, which had a major impact on what happened in 1613. The book will proceed more or less chronologically from this event to Princess Elizabeth's wedding and the stunning array of dramatic performances at court, and include the journey to her new home in Germany. As part of the year's cultural nexus, the narrative reaches into the Guildhall experience to explore the riches of the books that emanated from London's printers and to examine specifically the drama performed or published in 1613. The final major focus centres on the Carr–Howard wedding at the year's end, full of cultural activities and ripe with political significance. This book presents a biography of the poetics and politics of London in 1613, from Whitehall to Guildhall, that is, Shakespeare's London.

Prince Henry, heir apparent and Prince of Wales, deteriorated rapidly, being unable, for example, to attend the Lord Mayor's Show on 29 October. Instead, he lay desperately ill in his bed in St James's Palace. Despite well-intentioned, if somewhat grotesque, efforts of numerous physicians, Henry, at age eighteen, succumbed to death on 6 November. His death shocked the royal family and the country, manifested in a staggering outpouring of grief. The successor to James had died, and the 'hopeful seed' suddenly looked less hopeful. A month of official mourning paralysed the country, culminating as thousands watched Henry's coffin process through Westminster on 7 December, where at the Abbey church an impressive and moving service took place. The royal family would never be the same. Indeed, the country had a hard time shaking off the significance of this event, which disrupted royal succession. The country had met with 'things dying'.

Earlier in that same October, James had completed an apparent act of filial piety by reburying his mother, Mary, Queen of Scots. The king had her body exhumed from Peterborough Cathedral, where it had lain since 1587, and moved to Westminster Abbey, where it would reside in a magnificent tomb, itself a work of great artistic achievement. Mary's tomb, located in the Henry VII chapel – the quintessential final resting place for *English* monarchs – attempted to redirect attitudes if not history. The coffin moved mysteriously through London's streets one dark October evening on its way to the Abbey, a sober reminder of death and its commemoration.

Lingering beneath these death–funeral–reburial transformative moments of late 1612, the emerging plans for Princess Elizabeth's imminent wedding solidified. In fact, her future husband, Frederick, had arrived from Germany in that same October. But how can the court move from grief to rejoicing? Drama offers one of the answers. The time after Christmas up to the February wedding stirred with numerous Whitehall performances, allowing drama to provide an antidote to suffering. And then came the wedding itself – a moment of unparalleled celebration and artistic outpouring. The days before the wedding on the fourteenth included magnificent fireworks on the Thames and a fierce mock battle on the river between 'Turks' and 'Christians'. The wedding in Whitehall's Chapel Royal strained the bounds of extravagance with opulent and dazzling jewels. James, not surprisingly, did not limit expenditures. A masque by Thomas Campion followed that evening, and then, later in the week, masques by George Chapman and Francis Beaumont. A midweek tournament in the tiltyard beneath the Holbein Gatehouse rounded out the festivities. No royal child had been married in England for decades, and James seemed determined to show how it should be done. The excess surely helped assuage grief and turn the country in a new and reassuring direction. This 'hopeful seed' through her marriage now linked England to a solidly Protestant section of Germany. In this sense, one can refer to succession as having been restored, although Elizabeth's removal to the Continent made her seem more remote as a likely successor. But clearly the future looked brighter than it had in November 1612 – 'things new-born'.

Entertainments presented to Princess Elizabeth on the Continent and the ones performed for Queen Anne in western England during the spring and summer of 1613 also enlivened the cultural horizon. This auspicious year ended with the wedding of Frances Howard and Robert Carr on 26 December. Getting to the wedding proved problematic because first there had to be a divorce, namely, Frances Howard's divorce from her husband the Earl of Essex (they had married in 1606). A royal commission finally found in favour of the divorce in September after King James stacked the group so that the 'correct' decision would be made. Shortly thereafter the king conferred on his favourite Carr the title Earl of Somerset, helping make him worthy of Frances, at least in terms of rank.

By late December even the troubling death of Thomas Overbury in the Tower in September had been swept aside in the enthusiasm for this wedding. Queen Anne had come around to countenancing this event; hence, it took place in the Chapel Royal in Whitehall, presided over by Bishop James Montagu, who had also performed the ceremony for Frances' earlier marriage to Essex. James bore the expenses for this December wedding, a sign of his love for Carr. Five different dramatic events, beginning on 26 December and extending to 6 January, created extravagant celebration. On the evening of the wedding Campion's masque captured the court's imagination. The next day, the 27th, Ben Jonson's *A Challenge at Tilt* took place: first, the challenge, then the actual tournament on 1 January. Shakespeare's King's Men performed Jonson's *The Irish Masque* on 29 December and repeated it, at James's request, on 3 January. This strange masque at moments seemed clearly and intentionally to mock Campion's earlier one. But it closed with special praise for James, making him the fulfilment of favourable prophecies. On 4 January, the royal party and newly married couple went by procession to the Merchant Taylors' Hall in London for performances, which included Thomas Middleton's masque, unfortunately lost. Two days later, back in Whitehall, members of Gray's Inn performed the anonymous *Masque of Flowers*, which Francis Bacon financed. Heady days of cultural festivity rounded out this exceptional year, touching and resonating in both the court and London.

The Duke of Lennox's presence weaves palpably and inextricably within the events of 1613. He watched the procession that carried Mary's body to Westminster; he accompanied Prince Charles as chief mourner in Prince Henry's funeral procession. The Duke participated in all the festivities associated with Elizabeth's wedding, including the tiltyard event. Indeed, he accompanied her from the marriage ceremony, a sign of his deep devotion to her and her respect for him, qualities also shared by Queen Anne, who leaned on Lennox for advice. King James chose Lennox to go to south-eastern England to fetch the arriving Prince Frederick and bring him to London so that the royal family could meet this German prince. And the king chose Lennox to accompany Elizabeth as she left England in April with her husband to make her way to a new life in Germany. Leaving her behind in midsummer, Lennox went on to France, at James's request, in order to pursue marriage negotiations for the thirteen-year-old Prince Charles; these conversations proved futile. James rewarded Lennox in October 1613 by naming him Earl of Richmond, a highly regarded English title that complemented his Scottish ducal title and one that now allowed him to sit in the House of Lords.

Despite sometimes sparse evidence, a clear picture emerges of a Lennox who played a major role in the cultural and political activities of 1613. He may have resided in the Holbein Gatehouse, but obviously he did not stay there. He moved seamlessly through the highest corridors of power and feasted on the manifest cultural riches that the year afforded. As in the case of Shakespeare and the royal family, 1613 was a pivotal year for Lennox, this loyal friend and servant of the king, who many years earlier in Scotland had been called a 'paragon'. He had become the 'phoenix', who fulfilled the prophecy at the close of King James's elegiac and allegorical poem *Phoenix*.

James himself completed Cranmer's prophecy of a phoenix at the close of *Henry VIII*. Queen Elizabeth first and then James, coming from the north, would bring peace and prosperity to the kingdom. James would rise, Cranmer prophesied, phoenix-like from Elizabeth's ashes. The first recorded performance of *Henry VIII* in late June 1613 helps punctuate the middle of this extraordinary year. In many ways, the play offers Shakespeare's most self-conscious response to the current historical moment, given that James occupies the throne, the very one anticipated for him, and serves as patron of Shakespeare's acting company. The play comes across as possibly Shakespeare and Fletcher's response to February's royal wedding, which itself underscored the political issue of succession, wrapped in extravagant festivities. On that occasion, the court certainly resembled a play. Henry's death and Elizabeth's wedding changed the royal family's future, as these events similarly affected the country.

London's citizens a few months after the performance of *Henry VIII* had a different kind of cultural experience. On 29 September, a new waterway, called the 'New River', began to flow into north London in Islington, completing a decades-old project and providing at long last a major reliable source of fresh water for a growing city. City authorities chose the playwright Thomas Middleton to prepare an entertainment for this occasion. This slight show focused on the artisans who had built the 40-mile-long canal and on Sir Hugh Myddleton, Goldsmith, who successfully brought it to fruition. Artisans and artist celebrated this engineering accomplishment, achieving 'perfection', Middleton insists, as the city rejoiced in its new destiny, relieved, for a while at least, of its worries over a water supply. A 'new river' provided a 'new world' for London.

A month later, on 29 October, thousands of London's citizens lined the streets to witness the Lord Mayor's Show, sponsored by the Grocers, who hired Thomas Middleton to write the pageant, named *The Triumphs of Truth*, in honour of Thomas Middleton (no relation), the new mayor. The dramatist obviously built on Dekker's show of 1612, watched by Lennox and Prince Frederick. The 1613 civic pageant, moving through the city, provided an allegorical battle between Truth and Error, vying for the allegiance of the mayor. Elegant and symbolic costumes join with compelling speeches to produce a rich spectacle, which closes with fire that shoots from the head of Zeal, thereby setting on fire Error's chariot. Error does not rise from these ashes. Truth thus triumphs and welcomes the mayor into his new responsibility. Middleton has created the most spectacular and most expensive Lord Mayor's Show of the Jacobean and Caroline periods – another way in which 1613 stands out culturally. A fantasy might allow for the presence in London's streets of Lennox and Shakespeare, who has wandered from Blackfriars to Cheapside, a short distance, where much of the dramatic action took place. This October moment under the aegis of the Guildhall demonstrates compellingly as well as any in 1613 how civic entertainment and public theatres clearly rival and complement the performances at Whitehall, a reality understood from Holbein Gatehouse to Blackfriars gatehouse.

The Second Lord in Shakespeare's *All's Well That Ends Well* says: 'The web of our life is of a mingled yarn, good and ill together' (4.3.70–1). The year 1613 presents its own version of 'mingled yarn', in which life meets death, celebration meets grieving, funerals meet weddings, theatre meets publication. On a late June afternoon in 1613, a theatre caught fire and burned to the ground. Cultural resilience did not let this disaster triumph; instead, renewal prevailed. A royal family a few months earlier suffered a tragic loss, but it renewed itself through marriage. A mingled tapestry of the year thus emerges, full of shining, brilliant moments with splashes of gold, intermixed with muted hues of grey and black and everything in between. The lives of James, Henry, Elizabeth, Lennox, Shakespeare, and many others weave in and out of this fabric, which seems to stretch along a river from Whitehall to London. At moments this fabric must resemble one of Monet's 'water lily' paintings, which, rich in colour, look slightly different, depending on the viewpoint. Observed from afar, the Monet painting looks enormous with vibrant displays of colour; up close, it reveals its own brush marks. Throughout the imagined 1613 tapestry stunning examples of artistic achievement unfold, in drama, in pageant, in books, all helping render palpable the defining moments of this crucial year – for James and the royal family, for Lennox, for Shakespeare, for England. No other single year in James's reign matches this one for its cultural achievements and political significance.

Notes

1	This is James Shapiro's argument in his imaginative book *1599: A Year in the Life of William Shakespeare* (New York: HarperCollins, 2005), p. 7.

2	Documented in Andrew Gurr's 'Venues on the Verges: London's Theater Government between 1594 and 1614', *Shakespeare Quarterly* 61 (2010): 468–89.

3	Robert Ashton, *The City and the Court 1603–1643* (Cambridge: Cambridge University Press, 1979), p. 39. Ashton makes a compelling case for the economic reliance of the court on the city and its increasing economic power.

4	*The Works of Thomas Campion*, ed. Walter Davis (New York: Doubleday, 1967), p. 273.

5	Materials found in *Annals of English Drama 975–1700*, compiled by Alfred Harbage and revised by S. Schoenbaum (Philadelphia: University of Pennsylvania Press, 1964); and Yoshiko Kawachi, *Calendar of English Renaissance Drama 1558–1642* (New York: Garland, 1986). For all the many variables in trying to arrange such material and make sense of it, the *Annals* and *Calendar* are mainly in agreement, despite some variation in absolute numbers.

6	Martin Wiggins in association with Catherine Richardson, *British Drama 1533–1642: A Catalogue*, volume 6 (1608–1616) (Oxford: Oxford University Press, 2015). Unlike other surveys, Wiggins's focuses on the date of composition, as well as matters of attribution. Of course, Wiggins often has to settle for a favourite category: 'Best Guess'.

7 This information comes from the charts in John Astington's *English Court Theatre Court Performances 1558–1642* (Cambridge: Cambridge University Press, 1999). As with the information cited above, these numbers are relative, but the general picture is valid. All such evidence acknowledges that the compilers can deal only with the evidence that survives.

8 Richard Dutton in *Shakespeare, Court Dramatist* (Oxford: Oxford University Press, 2016) has recently argued that Shakespeare regularly revised plays in order to make them fit court performance. This practice explains some of the differences between texts of the same play. Dutton emphasises the importance of the court for Shakespeare. Indeed, Dutton claims in the last sentence of his book, 'The court is what made Shakespeare Shakespeare' (p. 290).

1

Fire and phoenix

On a bright, sunny, early summer day in 1613 hundreds of Londoners of various social and economic backgrounds began to make their noisy way to the Globe Theatre on the south bank of the Thames after their midday meal. They came from their shops and homes, walking along the streets of the City of London, through Cheapside and southward toward the medieval London Bridge where they could walk across its crowded surface to the theatre area; some more prosperous citizens hailed the readily available boats and engaged the watermen to transport them. Seasoned theatregoers moved among the bustling crowds. Others were coming to the theatre for the first time with keen anticipation. They knew the stellar reputation of the King's Men acting company and its leading playwright, William Shakespeare, who by mid-1613 had largely retired to Stratford and New Place where he lived with his family. But 1613 also found him, as noted, involved in London where, for example, early in the year he had purchased property in Blackfriars, joining his friends Richard Burbage, his chief actor, and Ben Jonson, a major playwright rival, there as property owner.

Shakespeare's financial stake in Blackfriars reinforces part of the setting for the afternoon's play, *Henry VIII*, which also had the title *All Is True*. Shakespeare and his collaborator John Fletcher dramatise the divorce and fall of Katherine of Aragon, Henry VIII's wife of some twenty years. Her trial took place in Blackfriars, which spectators might see from the Globe by glancing across the river towards St Paul's Cathedral. The audience members took their places in the Globe on 29 June, anticipating a play about early sixteenth-century English history, but knowing of the recent royal festivities involved with Princess Elizabeth's wedding in February 1613. The crowds jostled for position as they settled in, listening to music. As the play began, a momentary hush fell across the theatregoers, their attention fixed on the stage. Early in the performance, they saw a spark and then a blaze that ran along the upper reaches of the theatre. Suddenly, the Globe was on fire. Panicked, the audience rushed to the exits; fortunately, all safely escaped unharmed. Not the theatre itself, however, which burned to the ground.

Sir Henry Wotton, formerly Ambassador to Venice and a leading courtier, had returned to London in late 1612. Although he may not have been at the theatre on the 29th, he nevertheless recorded a response to its burning in a letter to his frequent correspondent Sir Edmund Bacon. On 2 July 1613, Wotton wrote:

> Now, to let matters of state sleep, I will entertain you at the present with what hath happened this week at the Bank's side. The King's players had a new play, called *All is true*, representing some principal pieces of the reign of Henry VIII, which was set forth with many extraordinary circumstances of pomp and majesty, even to the matting of the stage; the Knights of the Order with their Georges and garters, the Guards with their embroidered coats, and the like: sufficient in truth within a while to make greatness very familiar, if not ridiculous. Now, King Henry making a masque at the Cardinal Wolsey's house, and certain chambers [small guns] being shot off at this entry, some of the paper, or other stuff, wherewith one of them was stopped, did light on the thatch, where being thought at first but an idle smoke, and their eyes more attentive to the show, it kindled inwardly, and ran round like a train, consuming within less than an hour the whole house to the very grounds.[1]

Wotton added a final comment about the losses at the Globe that afternoon: 'This was the fatal period of that virtuous fabric, wherein yet nothing did perish but wood and straw, and a few forsaken cloaks; only one man had his breeches set on fire, that would perhaps have broiled him, if he had not by the benefit of a provident wit put it out with bottle ale.' Henry Bluett, a young merchant, confirms the basic details of Wotton's account, claiming that the play was 'new', having been performed no more than two or three times before. He indicates that all successfully escaped the burning theatre; only one man received a slight burn as he rescued a child.[2]

Wotton emphasises and interprets certain of the play's features, noting its splendour and verisimilitude, making 'greatness familiar'. He claims that the chambers fired during the masque at Cardinal Wolsey's York Place (the play's 1.4) set the theatre alight. Whatever the precise moment or cause, the theatre burned 'to the very grounds'. Wotton adds the episode of the man with his breeches set on fire, whereas Bluett cites a heroic story of escape. The harried, but safe, spectators looked back at the pile of glowing embers, the only remnants of the once-proud theatre building. These timbers, now rendered to ashes, had first stood proudly in The Theatre in the Shoreditch area of London until 1599 when members of the Lord Chamberlain's Men (Shakespeare's acting company) surreptitiously dismantled this first public theatre building, stored the timbers, and then floated them eventually across the Thames where on the south bank a new theatre emerged phoenix-like.

In his letter Wotton turns away from immediate court business and makes the transition: 'Now, to let matters of state sleep'. But of course matters of state cannot sleep, certainly not in this play or in the theatregoers' recollections. The Prologue opens the play by striking a note of seriousness, saying: 'Things now / That bear a weighty and serious brow, / Sad, high, and working, full of state and woe, / Such noble scenes as draw the eye to flow / We now present' (1–5).[3] If the spectators desire something amusing, they should look elsewhere. Perhaps the Prologue has in mind the light-hearted earlier play about Henry VIII's reign by Samuel Rowley, *When You See Me, You Know Me*, published in 1605 and reissued in 1613, possibly to tap into Shakespeare and Fletcher's play. Their *Henry VIII* represents the serious business of the disgrace and execution of the Duke of Buckingham, Katherine of Aragon's fall and eventual divorce, Henry's marriage to Anne Boleyn, the fall of Cardinal Wolsey, and at the end the birth of Elizabeth, complete with Archbishop Cranmer's prophecy about her and her successor, the current King James I. In Act 2 alone we find Buckingham's destruction, increasing complaints about Wolsey, and Katherine's trial in which she offers a rousing defence. Each situation seems to carry seeds of the other.

Act 3 focuses on Wolsey's fall, and scene 2 provides a riveting encounter between him and his accusers and eventually the king himself. This experience dooms Wolsey, whose breathtaking reach had extended across the country in its grasping thoroughness. But now his betrayal and deceit become obvious, thanks in part to letters and documents that reveal his mendacity and his exceptional wealth. These events pave the way for Anne Boleyn's rise to power, confirmed by her coronation as Queen in 4.1, Katherine having been set aside. Anne must fulfil the fundamental task of producing a male heir, something that Katherine had been unable to do after twenty years of marriage, hence Henry's desire to get rid of her on the grounds that God has been punishing him for having married Katherine, his deceased brother's wife. Anne indeed gives birth, the focus of Act 5, but she provides another female child, Elizabeth.

However disappointed, Henry nevertheless proceeds with the expected rituals, such as Elizabeth's christening, the business of 5.4, surrounded by all the apparatus of power and state: matters of state do not sleep. Cranmer speaks glowing words of prophecy about the future of this child: 'She shall be / … / A pattern to all princes living with her / And all that shall succeed' (5.4.20–3). She will embody all 'princely graces'; and 'Truth shall nurse her, / Holy and heavenly thoughts still counsel her' (28–9). Cranmer's vision extends far beyond this child: 'when / The bird of wonder dies, the maiden phoenix, / Her ashes new create another heir / As great in admiration as herself' (39–42). The Archbishop now refers to King James, the currently reigning monarch. In the year of James's arrival in England, John Fenton celebrated this event in his poem *King James His Welcome to London*, claiming, for example, that the peaceful transfer of power 'Was never matched since *Augustus* dayes'.[4] And, in what seems a precursor of the phoenix image in Shakespeare's play, Fenton writes: 'The *Phoenix* that of late fled to the skies / Hath left her ashes, from whence doth arise / Another *Phoenix*, rare, unmatcht, unpeered.'[5]

The play continues with Cranmer's prophecy: from Elizabeth's 'ashes of honor' shall rise James from the north (Scotland) 'as great in fame as she was' (46). Further, 'Peace, plenty, love, truth, terror, / That were the servants to this chosen infant, / Shall then be his' (47–9). James shall flourish, 'And like a mountain cedar reach his branches / To all the plains about him' (53–4). Small wonder that Henry VIII calls Cranmer an 'oracle of comfort' (66).

The play thus extends to the present moment, 1613, commemorating James's rule, despite being a play about the Tudors. Shakespeare and Fletcher make an obvious nod of gratitude toward their royal patron, the sponsor of the King's Men. The family of history becomes in the drama the family of art only in turn to become the current family of history. The play's Prologue says: 'Think ye see / The very persons of our noble story / As they were living' (25–7). But spectators at the Globe understood the living royal persons as part of the noble story. The Stuart royal family pervades their consciousness, whether in this fiction or in the rich realities of 1613.

Ludovic Stuart, Duke of Lennox, and cousin of King James, arrived back in London in August, fresh from accompanying the recently married Princess Elizabeth and her husband Frederick, Elector Palatine of Germany, on their journey to Germany, and a diplomatic mission to France on behalf of a possible marriage partner for Prince Charles. He learned of the Globe Theatre disaster and about the performance of *Henry VIII*. His mind scanned over the year's events and even farther because 1613 represented the thirtieth year of his departure as a nine-year-old child from his native France and his arrival in Scotland. Of theatrical matters, Lennox remembered his association with an adult acting company, which for several years, starting in 1604, bore his name, the Duke of Lennox's Men; this group mainly travelled through the countryside.[6] Lennox and his brother Esmé participated in numerous dramatic events.[7] Looking at the ruins of the Globe, Lennox (the title that he enjoyed from his earliest moments in Scotland, and one previously held by his father, also named Esmé Stuart) recalled the joys and sorrows of the previous months, especially a funeral and a wedding (see Figure 2).

For the moment Lennox resembles Prospero in Shakespeare's *The Tempest*. This Duke of Milan had lived on a remote Mediterranean island for twelve years before the play opens, but his experiences on that single day compelled Prospero to recall many years earlier, his time in Milan before his forcible expulsion. Like Prospero, Lennox has lived on a foreign island for thirty years, cut off from home in France; and, like Prospero who seeks to connect Ferdinand and his daughter Miranda in marriage arrangements, Lennox has been in France negotiating on behalf of Prince Charles. Although he does not have Prospero's magical powers, Lennox does have sufficient imagination and memory to recall why he has lived on this island and the deeds and events of the past thirty years. Like Prospero, Lennox sees 1613 through the prism of his earlier life. He had, after all, also seen a performance of *The Tempest* at court during the 1612–13 winter season.

As Lennox thought about *Henry VIII*, he could recall his negotiations with Queen Elizabeth and his encounter with her in 1601.

2 Portrait of Ludovic Stuart, Duke of Lennox, by Paul van Somer

These immediate, direct connections with the Queen, King James never had. And, of course, Lennox knows well her namesake, the Princess Elizabeth, King James's only surviving daughter, whose baptism he had attended in 1596 in Scotland. Lennox further recognises that in referring to the events of a certain year, a single year or date, he cannot understand that year without the perspective of all that has preceded it. The past is prologue, as Shakespeare observes in *Cymbeline*. Individual years may serve as convenient markers, but a single year does not stand alone. Prospero understood this, and so does Lennox.

Why did a nine-year-old boy from France leave his native land and come to Scotland in 1583? Lennox's journey began with his father, Esmé Stuart, D'Aubigny, who died in May 1583. Esmé had himself left France in 1579, as a thirty-seven-year-old French courtier, presumably at the request of the Scottish Privy Council who sought someone to guide their teenaged king (now thirteen years old); Esmé left behind a wife and five children. Arriving at Stirling Castle in September 1579, he received an immediate and enthusiastic welcome from the young King James VI. From that moment on their relationship deepened as James showered him with titles and gifts, including the title Duke of Lennox, the only duke in all of Scotland. A relationship of mutual love also developed, to the chagrin and worry of the Scottish nobles and Kirk and to the alarm of English authorities. Esmé was first cousin to James's father, Henry Stuart, Earl of Darnley. James had no brothers or sisters, and his mother, Mary, Queen of Scots, had been driven into exile when James was scarcely a year old. He would thus consciously know his mother only through letters and reports. The young king felt very much alone. Into this familial vacuum Esmé moved and eventually filled it with love, respect, and loyalty.

His motives remained suspect, as he established contact with Mary and sought to find help for her cause; such an overture to her became well known to both the Scottish lords and the English. Some imagined that he had come to Scotland to pave the way for more Catholics to enter the kingdom and for them to gain new liberties and power. Something slightly disingenuous, if not deceitful, lingered in his actions. But James did not care. He allowed Esmé to manage the royal household, put him in charge of many political operations, and listened attentively to his advice. Only one thing stood in the way of Esmé's complete sway over the young king: his religion. But Esmé soon took care of that, converting to Protestantism and thus outflanking the Scottish Church's opposition to him. James's love for him increased, for he understood this religious conversion as a sign of Esmé's love for him.[8]

Eventually the Scottish nobles and churchmen grew weary of Esmé's influence and political power, which had gone largely unchecked. When they could no longer batter him about his Catholicism, they devised other schemes to discredit him. In late summer 1582, the 'Lords Enterprisers', as the opposing group called itself, succeeded in literally separating James from Esmé as James hunted near Ruthven Castle at which the Earl of Gowrie persuaded him to rest. This 'Ruthven Raid' of conspirators in late August captured James and held him as prisoner for many months, despite his protestations. The Enterprisers believed that whoever gained possession of and maintained proximity to the king's body would secure the desired power. Removing Esmé from James's person suited their purposes perfectly. The Enterprisers claimed that they took James against his will in order to 'protect' him from Esmé's devious wiles. They regularly moved James, thereby pretending that he was not in fact a prisoner. They achieved by violence what they could not by persuasion and policy.

For the first time in nearly three years, James and Esmé experienced a breach in their relationship. James remained anxious for Esmé to rescue him, but Esmé was frustratingly powerless to save the king. The noblemen made clear that Esmé had only one option: to leave Scotland. Reluctant and guilt-ridden, James bent to their pressure and agreed to Esmé's exile. (This situation Christopher Marlowe a few years later unwittingly echoes in his play *Edward II* in which the king must agree to Gaveston's expulsion.) On 21 December, Esmé Stuart began his journey to France, going by way of England. Although many people, including James, assumed that he would return in a few months, that did not happen.

Esmé arrived in France a broken man, reviled by the French court and largely ignored by his wife, from whom he had been separated for three years. The surviving letters that he wrote to James just before his departure in December capture the poignancy of their situation, even as they document Esmé's devotion to and love for James. He writes: 'For whatever might happen to me, I shall always be your very faithful servant.' He insists that if his breast should be split open, James would find engraven on his heart the words 'fidelity and obedience', not 'words of inconstancy and disloyalty'.[9] He had served the king with his whole heart. In this state of brokenness, Esmé's health failed.

Letters moved back and forth from Scotland to France, but they could not conquer the separating space; indeed, nothing could assuage the loss that both men felt. As his health worsened and death loomed, Esmé's wife insisted that he should have the advantage of a Catholic funeral; but he steadfastly refused, pointedly claiming that he remained a Protestant. On the day of his death, 26 May 1583, Esmé 'at seven of the clocke … caused to write a writing to the King's Grace, shewing his Grace the estate he was at, desiring him to be good to his barnes [children], and to tak upon his Grace the defense of them'.[10] This letter James eventually received. But he also got something else: Esmé's embalmed heart. Calderwood reports, 'he was bowelled, the same night, his heart takin out, the bodie putt in a leadin kist [leaden coffin], … and on the morne conveyed away secreetlie'.[11] This action occurred without the widow's knowledge, even as she had violated Esmé's wishes by providing a Catholic funeral. In death, Esmé determined that his heart should be sent to James, rather than being left in France. This act powerfully testifies to and underscores his love for James, making literal what had been a metaphor.

The news of Esmé's death took a while to reach Scotland; it took the king even longer to accept it. For weeks no one at court dared broach the subject. But James did not wallow in grief for long; he decided instead to take action. First, he successfully escaped his captors in June 1583, just a month after Esmé's death. Second, he responded aesthetically by writing a poem, *Ane Metaphoricall Invention of a Tragedie called Phoenix*, typically referred to as *Phoenix*, which he published in his first volume of poetry, *The Essayes of a Prentise in the Divine Arte of Poesie* (1584). He thereby made public to a reading audience his recreated, imaginative version of desire. *Phoenix* offers a thinly veiled allegory of his love for Esmé Stuart. Through the covert allegory of this poem, James voices deep desire for his cousin, including homoerotic desire.

The poet's role in *Phoenix* bifurcates into narrator and participant; at moments they are, of course, the same. Another person lurks around this poem: namely, James the adolescent king, who poses as the narrator of a simple fiction about a phoenix. Within the poem the narrator becomes more than a conduit through whom the story flows: he expresses judgement, displays emotion, and responds with action, but all restricted by the confines of the allegory. By this beautiful Arabian bird of the poem James clearly intends Esmé, who like the bird endured attack and eventual death. Everything in the poem speaks of the narrator's desire for the bird: its beauty, its soaring power, its brightness that rivals the sun, its attractiveness perceived by others, and finally its helplessness as it comes to seek refuge from attack. The *Phoenix* thus forever links the two cousins in a fiction that adumbrates their personal lives; it recollects with lamentation and consolation the loving relationship of James and Esmé Stuart, including its sharp edge of desire.[12]

James closes the 280-line poem with a 'L'envoy' section of three stanzas, which serves as an address to Apollo and offers a way out of the tragedy that he has presented. The poet hopes that something may happen to assuage his grief; he urges Apollo: 'so heir / Let them be now, to make ane *Phoenix* new / Euen of this worme of *Phoenix* ashe which grew'.[13] If indeed a new Phoenix can emerge from the ashes of the former one, 'My tragedie a comike end will haue'. Ludovic Stuart will be the new phoenix in James's life. James completed his grief not only by escaping and writing a poem about his love for Esmé but also by inviting the young Ludovic to the Scottish court and into his life. By recalling the lost and dead love, he recuperates beauty, wonder, and desire in the poem. By summoning Ludovic, James enlarged his life, making it open to renewing and hopeful possibilities that point toward reassuring comedy. Phoenix can replace phoenix. Only new life can supplant and fulfil the *Phoenix*.

From early on the young Ludovic understood this poem, its relevance and resonance for his life, and his role as the new phoenix. With the Prologue's words at the beginning of *Henry VIII*, 'Think ye see / The very persons of our noble story / As they were living' (25–7), Ludovic could understand how James's poetic fiction rehearses the noble story of the king's love for Esmé. Cranmer's prophecy at the end of *Henry VIII*, 'her ashes new create another heir', opens the pertinence of the phoenix myth and Ludovic as the fulfilment of James's earlier wish. Just as the playwrights envision Queen Elizabeth as a phoenix who gives rise to her successor James, so Ludovic, the new heir, stands in for his father. The phoenix funeral pyre has yielded another phoenix.

In 1596, the Scottish poet John Burel dedicated his collection of poems to Ludovic, Duke of Lennox, great Chamberlain of Scotland, wishing for him long life and happy success. Burel writes further: 'And sen ze are, the onely sonne and hair, / Sprung from the synders, of that Phoenix rair', so must Ludovic serve God and their sovereign king.[14] Others revere his renown and acknowledge his descent from and perpetuation of the phoenix.

Apparently, this young phoenix, arriving into the presence of King James at Stirling Castle in November 1583, did not feel intimidated or daunted by his figurative and real responsibility as heir to his father. From the beginning, James showered him with most of his father's titles, including the crucial one, Duke of Lennox. He became a member of the King's Bedchamber, Privy Council, and Lord Chamberlain of Scotland for life. Heady recognition for this child. The scant evidence suggests that Ludovic handled these privileges and duties with equanimity, despite his youth and inexperience. Wrenched from his comfortable familial life in France, he suddenly stood at the centre of Scottish politics but embraced by the king's love. A few months after his arrival, Lennox carried the royal crown to the opening of Parliament in 1584, a sure sign of James's love for and confidence in him. Thomas Fowler reported back to England to William Cecil, Lord Burghley, a few years later on 28 March 1589 that the Duke 'is "so proper a youthe, so wy[se], stayed, active on horse and fote, cowrteows, of suche intertey[nment] and carryage of him selffe, so pleasynge to all men … [and] tr[uly] he is a parragon. The Kinge loves this Duke as him selffe".'[15] Robert Bowes captures a striking image of the king's reliance when he wrote to Robert Cecil on 13 April 1594: 'The King is now determined to pass quietly to-morrow to Stirling, taking with him the Duke alone.'[16] This paragon of a phoenix had become confidant and trusted adviser to the king, who took refuge in his loving and pleasant company.

Caught in the ebb and flow of political and cultural events, Ludovic did not remain alone; his siblings eventually also came to Scotland, as they in turn abandoned their mother in France. As early as July 1583, even before Ludovic's own arrival, the possibility of marriage of Henrietta, Lennox's oldest sister, surfaced in Ambassador Robert Bowes's letter back to Francis Walsingham in England in which Bowes noted that the Earl of Huntly 'shall be pressed to accept Lennox's [Esmé Stuart's] daughter in marriage, and misliking presently to bound thereto, he is purposed to put the matter over by all fair means he can'.[17] In 1584, negotiations for the marriage of Henrietta to George Gordon, Earl of Huntly, intensified. The Frenchman M. Fontenay reported to Queen Mary that 'it may please your majesty to work for his [Lennox's] friends by an alliance which could be made for the marriage of his three sisters, that is to say, the eldest with the Earl of Huntly'.[18] Finally in 1588, the wedding took place, for which James himself wrote a masque-like entertainment. Henrietta thereby married arguably the most powerful lord in Scotland and one who because of his Catholicism (regularly disavowed) and serious political ambitions caused James endless problems. Both Huntly and Henrietta, however, became mainstays of the Scottish court, except when Huntly was out of favour; and they enjoyed a long and apparently successful marriage. Ludovic and King James both felt a strong attachment to Huntly, thus assuring that his occasional banishment from court did not last long.

The second sister, Marie, also came to Scotland and in 1592 married another powerful nobleman, John Erskine, Earl of Mar. The third sister, Gabrielle, was betrothed to Hugh Montgomery, Earl of Eglinton, in 1598; but she chose to return to France and there entered a convent. Ludovic himself married twice in Scotland, first in 1591 to Lady Sophia, daughter of William Ruthven, first Earl of Gowrie, a marriage dissolved by Sophia's death in 1592. In 1598, he married Jean, daughter of Sir Matthew Campbell; they produced two children who died in childhood. Jean herself died in 1610, but before then the marriage had essentially collapsed. Ludovic's only brother, named Esmé for their father, eventually came to Scotland, leaving behind in France their father's lands but bringing the title of Seigneur D'Aubigny. Esmé would journey to England with Lennox and the king's party in 1603; the brothers would spend the rest of their lives in England.

In 1589, the twenty-three-year-old James decided to marry, and his attention turned to Anne of Denmark, daughter of King Frederick II and his wife Sophia. Clearly, James had begun to feel some pressure to fulfil this expectation of kingship and provide an heir. Lennox had himself been declared the presumptive heir apparent to the Scottish throne and would so remain until the birth of Prince Henry in 1594. On 22 October 1589, James began his journey to Denmark because Anne's attempts to arrive in Scotland had been thwarted by bad weather at sea. Boldly and unexpectedly, the king set sail, having never left his kingdom until this moment.

He declared himself desperately in love with Anne, whom, of course, he had not met.

James left behind two extraordinary documents. The first, addressed to the people of Scotland and not vetted by his advisers, lays out his reasons for marrying and claims that he has made this decision alone. James poignantly explains why he seems to have delayed in marrying: 'The reasons were that I was alone, without father or mother, brother or sister, king of this realm and heir apparent of England.'[19] He acknowledges that his failure to marry created a 'nakedness' that made him appear 'weak' and emboldened his enemies. Some have apparently wondered if James 'were a barren stock'. He denies this possibility and adds: 'God is my witness I could have abstained longer nor the weal of my patrie could have permitted.' He thus approaches marriage out of duty, not passion. James even specifies where he made his decision: 'The place that I resolved this in was Craigmillar, not one of the whole Council being present there.' A certain self-satisfaction runs through this statement. James also assures his people that he will not be gone long, a matter of a few weeks; in fact, he did not return until the following May, having thoroughly enjoyed his time in Scandinavia.

The other document, also dated 22 October, confronts the issue of government: how will Scotland function with the king away? Given the precarious and turbulent nature of Scottish politics, this question resonates with anxiety. But James has thought this through. He leaves behind a structure for governing: 'That the Privy Council shall reside continuously in Edinburgh under the Duke of Lennox as President, who shall have [Earl] Bothwell continually associated with him.'[20] Lord John Hamilton shall govern over the southern border area. Should questions arise, the councillors will meet with Lennox to deliberate and 'take steps to do whatever they consider needful for the King's service and the public welfare'.[21] James also urges that 'the ministers pray earnestly for the success of the journey, admonish the people of their duty to God and the King, and live in harmony among themselves'. To the surprise of everyone, this system worked exceptionally well as Scotland settled into an unusually peaceful time. Surely Lennox must take some credit for this good fortune, which offers testimony to his political and personal skill, all the more remarkable because in 1589 Lennox was but fifteen years old, having been in Scotland a mere six years and yet having mastered the language and the country's politics. Yet he ranked above all the seasoned and powerful lords of the Privy Council – a certain sign of the king's trust in him. Lennox indeed seemed to merit the designation of 'paragon', given to him by Thomas Fowler earlier in 1589. He would remain indelibly linked to James and the political and social courtly life.

Thus, Lennox greeted the returning king and new queen in May 1590 in Edinburgh. For her entry into the city he and James rode on horseback alongside Anne's silver coach, sent over by the Danes for the occasion. Lennox also assisted in the plans and preparation for Anne's coronation as queen, including bearing her crown for the ceremony, an event resisted by some leaders of the Scottish Kirk. But crowned she was in Holyrood Abbey on 17 May in an elaborate seven-hour-long ceremony that some ministers found 'popish', especially the act of anointing her body with oil. As the coronation closed, Lennox, along with other nobles of the estates, knelt and pledged fidelity to Anne. Two days later on 19 May, Queen Anne made an official royal entry through Edinburgh in a pageant that Lennox had helped arrange. Escorted by Danish and Scottish lords on horseback, Anne moved again in a chariot through the excited city. She encountered an Angel who descended to welcome her, saw on one scaffold an array of the Nine Muses, and then the Four Cardinal Virtues who, emblematically costumed, greeted the queen. Several globes burst to reveal various characters. One scene included representations of all the previous rulers of Scotland; another displayed the seven planets from which a box covered with purple velvet and embroidered with the letter 'A' appeared, this letter set about with diamonds and precious stones as a gift from the city. At Nether Bow, Anne saw a tableau that depicted her marriage to James, a scene that rounded out this day of celebration and adulation. Like James, Anne came to rely on Lennox, whom she trusted; she also became a close friend with his sister Henrietta.

On 19 February 1594, Anne produced the much-desired male heir, Prince Henry Frederick. His baptism, however, did not take place until 30 August, delayed by necessary renovation and construction at Stirling Castle and difficulty in rounding up all the various foreign ambassadors. Queen Elizabeth, through a proxy, served as godmother to the new prince. One might conclude that the baptismal events were well worth the wait, so extravagant were they; a report indicates: 'those exercises that were to be used for decoration of that solemnitie, were to be devided both in field-pastimes with martiall and heroicall exploits, and in household with rare shewes and singular inventions'.[22] Lennox appeared everywhere, from dramatic activities in the field to the sacred rites of the baptism itself. On the first day, for example, he came as one of three Turks, set in opposition to three Christian Knights, led by James himself. A group of Amazons, 'in women's attire, very sumptuously clad' (356), rounded out the arrangement; this group improbably included the Abbot of Holyrood. Following strict rules, the would-be warriors on horseback began to run at the ring. Queen Anne promised a reward of a 'rich ring of diamonds' to the winner. 'The victorie fell to the Duke of Lennox; who, bringing it to his side and partie, had the praise and prise adjudged to himself' (357).

Amidst much pomp and circumstance the baptism finally took place. Ambassadors from many countries attended the ceremony in the Chapel Royal at Stirling. In his chamber the infant Prince Henry lay 'on his bed of estate, richly decored, and wrought with brodered worke, containing the story of Hercules and his travels' (359). (One might have expected a Biblical story.) The old Countess of Mar, who had taken care of James when he was a child, lifted the baby from his bed, 'and delivered him to the Duke of Lennox', who in turn handed him to the Earl of Sussex, the Ambassador of England, who then carried the prince into the chapel. These people underscored the past, present, and anticipated and desired future. 'The Prince's robe-royall, being of purple velvote, very richly set with pearle, was delivered to the Duke of Lennox, who put the same about the Prince.' Several other such transfers of the prince occurred, all involving Lennox, such as the approach to the pulpit for the actual baptism when Lennox received the baby from the Countess of Mar and delivered him to the English Ambassador.

Afterwards in the King's Hall 'the Duke of Lennox received the Prince from the Ambassador of England, and presented him to the King's Majestie, who addubbed him knight' (361). Through these procedures the Scottish King made clear the prominence he assigned to the English court, even as he certified his love for and dependence on Lennox. The banquet that followed included an extraordinary array of figures, such as a Moor, Neptune, Thetis, Arion, Ceres, Fecundity, Faith, Concord, Liberality, and Perseverance. During the event a large ship (18 feet long) appeared in the hall, commemorating the king's journey to Denmark and the royal couple's safe return in 1590.[23] Lennox watched the extravaganza, enjoying this glorious moment in Scottish history and rejoicing in his role. He felt similarly when participating in the baptisms of Princess Elizabeth in 1596 and Prince Charles in 1600, although they were understated events by comparison.

Glittering coronations and baptisms did not define the whole experience in Scotland for Lennox. On 5 August 1600, a very strange episode took place that involved the king and Lennox, along with others. (To this day scholars remain puzzled about what exactly took place and why.) Apparently, Alexander Ruthven and his brother, the Earl of Gowrie, encouraged James to leave his hunting near Falkland and follow them to their castle because supposedly some curious treasure had been found. The king dismissed Lennox and went along with Alexander. (This same family had been involved with separating Esmé Stuart from James in 1582, and yet this somehow did not raise James's suspicions.) After dinner with the Earl of Gowrie, the king followed Alexander to a remote upper part of the castle, Alexander locking every door behind him as they ascended. In a dark room James suddenly encountered an armed stranger, whose precise identity remains uncertain. James finally realised that he stood in danger of being killed; he struggled with the stranger and Alexander and finally cried out. Eventually James's pages found him and came to his aid, killing Alexander and the Earl, who had ascended the steps for some unknown reason. Lennox and the Earl of Mar finally discovered what had happened, and they promptly went into the village to calm any possible uprising or disturbance.

James insisted to one and all that the Ruthvens had wanted to murder him, and so he gave out this official version of the story, which the ministers in the Scottish Kirk in Edinburgh – and Queen Anne – refused to believe. All the recalcitrant ministers James sent away from Edinburgh until they recanted. Robert Bruce, who refused to relent, James banished from Scotland on pain of death. The whole story has many bizarre elements. Was it another attempted kidnapping of James, or was it James's plan to destroy the Ruthven descendants of those who had imprisoned him in 1582? Whatever had happened, James established 5 August as an ongoing day of celebration in honour of his escape from possible murder by the 'Gowrie Conspirators'. By the next day, 6 August, James sent word to Edinburgh, ordering the Privy Council to instigate general rejoicing for his divine deliverance. Lennox accepted the king's version of this frightening event, whatever doubts he might have harboured.[24] After all, in a flash he could imagine a potentially bleak, if not dangerous, future for himself, had James been killed.

In 1613, Lennox also remembered his first diplomatic mission to England in 1601, which followed a similar trip to France that had included a visit with his mother for the first time in eighteen years. In late July, Lennox went to France at James's bidding with no particular diplomatic agenda, but 'rather for confirming the old amity and friendship'.[25] He had an audience with the King of France 'and was very kindly accepted. A few days after, the king went to Fontainebleau, where the queen was to lie of childbirth.' Lennox followed 'and was entertained with hunting and the like sports unto the queen's delivery', which occurred on 17 September. After visiting the king and queen, Lennox then went to see his mother. According to Thomas Douglas in a letter to Robert Cecil (10 February 1601), Lennox's mother had objected to his official trip to France 'unless he has greater sums of money with him than Scotland can afford at this time'.[26] Douglas, presumably quoting the mother, reports her saying: 'I rather ye should stay in Scotland with the title (only) of a duke than in France not to perform the part of an ambassador.' Somehow she thought that her son would travel without sufficient money and recognition; perhaps she did not understand his superior position in the Scottish court. What she and her son discussed after many years' separation remains unknown. Doubtless he brought reports of Henrietta and Marie, his sisters, and their good political fortunes, as well as his own. In the intimacy of their conversation, did Lennox explain his relationship with King James and his prominence in Scotland?

Lennox then made his way to London, arriving in the beginning of November 1601. Spottiswoode reports: 'his commission indeed was no other but to salute the queen in the king's name, and let her know the kind and filial affection he carried unto her, whereof he should be willing to give proof at all occasions'.[27] Sir Robert Cecil, Elizabeth's chief counsellor, had written to Patrick Master of Gray in Scotland, acknowledging the preparations for Lennox's visit and the queen's willingness to accept him.[28] Lennox and the queen had carried on a correspondence for some time, and she understood thoroughly his importance. In the background of this 1601 visit lay many transactions and negotiations between Cecil and others with King James, paving the way for his eventual succession to the English crown; these plans remained unknown to the queen, but they resided very much in Lennox's mind as he met Cecil and other members of the English Privy Council. Spottiswoode observes: 'The duke, after three weeks' stay, being feasted by the queen and entertained with all compliments of amity, returned home, and came to Edinburgh in the end of December.'[29] Elizabeth herself wrote to James on 2 December about her meeting with Lennox: 'your faithful and dear Duke has at large discoursed with me as of his own knowledge what faithful affection you bear me and has added the leave he has received to proffer himself for the performance of my service in Ireland'.[30] She confirmed James's high opinion of Lennox: 'Sure, dear brother, in my judgment for this short acquaintance that I have had with him you do not prize with better cause any near unto you. For I protest without feigning or doubting I never gave ears to greater laud than such as I have heard him pronounce of you.' Did not Thomas Fowler call Lennox a 'paragon'? With great joy and eagerness, King James conversed with Lennox long into the night about impressions of Elizabeth, who retained supreme political importance for James. This renowned ruler he had never met, but he would become her successor in England.

In the cool of early morning 24 March 1603, the lives of James and Lennox changed forever: Queen Elizabeth drew her last breath, and the path to the English crown opened for James finally and irrevocably (see Figure 3). By that night Sir Robert Carey, in a surreptitious, frantic, and impressive journey, reached Edinburgh and entered Holyrood Palace, where servants awoke James, and Carey told him of Elizabeth's death. Everything that James had hoped for, dreamed about, and angled for since childhood, had now become a reality. In fact, as early as 1600, James had written to various Scottish lords about his plans to 'possess us in the crown of England according to our just and undoubted title'.[31] He also promised these lords that 'we shall, within the space of a year thereafter, thankfully pay and content every one of these persons that have advanced us at this time with such sums as the Duke of Lennox has in ticket'. Apparently Lennox had the job of keeping tabs on who had lent what to the king. In 1603, James would leave behind the stark, rough world of Scotland and enter the Promised Land, full of wealth and security. By the next day James received the official word from the English Privy Council that he had been proclaimed King

3 Engraving of King James I by Simon van de Passe from
The Workes of King James (1616)

of England, Scotland, Ireland, and France. He would de facto unite Scotland and England. He thus anticipated the prophecy at the end of *Henry VIII* by being the new phoenix from the north, succeeding Elizabeth, arising from her 'ashes of honor'. The bleakness of the Edinburgh sky gave way to the glittering hope of a new day and life that awaited him in the southern kingdom. James's thoughts also turned to the ponderous task of actually going to London.

One thing he knew for certain: he wanted Lennox to accompany him on the journey and to remain with him in the new kingdom. Thus, on 27 March he wrote to Lennox, informing him that Elizabeth had died and requesting that he prepare himself for service: we 'desire you to addresse yourself hither to us in your maist cumelie and decent maner, to attend upoun and accompany us … as you tender our plesour and service'.[32] Lennox responded affirmatively and enthusiastically. Unlike James, Lennox had, of course, visited England; but he had no way of anticipating what living there would entail. The chapter of his life that began as a nine-year-old arriving in Scotland and remaining for twenty years would now close, as a new, exciting chapter emerged. In 1613, he would have much reason to recall and assess his first ten years in England.

On Sunday 3 April 1603, the king went to St Giles's church in Edinburgh where he addressed the people of Scotland, assuring them of his continuing devotion and promising to return for a visit at least every three years. (On the latter point, he made only one trip back to Scotland, that in 1617.) He was, he insisted, merely travelling to another part of his kingdom. His heart-felt sentiments moved some Scots to tears. On Tuesday 5 April, he bade farewell to his queen in a public display of emotion as both shed tears. (Anne was pregnant and would follow later.) With Lennox, his brother Esmé Stuart, and others accompanying, James then began his arduous but exciting trip to England, moving along the Great North Road through places great and small, not reaching London until 7 May.[33]

This somewhat leisurely pace served several purposes. First, it enabled James to avoid London in the time of official mourning for Elizabeth and her funeral on 28 April (James never attended a funeral). Further, it provided ample opportunity for him to see great stretches of the countryside and to meet his new English citizens, including those with political power. Crowds of people presseded against the king, to his chagrin, their enthusiasm unparalleled. Later he recounted in his first speech to Parliament on 19 March 1604 something of his trip southward: 'Shall it ever bee blotted out of my minde, how at my first entrie into this Kingdome, the people of all sorts rid and ran, nay rather flew to meet mee? their mouthes and eyes flaming nothing but sparkles of affection.'[34] In addressing Parliament in 1607, James likened his first three years of English rule to 'Christmas'. On the 1603 journey he spent, for example, near the end of the trip, profitable time with Robert Cecil at his house at Theobalds, where they and members of the Privy Council discussed major issues of transition and governing. About the latter, James made two early decisions: to reconfigure the Privy Council with equal numbers of Scots and English, and to elevate the importance of the Bedchamber. Lennox became the honorific head of the Bedchamber, corresponding to his political prominence in Scotland. This small group of men (at first all Scots) had complete access to the king and therefore extraordinary power, which diminished the importance of the Privy Council. Esmé also joined this group.[35] A few months after arriving, James inducted Lennox into the Order of the Garter, the most prestigious knighthood in England. Lennox became the only non-royal Duke in all of Scotland and England.

But in the transition from Scottish rule to English rule, not all went smoothly. James had to request that Lennox help resolve the problem of an intractable Queen Anne, who insisted, against James's wishes, on collecting Prince Henry from the oversight of the Mars at Stirling. James and Anne had fought over the rearing of their children since the birth of Henry in 1594.[36] (Anne had grown up with a different kind of familial arrangement in Denmark.) Anne had not seen her son in five years, making plausible her desire to be with him and to travel with him to their new kingdom; thus, she went to Stirling to get Henry. But the Earl of Mar's family, which had taken care of royal children for decades, had a clear mandate not to turn over Prince Henry's care to anyone, including the queen.

In early May, Anne made her move, only to be rebuffed by the old Countess of Mar and her son. The queen created such a scene that she had a miscarriage. As David Calderwood reports: 'The queene went to bed in an anger, and parted with childe the tenth of May.'[37] James first sent the Earl of Mar to placate her, but, Calderwood adds, 'the queene would not looke upon him'. When James got word of this response, he decided to dispatch Lennox, who arrived on 19 May. After much negotiation, the Council concluded: 'It was thought good that the Erle of Marr sould deliver the prince to the duke, and that the duke again deliver him to the counsell. The counsell, to pleasure the queene, delivered him to her and the duke, to be transported, and to be delivered by them to the king.' This sounds strangely reminiscent of the baptismal ceremony in 1594 in which Lennox passed the infant Henry to the English Ambassador, only to have him returned. On 17 May, James had written to the Earl of Mar: 'In all other thinges concerning the transporting of our sone yee shall dispose your selfe (according as our cousin the Duke of Lennox will particularely acquaint yow) to that whiche is our plesour; and advise with him carefully upon our honour and his surety.'[38] In triumph, Anne appeared in Edinburgh on 28 May with Henry in tow. 'Upon Tuisday, the 31st of May, the queen and the prince came from the palace of Halyrudhous, to the Great Kirk of Edinburgh, ryding in a coache, and accompanied with manie English ladies in coaches.'[39] Anne had won; it took Lennox to smooth out this very rough spot as he travelled with her and the prince towards London.

Unfortunately, the virulent eruption of the plague curtailed some of the more elaborate coronation activities, but the coronation took place on St James's Day, 25 July, as James and Anne took their oaths, Anne becoming the first crowned consort since Anne Boleyn. On that rainy late July day, the streets were desolate and Westminster Abbey half empty, yet the Protestant ceremonies took place, fulfilling expectations. Lennox and other lords attended and pledged their loyalty and support, completing the coronation. Not until 15 March 1604, however, did the royal family experience the official pageant commemorating their new reign. Financed by the City of London with the participation of Italian and Dutch merchants living in London, this royal entry outstripped anything previously seen in England. James, Anne, Henry, and Lennox moved from the Tower of London westward, making several stops for dramatic entertainment. The streets of London filled with thousands of people, who saw seven extravagant triumphal arches constructed for the occasion, which the artificer Stephen Harrison had prepared. He subsequently put together *The Arches of Triumph* (1604 and reissued in 1613), which contains magnificent engravings of the arches. The first arch located at Fenchurch offered, for example, a representation of the City of London carved atop the arch; Ben Jonson prepared the dramatic scene, which included a speech by the Genius of the city, portrayed by Edward Alleyn, one of the most highly regarded professional actors. Thomas Dekker and Thomas Middleton, Shakespeare's playwright rivals, joined Jonson in creating a spectacle that surpassed any such royal entry pageant.[40] Shakespeare and his fellow members of the King's Men appeared in their scarlet livery as servants of the royal household. The honoured party and spectators might all agree with one of the final arches that depicted a New World, complete with spectacular globe that turned. London certainly looked like a new creation to the royal family. Four days later (19 March) James made his first speech to Parliament, which, like the pageant, emphasised the theme of peace and prosperity that he had ushered into the kingdom.[41]

The king's principal residence was Whitehall Palace in Westminster, the property acquired by Henry VIII in 1529 after the disgrace of Cardinal Wolsey, who had lived in York House, the precursor of the palace. After Henry VIII, English monarchs used Whitehall as the official residence and seat of government. As a complex of buildings the palace evolved over the decades, not always adhering to a coherent plan. James himself oversaw the construction of a new Banqueting House (1606–9), the site of most of the court masques. In 1613, he added a new library and had earlier remodelled space for Prince Henry. James also decided to place Lennox in the Holbein Gatehouse, originally built in 1531–32, to which Hans Holbein had no apparent connection; but the name stuck. This impressive gate, resembling the one at Cripplegate in London Wall, contained on its upper floor residential space, which Lennox began to occupy.[42] What this location lacked in comfort it more than made up in prestige. This fortress-like structure on the west side of the palace complex recalled a chivalric tradition in its design. From this gatehouse Lennox could look southward to the large tiltyard, where he spent much time engaged in chivalric endeavours. The location also gave Lennox relatively close proximity to James's private lodgings. In a word, the Holbein Gatehouse underscored Lennox's exceptional position and the king's regard; and, as suggested, it can epitomise Whitehall culture.

George Marcelline aptly writes of Lennox's central position in James's life: 'You wise and prudent *Lodowicke*, honoured so many times with royall honors of *Lenox*, *Grace of Graces*, that have left *France* (your Native Country) to be alwaies by and at the right hand of *Our King*, as not able to loose the sight of him; neither be further off from his Majesty, then the Sun from the Eccliptick line.'[43] The Venetian Ambassador, Giovanni Carlo Scaramelli, reports in late June 1603: 'Although it has been customary for your Serentiy to send letters of credence to four or six of the principal ministers, it will be best on this occasion to address the Duke only.'[44] In an audience with James in July, Scaramelli noted the presence of Lennox: 'The Duke of Lennox was present all the time', fully aware of the business with the king. Lennox also addressed Scaramelli and James directly: '"Sire, I pledged myself to send to this good gentleman the portraits of yourself, the Queen, and the Princes, but I could not keep my promise for lack of artists in Scotland; now, however, I will not fail to send them by your Majesty's resident".'[45] This same Venetian Ambassador in a dispatch on 22 October concluded: 'Lennox is the person deepest in the King's confidence, and has some time ago been named the nearest to the Crown.'[46] Although now transplanted from Scotland, Lennox continued to enjoy the king's favour and confidence, sustaining an unusual closeness with James and remaining of exceptional value to him, all underscoring that which others had seen in him, this 'paragon'.

But, if Scotland lacked artists, as Lennox asserted, England did not, especially theatrical arts. Thus, court drama flourished in the Jacobean period, particularly the masque, a form sponsored in large measure by Queen Anne, who seems to have found a comfortable niche and purpose in England. She allied herself first with Samuel Daniel and then Ben Jonson for writing such entertainments, and they secured the services of Inigo Jones, England's most distinguished architect in order to create unsurpassed court spectacle. Having participated in the entertainment for his sister's wedding in 1588, having arranged the royal entry pageant for Anne in Edinburgh in 1590, and having served as a 'Turk' and run at the ring for Henry's baptism in 1594, Lennox was no stranger to such dramatic events, as spectator and participant. That he planned the first Jacobean masque, therefore, occasions no surprise.

Evidence for the masque derives from Dudley Carleton's letter to John Chamberlain, written 15 January 1604. No text of the masque exists, which some have named *Masque of the Orient Knights*, performed at Hampton Court on New Year's Day.[47] Carleton writes of the court's activities in this first Christmas season: 'The first holy days we had every night a public play in the great hall, at which the king was ever present and liked or disliked as he saw cause, but it seems he takes no extraordinary pleasure in them. The queen and prince were more the players' friends.'[48] On that night the court first saw a 'play of Robin Goodfellow and a mask brought in by a magician of China'. Carleton describes the setting: 'There was a heaven built at the lower end of the hall out of which our magician came down. … he said he had brought in clouds certain Indian and China knights to see the magnificency of this court.' Lennox apparently organised the masque and led the all-male corps of eight masquers, who danced and 'called out' a comparable group of women, beginning with Anne and those of her inner circle. 'To be included, then, by the organizer in this masque either validated one's own current court status or, at the very least, augured well for one's court future',[49] apparent in their names: Lennox, Esmé Stuart, William Herbert (Pembroke), Sir Thomas Somerset, Philip Herbert, James Hay, Richard Preston, and Sir Henry Goodyere. In choosing the women to be honoured, Lennox sought to compliment the queen. Even if everything did not go perfectly – Carleton says that 'Their attire was rich but somewhat too heavy and cumbersome for dancers, which put them beside their galliards'[50] – Lennox had made an additional and indelible mark on the world of court entertainment.

On 8 January, he also danced in the masque arranged by Queen Anne and written by Daniel, *The Vision of the Twelve Goddesses*, which Carleton also describes in the same letter. In this masque, women led the way under the guidance of the queen, attired, Carleton writes, in 'loose mantles and petticoats, but of different colors, the stuffs embroidered satins and cloth of gold and silver, for which they were beholden to Queen Elizabeth's wardrobe', Anne apparently having found some five thousand gowns among the late queen's things.[51] The women called out the men for dancing, beginning with Lennox. Thus, within a few days the court experienced first a male-oriented masque under the aegis of Lennox and then the female-dominated one under the queen's oversight. These events underscore not only interest in drama but also a politically aware court with complementary centres of power and influence.

Daniel dedicated the text of *The Vision* to Lucy Russell, Countess of Bedford, who served as a Lady of Queen Anne's Bedchamber. In fact, the dedication occupies twice as much space as the text of the masque itself. Continuing in 1605 with the *Masque of Blackness* by Ben Jonson, Anne developed a pattern through 1612 of sponsoring masques – a total of seven – and participating in their performance. She had gathered around her a group of accomplished English ladies, headed by the Countess of Bedford, all renowned for their patronage of the arts. They supported Jonson, Inigo Jones, George Chapman, Daniel, John Donne, to name a few. Anne's court 'became a crucial center for early Stuart high culture'.[52] The masques formed only one part of the cultural investment of the queen and her retinue. Such support of the arts helped delineate and solidify Anne's position as a power in her own right.

Beyond an auspicious beginning in the new Jacobean court, Lennox might well recall other appearances in masques, such as Jonson's *Hymenaei*, performed on 5 (masque) and 6 (barriers) January 1606, in honour of the marriage of the Earl of Essex and Frances Howard, a marriage apparently not made in heaven. Lennox appeared in the second part of the entertainment, the indoor tilt or barriers. Jonson writes: '*On the next night … there appeared at the lower end of the hall a mist made of delicate perfumes, out of which, a battle being sounded under the stage, did seem to break forth two ladies, the one representing Truth, the other Opinion.*'[53] Out of their intense dialogue emerged sixteen knights who represent champions for Truth. Jonson describes them: '*sixteen knights armed with pikes and swords, their plumes and colors carnation and white, all richly accoutred*' (103). Lennox led the group of sixteen who support Truth; they all fought vigorously against Opinion's supporters until suddenly a '*light seemed to fill all the hall, and out of it an angel or messenger of glory appearing*' (104). This Angel confirms the triumph of Truth against Opinion, who can only resemble Truth. This victory underscores Jonson's point that 'though their voice [the participants'] be taught to sound to present occasions, their sense or doth or should always lay hold on more removed mysteries' (76). Similarly, on 9 February 1608, Lennox, along with his brother Esmé Stuart and others, danced in Jonson's *The Haddington Masque*, in honour of the marriage of John Ramsey, Viscount Haddington, to Elizabeth Radcliffe, daughter of the Earl of Sussex. Jonson characterises the masquers' performance as '*magnificent and illustrious*'; and he describes their costumes: '*The colors carnation and silver, enriched both with embroidery and lace. The dressing of their heads, feathers and jewels, and so excellently ordered to the rest of the habit as all would suffer under any description after the show*' (118). Clearly, the arrangers for such masques sought out Lennox as performer and as an important political figure, capable for the present occasion whatever 'more removed mysteries' he may have evoked.

In the midst of these various entertainments, Anne also gave birth in 1605 and again in 1606 (she had danced in some of the masques while pregnant). On 8 April 1605, Anne gave birth to a daughter, named Mary in honour of James's mother. Excitement reigned at court: this was the first birth of a royal child in England since Jane Seymour in the sixteenth century (1537) gave birth to the child who became Edward VI. James and Anne now had an 'English' child. Mary's baptism took place on 5 May, amid much pomp and display at Greenwich. There had been considerable scurrying about and perusing of historical records in order to recall how a royal child should be baptised. At the ceremony Lennox served as one of the godparents; the other was Anne's brother, the Duke of Holstein – a further measure of the respect and friendship that Anne held for Lennox. On 22 June 1606, at Greenwich Anne gave birth to Sophia, named in honour of her mother. Unfortunately, the child lived only a few hours. Three days later a barge carried Sophia along the Thames to Westminster Abbey for burial. The daughter Mary died later, on 16 September 1607, having lived only two years. After seven births and three miscarriages, there would be no more royal births for James and Anne, who sank into depression after Sophia's death.

Only the arrival of Christian IV, her brother, in mid-July 1606 broke the queen's melancholy. When James learned that Christian had arrived by boat on the Thames, he 'sent the Duke of Lennox to welcome him; and the day following his Majesty, the Prince, and a large suite went in many boats to meet the King'.[54] The Venetian Ambassador, Giustinian, adds: 'I accordingly sent my secretary to offer my services to the King of Denmark. The Duke of Lennox procured him an audience, and the King graciously said that on his arrival in London he would gladly receive me.' On 31 July, the City of London offered a pageant in honour of King Christian, who rode with James and Lennox through the city. Although rushed in preparation, the pageant did not lack the essential devices of welcome. The conduit in Cheapside, for example, took the form of a garden, adorned with fruit of all kinds. Nearby stood a triumphal arch covered with sea scenes, including a representation of Neptune. Atop the arch stood Concord, who descended and addressed the two kings (in Latin, their common language). The Venetian Ambassador concludes: 'The ceremony was a magnificent and noble one, both on account of the great gathering of personages, the richness of their robes, and the trappings of their horses.'[55]

Lennox 'was at the head of a plan to honour the visit of King Christian by a challenge to be issued by certain knights of the Fortunate Island' throughout Europe.[56] This ambitious plan got scaled back to England only, proclaimed 'in the royal presence and the public places of Greenwich, on 1 June'. The death of Sophia further dampened this project, but Christian did participate in a tilt on 5 August, absent the full romantic possibilities that Lennox had envisioned. Perhaps this robust tilting could overcome the disastrous evening at Robert Cecil's place at Theobalds. A famous letter from John Harrington recounts the would-be masque for James and Christian, who seemed to be intent on matching each other in drinking.[57] The person representing the Queen of Sheba fell into the Danish king's lap; then James arose to dance with this queen, but he fell down and servants carried him out. The Theological Virtues, Faith, Hope, and Charity, appeared, all rendered helpless by alcohol, as for example, Faith, who left the court in a staggering condition. And so the night went – on this present occasion no removed mysteries.

At the intersection of court and city life, Lennox accompanied James twice in the summer of 1607 to more sober events in the City of London that honoured the city's guilds. On 12 June, they, along with others, went to the Clothworkers' Hall, where they dined with the Lord Mayor and members of the guild, who presented the king with a purse filled with gold. James also accepted membership in the guild, thereby becoming 'free' of the Clothworkers. John Watts, the mayor, 'humblie besought his Majestie, of his most especiall grace and favour to the Cittie in generall, and to that Societie in perticuler that hee would be pleased to be free of the Clothworkers'.[58] James accepted and generously promised: 'I doe here give unto this Company two brace of buckes yearely for ever.' The Master and Wardens of the guild humbly accepted the king into their brotherhood, thereby conferring of James the designation of 'citizen of London'.

A month later King James, Prince Henry, and Lennox went together to the Merchant Taylors' Hall for a similar occasion on 16 July. The guild's records reveal that members instructed Sir John

Swinnerton 'to conferr with Mr. Benjamyn Johnson, the Poet, about a Speech to be made to welcome his Majesty, and for Musique and other inventions'.[59] The records note further: 'At the upper end of the hall there was sett a chayer of estate where his Majesty sate and viewed the hall, and a very proper child well spoken being clothed like an Angell of gladnes, with a taper of francinnsence burning in his hand, delivered a shorte speech contanying xviii verses, devised by Mr Benjamn Johnson the Poet which pleased his Majestie marvelously well.'[60] John Rice (later a member of the King's Men) was the speaker, as the guild records indicate. Jonson, no stranger to the guilds, had prepared the first Lord Mayor's Show of the Jacobean era (1604), unfortunately lost, like the speech given here in 1607.[61] The renowned organist John Bull performed, and Nathaniel Giles led the Children of the Chapel in singing (both Bull and Giles were members of the Merchant Taylors). Seven lute players and other singers filled the hall with music. The banquet itself strains the imagination what with its 417 chickens, 1,300 eggs, and 441 gallons of wine. Small wonder that the presentation 'pleased his Majestie marvelously well'.[62] Finally, King James 'came downe into the greate hall, and sitting in his chayre of state, did heare a mellodious song of farwell song by the three men in the shipp' (170). The king noted that he was already a member of a London guild, and he suggested that the Merchant Taylors offer such to Prince Henry and Lennox, which they readily did. At considerable expense, estimated at £1,000, the Merchant Taylors had demonstrated their love to the king, prince, Lennox, and other noblemen, erasing for the moment boundaries between court and city.

Lennox actively participated in the various tilts that took place in the early years of James's reign, such as the regular Accession Day tilts (each 24 March). From his lodging in the Holbein Gatehouse, he could look out on to the tiltyard where these events took place. 'The most prominent man-at-arms, during the earlier years of the reign, was James's cousin, Ludovic Stuart, Duke of Lennox.'[63] He took part in the Accession Day tournament in 1606, although one account complains of lacklustre performance and the lack of stunning costumes.[64] That could not be said of the 1610 tournament in which the tilters tried to outdo one another. This joust at Whitehall included triumphal chariots that conveyed allegorical characters who delivered speeches of compliment to the king. A contemporary account describes the costume: 'The Duke of Lennox exceeded all in feathers; the Lord Walden in followers; and Sir Richard Preston in a pageant, which was an elephant with a castle on his back.'[65] Lennox had also been active in Prince Henry's Barriers on 6 January 1610, for which Jonson wrote the speeches. Here Lennox served as one of six who assisted the prince in his martial feats against all comers.

Similarly, he participated in the festivities later that summer for the investiture of Henry as Prince of Wales, a several-day extravaganza, which included a water pageant, written by Anthony Munday and containing performances by Richard Burbage and John Rice, members of the King's Men (31 May); the actual investiture ceremony (4 June); Daniel's masque *Tethys' Festival* (5 June); and concluding with an afternoon tilt and an evening sea battle and fireworks (6 June).[66] The contemporary Edmund Howes captures the scene in the tiltyard: 'there were divers Earles, Barons, and others being in rich, and glorious Armorure, and having costly Caparisons, wondrous curiously Imbroydered with Pearle, Gould, and Silver, the like rich habiliments'.[67] These knights presented their 'devices' to the king and prince and then ran at tilt, 'where there was a world of people to behould them'. Another account names Lennox as one of the tilters and comments on the costumes: 'Embroidered suits were so common, as the richest lace which was to be gotten seemed but a mean grace to the wearer.'[68] Perhaps Lennox also brought along a few feathers left over from earlier in 1610. For a court much given to extravagant display, these tournaments fit right in: celebrations of James's accession to the throne, to be sure, but also occasions to show off in various ways – a fading blush of chivalric hope and indulgence.

Although the tilt for King Christian lacked the romantic lustre that Lennox had intended, a version of it survives in John Ford's *Honor Triumphant* (1606), which includes the challenges that four knights would have given. Indeed, Ford dedicates the first section to 'To the Right Noble Lord, the Duke of Lennox his Grace'.[69] Lennox represents the chivalric argument that 'Knights in Ladies service have no free-will'. Thus, a knight 'ought not to be their owne, nor subject to their owne pleasure, unlesse to please themselves in the recreation which tendeth to their ladies honor' (B3v). This dedication calls attention to the slightly over twenty texts that various writers dedicated to Lennox, only two before his arrival in England. Burel's volume of poetry (1596), as cited earlier, was the first.

These epistles dedicatory seek patronage of some sort, or they simply acknowledge Lennox's prominence. Walter Quin, responding to the Gowrie Plot of 1600, addressed Lennox: 'thou him [James] hardst complaining in the snare, / Thy grief did then thy faithfull love declare: / Thy running eke with speed to make him free; / Wherein thow didst no paines, nor peril spare'.[70] Similarly, John Davies celebrates the close relationship of king and duke: 'Thou like the Moone, among heav'ns lamps dost shine, / While Sol thy Sov'raigne goest to the Globe about'.[71] Gervase Markham dedicates part of his *Cavalarice* to Lennox and praises his skill as a horseman, citing also 'the noble favours which you extend to your admirers'.[72] In 1605, James appointed Lennox as the king's aulnager (inspector of woollen cloth); in recognition of that office, John May dedicates his book on clothing to him, insisting that no cause can obscure May's 'love and duty' to Lennox.[73] Late in his life, Lennox even became the recipient of a dedication in a book in Spanish about learning this language.[74] Through these dedications Lennox emerges as a noble and heroic figure, a close companion to the king. In a sense they only acknowledge, albeit in glowing, idealised terms, what most people recognised: Lennox as paragon, in the tiltyard, on diplomatic missions, in political negotiations, and in books.

This accomplished, well-recognised, and admired man could in 1613 think back over an already rich life, full of political esteem, personal wealth, and cultural pleasure. Looking at the burned-out hulk of the Globe Theatre and thinking about *Henry VIII*, Lennox had occasion to recall another Shakespeare and Fletcher collaboration: *Two Noble Kinsmen*, their take on Chaucer's 'Knight's Tale'. The earliest printed text of this play (1634) refers on its title page to performances by the King's Men at the Blackfriars Theatre, first acquired by this acting company in 1608, offering the group an indoor theatre to complement the Globe. Of course, the play may well have also been performed at this public theatre. In all likelihood, the first performances occurred in 1613, especially given that the morris dance in 3.5 of the play reproduces one of the antimasques of Francis Beaumont's *Masque of the Inner Temple and Gray's Inn*, presented at court on 20 February 1613 for the wedding festivities for Princess Elizabeth and Frederick Elector Palatine. The Prologue to *Two Noble Kinsmen* closes by saying: 'If this play do not keep / A little dull time from us, we perceive / Our losses fall so thick we much needs leave.'[75] The speaker probably alludes to the 'loss' of the Globe Theatre. But the play has even greater resonance than this for Lennox.

The play focuses on funerals and weddings, a subject and reality powerful in any recollection of 1612–13. As the play opens, Theseus and Hippolyta move towards their wedding, only to be interrupted by Three Queens who have suffered the deaths of their husbands and resent the unwillingness of Creon to allow them to bury them: '*Enter three Queens in black, with veils stained, with imperial crowns*' (1.1.25 SD). They fall down at the feet of Theseus, Hippolyta, and Emilia, entreating them for help. Theseus claims that he has been 'transported' with their speeches. The Second Queen poignantly asks: 'We come unseasonably; but when could grief / Cull forth, as unpanged judgement can, fitt'st time / For best solicitation?' (1.1.168–70). Grief, Lennox powerfully remembered, intruded in the royal family's anticipated happiness and shocked the nation. But the marriage procession in the play moves forward, having promised help to the Queens, who appear again briefly in 1.5 with their dead husbands '*in a funeral solemnity*'. The Third Queen says: 'This world's a city full of straying streets, / And death's the market-place, where each one meets' (15–16).

The struggle between Palamon and Arcite, adapted from Chaucer, for Emilia's love finds its focus in a tournament, the likes of which Lennox would have recognised, except here the tilters face real danger and possible death. But the ceremony and formality ring true. The two knights enter in 5.1 with their accompanying three knights. Three altars stand ready for attention and adoration: Mars (Arcite), Venus (Palamon), and Diana (Emilia). Seeming to come straight out of a masque, the stage directions at the Venus altar, for example, say: '*Here music is heard; doves are seen to flutter; they fall again upon their faces, then on their knees*' (5.1.129 SD). Emilia '*in white, her hair about her shoulders, and wearing a wheaten wreath*' enters and does obeisance to the Diana altar. The actual battle takes place offstage in 5.3 with only noise and reports of the action. Arcite triumphs and enters victorious. But the victory rings hollow as he dies accidentally, having fallen from his horse; and Theseus awards Palamon to Emilia in marriage (5.4). Palamon laments Arcite's death: 'O cousin, / That we should things desire which do cost us / The loss of our desire!' (5.4.109–11).

Funerals and weddings intermix, as the royal family and Lennox understand well, given his thirty years on this island. Indeed, such events define his compelling memory of 1613. Mourning clothes and wedding garments mingle in an unsettling way, each struggling to define life and its potential for happiness. Which offers the greater reality? Lennox might recall the haunting words of the Second Lord in *All's Well That Ends Well*: 'The web of our life is of a mingled yarn, good and ill together' (4.3.70). Much in 1613 reinforced this truthful observation.

Meanwhile, the King's Men, assessing the loss of the Globe Theatre to that summer fire, decided to rebuild. From the ashes of 1613, a new theatre arose, like a phoenix, in 1614. The consumed artefact gained new life. Out of tragedy, the court and London had to seek renewal. The year 1613 offers abundant evidence of a trajectory that moves away from tragedy towards life-affirming restoration.

Notes

1 *The Life and Letters of Sir Henry Wotton*, ed. Logan Pearsall Smith (Oxford: Clarendon Press, 1966; originally published 1907), 2: 32–3. Gordon McMullan in his Arden edition of *King Henry VIII* provides all the primary documents and an extensive interpretation of Wotton's account (London: Arden, 2000), pp. 57–62.

2 Found in McMullan's edition, p. 58.

3 All quotations come from *Henry VIII*, ed. Jonathan Crewe (New York: Penguin, 2001).

4 John Fenton, *King James His Welcome to London* (London, 1603), sig. A3v.

5 Fenton, *King James*, sig. B3.

6 See E. K, Chambers, *The Elizabethan Stage*, 4 vols (Oxford: Clarendon Press, 1923), 2: 241.

7 Ian Donaldson claims that the brothers were keen theatregoers in his biography of Ben Jonson, *Ben Jonson: A Life* (Oxford: Oxford University Press, 2011), p. 186. For additional information about their involvement, see my 'The Stuart Brothers and English Theater', *Renaissance Papers 2015* (2016): 1–12.

8 I discuss their relationship extensively in my *King James and Letters of Homoerotic Desire* (Iowa City: University of Iowa Press, 1999), pp. 32–64.

9 Bergeron, *King James and Letters*, p. 51.

10 Quoted in Bergeron, *King James and Letters*, p. 63, from an account in David Calderwood's *The History of the Kirk of Scotland*, ed Thomas Thomson (Edinburgh: Wodrow Society, 1845), 8:243.

11 Qtd in Bergeron, *King James and Letters*, p. 63.

12 See my discussion of the poem in *King James and Letters*, pp. 53–64.

13 I quote from the edition of the poem included in my *King James and Letters*, pp. 220–9.

14 John Burel, [*Poems*] (Edinburgh, 1596?), sig. A2v.

15 *Calendar of State Papers Relating to Scotland and Mary, Queen of Scots 1547–1603*, 13 vols (Edinburgh: HM General Register House, 1898–1969), 10: 17. Hereafter cited as *Calendar of Scottish Papers*.

16 *Calendar of Scottish Papers*, 11: 310.

17 *Calendar of Scottish Papers*, 6: 552.

18 *Calendar of Scottish Papers*, 7: 272.

19 *The Letters of King James VI and I*, ed. G. P. V. Akrigg (Berkeley: University of California Press, 1964), p. 98. All quotations from James's letters come from this edition.

20 *The Warrender Papers*, ed. Annie I. Cameron (Edinburgh: Scottish History Society, 1932), 2: 111.

21 *The Warrender Papers*, 2: 112.

22 From the account in John Nichols, *Progresses of Queen Elizabeth* (London, 1823), 3: 355. All quotations regarding the baptism come from this edition by Nichols. The first publication came in 1603 in London.

23 For additional information about the coronation and pageant and for the Danish account of these events see David Stevenson, *Scotland's Last Royal Wedding* (Edinburgh: John Donald, 1997).

24 For an excellent account of this Gowrie Plot, see Alan Stewart, *The Cradle King* (New York: St Martin's, 2003), pp. 150–9. *Calendar of Scottish Papers* has some wonderful, slightly contradictory reports; see 13: 678–89.

25 John Spottiswoode, *History of the Church of Scotland*, 3 vols (Edinburgh: Oliver & Boyd, 1851), 3: 100.

26 *Calendar of Scottish Papers*, 13: 769.

27 Spottiswoode, *History of the Church*, 3: 101.

28 *Letters and Papers Relating to Patrick Master of Gray* (Edinburgh, 1835), pp. 192–3.

29 Spottiswoode, *History of the Church*, 3, 101.

30 *Calendar of Scottish Papers*, 13: 904.

31 *Letters of King James*, ed Akrigg, p. 166.

32 A slightly modernised version of the letter found in the *Third Report of the Royal Commission on Historical Manuscripts* (London, 1872), p. 396.

33 For an excellent discussion of the whole period of transition from Scotland to England, see Leanda de Lisle, *After Elizabeth: The Rise of James of Scotland* (New York: Ballantine, 2005). On p. xxvi, she

includes a helpful map of the actual route that James travelled with its sixteen-plus stops.

34 Quoted in my *Royal Family, Royal Lovers: King James of England and Scotland* (Columbia: University of Missouri Press, 1991), p. 68.

35 For a thorough discussion of this new development, see Neil Cuddy, 'The Revival of the Entourage: The Bedchamber of James I, 1603–1625', in *The English Court from the Wars of the Roses to the Civil War*, ed. David Starkey (London: Longman, 1987), pp. 173–225.

36 See the discussion in my *Royal Family, Royal Lovers: King James of England and Scotland*, pp. 51ff.

37 David Calderwood, *The History of the Kirk of Scotland*, 8 vols, ed. Thomas Thomson (Edinburgh: Wodrow Society, 1845), 6: 231.

38 *Report of the Manuscripts of the Earl of Mar and Kellie* (London: HMSO, 1904), 1: 51.

39 Calderwood, *History of the Kirk*, 6: 231.

40 For a full discussion of this pageant, see my *English Civic Pageantry 1558–1642*, revised edition (Tempe: Arizona State University Medieval and Renaissance Studies, 2003).

41 For a discussion of the links between the pageant and the speech, see my 'King James's Civic Pageant and Parliamentary Speech in March 1604', *Albion* 34 (2002): 213–31.

42 Simon Thurley, *Whitehall Palace: An Architectural History of the Royal Apartments, 1240–1698* (New Haven: Yale University Press, 1999).

43 George Marcelline, *The Triumph of King James the First* (London, 1610), p. 75.

44 *Calendar of State Papers Venetian, 1603–1607*, ed. Horatio F. Brown (London, 1900), 10: 56.

45 *Calendar of State Papers Venetian*, 10: 72.

46 *Calendar of State Papers Venetian*, 10: 106.

47 The suggestion made by Leeds Barroll in his *Anna of Denmark, Queen of England: A Cultural Biography* (Philadelphia: University of Pennsylvania Press, 2001), p. 83. Barroll calls Lennox the *rector chori* for the masque (p. 81). Barroll's incisive analysis of this masque, based on Carleton's letter, occurs on pp. 81–9.

48 *Dudley Carleton to John Chamberlain 1603–1624: Jacobean Letters*, ed. Maurice Lee, Jr (New Brunswick: Rutgers University Press, 1972), p. 53. All quotations from this letter are from this edition.

49 Barroll, *Anna of Denmark*, p. 81.

50 *Dudley Carleton to John Chamberlain*, p. 54.

51 *Dudley Carleton to John Chamberlain*, p. 55.

52 Barroll, *Anna of Denmark*, p. 37. Barroll adds: 'I shall be arguing that patronage of the arts during the first decade of James's reign flour-

ished first around Anna.' Barroll's is the most extensive investigation of Anne's personal cultural power.

53 *Ben Jonson: The Complete Masques*, ed Stephen Orgel (New Haven: Yale University Press, 1969), p. 98. All quotations will be from this edition.

54 *Calendar of State Papers Venetian*, 10: 383, the report of Zorzi Giustinian.

55 *Calendar of State Papers Venetian*, 10: 384.

56 E. K. Chambers, *The Elizabethan Stage*, 1: 147.

57 John Nichols, *The Progresses, Processions, and Magnificent Festivities of King James the First* (London, 1828), 2: 73.

58 The report of Edmund Howes, reproduced in Nichols, *The Progresses of James*, 2: 132.

59 Information comes from Nichols, *The Progresses of James*, 2: 136.

60 *Collections III: A Calendar of Dramatic Records in the Books of the Livery Companies of London 1485–1640*, ed. Jean Robertson and D. J. Gordon (Oxford: Malone Society, 1954), pp. 169–70. Nichols also includes a report of this entertainment in *The Progresses of James*, 2: 136–43.

61 Recent research has unearthed what may be three songs, written by Jonson for this occasion. See Gabriel Heaton and James Knowles, '"Entertainment Perfect": Ben Jonson and Corporate Hospitality', *Review of English Studies* 54 (2003): 587–600. They found the documents among the Cecil Papers at Hatfield House.

62 Nichols, *The Progresses of James*, 2: 138.

63 Chambers, *Elizabethan Stage*, 1: 146.

64 See Alan Young, *Tudor and Jacobean Tournaments* (London: George Philip, 1987), p. 41. Young includes a list of all the tournaments during this period.

65 A report from Dudley Carleton, quoted in G. P. V. Akrigg, *Jacobean Pageant, or The Court of King James I* (London: Hamish Hamilton, 1962), p. 162.

66 For a discussion of the pageant and masque, see my 'Creating Entertainments for Prince Henry's Creation (1610)', *Comparative Drama* 42 (2008–9): 433–49.

67 Edmund Howes, continuation of John Stow, *The Annales or Generall Chronicle of England* (London, 1615), p. 907.

68 An anonymous account cited in Nichols, *The Progresses of James*, 2: 361.

69 John Ford, *Honor Triumphant* (London, 1606), sig. B1.

70 Walter Quin, *Sertum Poeticum* (London, 1600), sig. F2.

71 John Davies, *Microcosmos. The Discovery of the Little World* (Oxford, 1603). I quote from the 1607 edition, p. 255.

72 Gervase Markham, *Cavalarice, or, The English Horseman* (London, 1607), sig. Xx2.

73 John May, *A Declaration of the Estate of Clothing Now Used within this Realme of England* (London, 1613), sig. A3.

74 Juan de Luna, *Arte Breve* (London, 1623).

75 Shakespeare, *Two Noble Kinsmen*, ed. Eugene M. Waith (New York: Oxford University Press, 1989), ll. 30–2. All quotations will be from this edition. For discussion, see Peter C. Herman, '"Is This Winning?": Prince Henry's Death and the Problem of Chivalry in *The Two Noble Kinsmen*', *South Atlantic Review* 62.1 (1997): 1–31.

2

Two noble kinsmen and a funeral

Sitting in a solitary chamber in the Holbein Gatehouse in early 1613, suffused with memories, the Duke of Lennox recalled the haunting words of the Third Queen in *Two Noble Kinsmen*: 'The world's a city full of straying streets, / And death's the market-place where each one meets' (1.5.15–16). As he awaited additional plans for Princess Elizabeth's wedding, Lennox allowed his mind to stray to those streets of memory that led to death's marketplace. With a pain still raw, Lennox thought of Prince Henry's death of just a few months earlier. The ferocious wind outside that lashed at his chambers in this the harshest winter of recent times coincided with sober and sombre reflections. Lennox's mind wandered back as it had many times to October 1612.

He remembered the ominous rainbow, noted by Charles Cornwallis, writing about the events of 29 October 1612: 'This evening there appeared a fatall signe about two houres or more within the night, bearing the colours and shew of a *Rainbow*, which hung directly crosse and over Saint *Jameses* House.'[1] This strange rainbow had first appeared at seven o'clock. Lennox and many others saw it and pondered its meaning as it lingered over St James's Palace where lay the critically ill Prince Henry.

Earlier on that same day, the streets of London had vibrated with thousands of spectators watching attentively and excitedly the Lord Mayor's Show that celebrated the inauguration of Sir John Swinnerton, Merchant Taylor, as the new mayor. Not even the lingering chill from yet another storm could dampen the crowd's enthusiasm. Lennox watched from a privileged place, along with other distinguished guests. The playwright Thomas Dekker, with assistance from John Heminge of the King's Men, wrote this civic pageant, which he entitled *Troia-Nova Triumphans*, capturing

London's supposed link to ancient Troy. He filled it with drama, music, allegory, and rich spectacle. Indeed, the sponsoring guild spent extravagantly, anticipating the appearance of two noble kinsmen.

The Merchant Taylors expected Prince Henry and his future brother-in-law, Frederick V, Count Palatine of the Rhine and Elector of the Holy Roman Empire. Frederick had arrived in England on 16 October, eager to become the husband of King James's only daughter, Elizabeth. After a period of intense negotiation, James had finally settled on Frederick as being suitable, to the chagrin of Queen Anne but with the support of Henry, who longed for such a stalwart Protestant to marry into the Stuart royal family. In the negotiations, James offered a dowry of £40,000, and an allowance; the Germans responded with an offer of £1,500 per annum for Elizabeth, and provided for the princess's retinue of thirty-six men and thirteen women. 'If she were widowed, Elizabeth would receive an income of £10,000 and be able to live where she chose.'[2] Although a somewhat minor German prince, Frederick found favour in James's eyes as the king envisioned some kind of pan-Protestant union across Europe. Frederick, not incidentally, offered attractive monetary terms.

In order for Frederick to be received correctly and with good taste, James entrusted the Duke of Lennox with the task, and he set out to retrieve the prince. As the Venetian Ambassador Antonio Foscarini reports: 'The Duke of Lennox and other nobles have left in haste to receive him.'[3] The ambassador adds: 'The Elector will be received in great state. The arrival of the Palatine with so large a following, the fêtes which are being prepared, the expenditure in dresses and liveries, have attracted an extraordinary number of people to London and caused a great rise in the price of everything.' Lennox met Frederick at Gravesend and greeted him in French, the Duke's native tongue and one that the prince had learned (he did not know English). The young prince, like Elizabeth born in 1596, understood Lennox's importance and accepted this kingly gesture of confidence and compliment. From Gravesend, Lennox led the prince and his entourage towards London in a flotilla of at least 150 boats. According to the Venetian Ambassador, this group passed straight to Whitehall, and 'was saluted on [its] way by upwards of two hundred guns from the Tower of London, as well as by an infinity of salutes from the shipping, with which the river was full'.[4] The only disadvantage was the weather: 'the coldest day that came this winter, and yet he [prince] caried himself with … assurance'.[5]

When Frederick arrived at Whitehall, he entered the great hall and found the king and queen seated on a dais, surrounded by Prince Henry, Prince Charles, and Princess Elizabeth, the hall itself 'thronged with Lords and Ladies in the richest robes and laden with jewels'.[6] The ambassador adds: 'The Duke of Lennox walked with Prince Henry and all preceded the Palatine', who made his reverences to the King, who then embraced him: 'the King was extremely pleased … and tenderly embracing him he said he took him for his son'. Frederick next greeted the queen, 'who looked favourably on him'; then the prince approached Elizabeth 'and boldly kissed her'; she blushed at his assertiveness. In the days to come, Frederick focused his attention almost exclusively on the princess, ignoring opportunities for running at the ring, playing tennis, or riding with Prince Henry.

Foscarini, the Ambassador, notes Frederick's daily visits to Elizabeth 'with whom he is now very familiar' (444). He describes the prince as being 'very handsome [and] of pleasant speech'. Foscarini also notes Frederick's extravagant clothing and entourage: 'He changes his dress every day, and one is richer than another. All the gentlemen he has with him are covered with gold, chains and jewels. He has fifty pages and grooms in crimson velvet liveries embroidered with gold, silver-brocade doublets.' In a fashion-conscious court, Frederick's appearance held much appeal. These two young people rivalled one another in dazzling array and satisfied everyone with their growing and comfortable intimacy. Chamberlain reports that Elizabeth invited Frederick to a supper and a play, 'and they meet often at meales without curiositie of bidding'.[7]

In a clear sign of the conjunction of Holbein Gatehouse and Blackfriars gatehouse, the Merchant Taylors invited Frederick and Prince Henry to the Lord Mayor's feast, and 'great preparation was made for them'.[8] Chamberlain writes: 'the Count Palatine and his companie after they had seene the shew in Cheapside (which was somwhat extraordinarie with fowre or five pageants and other devises) went to Guild-hall, and were there plentifully feasted and welcomed by Sir John Swinerton the new Lord Mayor'. The Duke of Lennox accompanied Frederick, along with other earls and barons, but not the ill Prince Henry.[9] The guild and the City of

London presented Frederick a fair standing cup, a basin and ewer, with two large livery pots, valued at £500. Howes observes that the pots had the term *Civitatis London* engraved on them.[10] The merchants had sent the prince some wine a few days earlier. Clearly the city revelled in his presence.

Their 'great preparation' for the two noble kinsmen included Dekker's pageant, as Chamberlain's report makes clear. Dekker writes in the opening lines of his text: '*Tryumphes*, are the most choice and daintiest fruit that spring from *Peace* and *Abundance*; *Love* begets them; and *Much Cost* brings them forth.'[11] The entertainment will taste 'sweetly' for everyone, including 'the *Noblest strangers*', meaning Frederick, Lennox, and others in his party. Dekker adds: 'none but our *Soveraigne King* can bestow *Royall welcomes*; yet shall it be a *Memoriall* of an *Exemplary Love* and *Duty* (in those who are at the *Cost* of these *Triumphs*) to have *added* some *Heightning* more to them then was intended at first, of purpose to do honor to their Prince and Countrey' (230–1). *Troia-Nova Triumphans* honours not only the new mayor this day but also the visiting prince – hence the unusual expenditures. In the swirl of action and spectacle Dekker produced a show that rivalled royal welcomes, therefore worthy for two princes.

The procession of the mayor arrived at one of the allegorical pageant devices that included the 'house of Fame' where she sits 'crowned in rich attire, a Trumpet in her hand' and several places reserved for former kings and princes who have been free of the Merchant Taylors. 'A particular roome', Dekker writes, 'being reserved for one that represents the person of *Henry* the now Prince of *Wales*' (240). (Henry had gained the freedom of this guild in 1607.) In a lengthy speech Fame addresses the new mayor, reminding him that 'In this Court of *Fame* / None else but *Vertue* can enrole thy *Name*'. And Fame calls attention to Henry: 'A Sprig of which Branch (Highest now but One) / Is *Henry Prince of Wales*, followed by none: / Who of this *Brotherhood*, last and best steps forth' (241). A particular room in the House of Fame contained a special place for Prince Henry, who, they expected, would be present and see this device, lending resonance for the concept of virtue's triumph. But his absence underscored the terrible fact that he remained in another particular room, one in St James's Palace where he lay gravely ill. No House of Fame on 29 October 1612; rather, an ominous rainbow arched over his residence.

Lennox remembered vividly the events of Henry's life that led up to Dekker's Lord Mayor's Show and its House of Fame with a vacant room. The Duke had, of course, been much involved in the prince's baptism in 1594 in Scotland. Lennox had also served as the king's personal representative in the tense negotiations that allowed Queen Anne to lay claim to her son and secure his presence in 1603; and he in fact travelled with mother and son to England, where they joined King James. Lennox had watched Henry develop into a vigorous young man, readily preparing himself for the role of heir apparent, thereby supplanting Lennox's own former position in royal succession. The duke observed approvingly as Henry established his own household at St James's Palace, a household noted for its orderliness, sobriety, and discipline – qualities mainly lacking in the king's own household. And Lennox actively participated in the prince's *annus mirabilis* (1610); this year included the formal investiture as Prince of Wales, what commentators at the time referred to as the prince's 'creation'.

But first, English culture had to recuperate and even create the narrative and 'liturgy' of the actual investiture ceremony. No royal son had been created Prince of Wales since 1504, when Henry, son of Henry VII and later himself Henry VIII, at the age of thirteen experienced the official installation. While authorities began extensive research, Robert Cecil began the necessary quest for funding, first approaching Parliament in February 1610 and then later in April gratefully accepting the loan of £100,000 from the City of London, underscoring the reciprocal relationship of Whitehall and Guildhall.[12] A view of the year in terms of drama, experienced by Lennox and many others, shows it as bookended by two masque or tilting entertainments written by Ben Jonson: *Speeches at Prince Henry's Barriers* (6 January 1610) and *Oberon* (1 January 1611). These entertainments, full of romance elements, celebrate Henry in idealising, myth-making ways. They do not, however, specifically or immediately connect to the investiture, which takes place in mid-year, but they underscore several themes that run through the celebrations that acknowledge Henry's new status.

Prince Henry's challenge in late December preceded the actual Barriers on 6 January. Under the name of Meliadus of Arthurian legend, presumed lover of the Lady of the Lake, Henry issued the challenge to all the knights of Great Britain, 'accompanied with Drummes and Trumpets in the Chamber of presence, before the

King and Queene, and in presence of the whole Court'.[13] In a speech to the king, Henry hoped to present to the king 'the first fruits of his chivalry at his Majestyes feete'.[14] A short speech to the queen followed as the prince laid out the procedures of the barriers. Thereafter followed days of intense preparation as time drew nigh for Henry to make his first public mark as a chivalrous knight, full of valour and strength. Not surprisingly, he chose the Duke of Lennox as one of his six 'assistants' to ward off the fifty-six defendants. With the others, Lennox fulfilled the report of Marc Antonio Correr, the Venetian Ambassador: 'All this week the Prince's six defenders have kept open table in the Prince's apartments; some of my suite have been invited more than once.'[15] Such hospitality graciously paved the way for the Barriers on the day of Epiphany.

Howes sets the stage for the event: 'The sixt of January, at the pallace of white-hall in the presence of the Kinge and Queene, and the Ambassadours of Spayne, and Venice, and of al the peeres & great Ladies of the land with a multitude of others: in the great banqueting-house all these were assembled, at the upper end wherof was the kinges Chaire of State'[16] (see Figure 4). From a sumptuous pavilion, Henry and his assistants descended into the middle of the room, and 'there the Prince performed his first feats of armes'. Every challenger fought with eight defendants 'two several combats at two several weapons, viz. at push of the pike, and with single sword'. They performed this across a bar set in the middle of the room. According to Howes, 'These feates of armes with their triumphal shewes began before ten a clocke at night, and continewed there untill the next morning'. Henry, 'to the great wonder of all the beholders, did admirably fight his part, giving and receiving that night 32. pushes of Pikes, and above 360. of strookes with swordes, which is scarce credible in so young yeares, enough to assure the world that great Britaines brave Henry aspired to immortality'.[17]

Before the formal fighting began, Lennox and the prince participated and enjoyed the scenes and speeches devised by Ben Jonson and Inigo Jones, England's greatest architect and designer. Surviving drawings show Jones's sketch for the House of Chivalry and St George's Portico, as well as the costume for Merlin.[18] Jonson established an Arthurian setting as the entertainment began with the speech of the Lady of the Lake, situated near Merlin's tomb. She praises the kingdom's renewal under King James, who has laid claim to Arthur's seat. Arthur, celebrating 'the union of this isle',

4 Engraving of Prince Henry from Michael Drayton's *Poly-Olbion* (1612)

appears '*as a star above*'.[19] He offers a shield 'wherein is wrought / The truth that he [Henry] must follow' (146). The Lady of the Lake summons Merlin, who arises out of his tomb and calls forth 'fair Meliadus'; at which point '*Meliadus and his six assistants here discovered*' (147), residing in St George's Portico. Merlin redefines 'romance' so that it does not confine itself to antique knights who rescue ladies and slay giants. Rather, Henry must accept the task of governing and giving laws. After reviewing the history of many of Henry's predecessors, Merlin closes by commenting on the uniting of the kingdoms. Immediately before the 'Barriers', Chivalry appears, claiming that Henry has revived his spirit and orders that the 'rusty doors' be thrown open: 'and from the shores / Of all the world come knighthood like a flood / Upon these lists to make the field here good' (157). After the jousting, Merlin again speaks, prophesying Henry's bright fortune, 'Which shall rise brighter every hour with time' (158). Among the spectators stood Phineas Pett, Master Shipwright, and friend of Henry's, who reported: 'The supper was not ended till after ten at night, from whence they went to the Play, and, that ended, returned again to a set banquet, … and it was 3 of the clock in the morning before all was finished.'[20] The long night had ended on a triumphant note. Surrounded by Lennox and others and on full display to the court and ambassadors, Henry took a giant step in establishing his status as a true knight, wrapped in Arthurian mystique and confirmed by his physical strength in the barriers. Chivalry welcomes him, this prince who restores the decrepit House of Chivalry.

Not to be outdone by such festivity, the citizens of Chester presented a pageant in Henry's honour as Earl of Chester on St George's day, 23 April. Richard Davies and Robert Amerie collaborated in designing this street entertainment, which had a processional form as devices moved through the city. The pageant contained multiple speeches, including the dramatic dialogue between Envy and Love. The compilers of the text enumerate some twenty 'particulars' of the triumph, different riders on horseback representing mainly allegorical figures, St George, and Mercury, all appropriately costumed. Fame, for example, with a trumpet in her hand, speaks in praise of the day; a song follows urging the descent of Mercury, who obliges by 'descending from heaven in a cloud, artificially Winged, a wheele of fire burning very cunningly, with other Fire-workes'.[21] Mercury insists that he has descended from the throne of the immortal gods in response to their commandment to honour Prince Henry. Peace offers promises: 'I'le send pale Envie downe to hell with speed, / Where she upon her Snakes shall onely feed' (C2v). This cues the gruesome appearance of Envy, 'with a Wreath of Snakes about her head; another in her hand, her face and armes besmeard with blood' (A4v). Love, however, counters Envy and engages in emphatic exchanges with her; she eventually exits after the scathing words of Joy, who joins in this battle against Envy. The dramatic centre of this civic pageant in a provincial city focused on the ageless struggle between virtue and vice; the victory of the virtuous forces cleanses the city and creates a new, harmonious place for the prince, possibly a new St George. No evidence exists, however, to document Henry's actual presence in Chester, but he would soon have had access to the printed text of this pageant.

The loan from the City of London in late April, secured by Cecil, accelerated the pace for the official investiture of Henry. But two other events determined the timing: the ongoing effects of the plague, which had begun in July 1608 and did not end until November 1610, resulting in part in the closing of the public theatres; and the startling and frightening assassination of Henry IV of France on 4 May 1610. Prince Henry had maintained a close alliance with King Henry; indeed, he thought of the French king as another 'father'. The news of this murder devastated the young prince. The security and safety of the prince thus emerged as an important consideration for the public nature of the 'creation' festivities. Therefore, court authorities settled for a late-May beginning of the events, opting to have the main public pageant on the river Thames, possibly for security reasons. But perhaps something else lay behind not having an extravagant pageant through London's streets, as the Venetian Ambassador implies: 'The King would not allow him on this occasion, nor yet on his going to Parliament, to be seen on horseback. The reason is the question of expense or, as some say, because they did not desire to exalt him too high.'[22] This same ambassador, Marc Antonio Correr, just a few days after the festivities, added: 'It seems that the King has some reasonable jealousy of the rising sun; and indeed the vivacity of the Prince grows apace, and every day he gives proof of wisdom and lofty thoughts far in advance of his years.'[23] If James felt threatened by Henry's allure, he gave no public evidence. Thus, with considerable haste the City of London began to make its plans for a river pageant; and it hired Anthony Munday, already known as a writer of Lord Mayor's Shows, to put together a suitable entertainment. It took place on 31 May, the first of multiple events that unfolded over the next several days, including the formal investiture on 4 June.

Prince Henry, who had purposely gone to Richmond the day before, made his way from there downriver first to Chelsea and then to Whitehall, there to be received by his royal parents, Charles, Elizabeth, and Lennox. Munday writes that by eight in the morning of the 31st, 'all the worshipfull Companies of the Cittie, were readie in their Bardges upon the water'.[24] Gloriously and festively decorated, these boats moved along the river 'with such a chearefull noyse of Hermonie, and so goodlie a shewe in order and equipage, as made the beholders and hearers not meanely [moderately] delighted' (39). It seemed, Munday insists, that Neptune presided over the occasion and granted his favour to this pageant. Charles Cornwallis reports: Henry moved along the river, encountering the barges 'with all the joy, love, and kindnesse possible, to the wonder of the World; all eyes were bent towards so joyfull and desired a sight'.[25]

Beyond such generalised spectacle, Munday arranged for two speakers: Corinea, Queen of Cornwall, on the back of a 'huge Whale', and Amphion, representing Wales, on a dolphin. Neptune's good will presumably prompted these figures and the sea creatures to appear on the Thames. At Chelsea, Corinea greeted and spoke to the prince. Appropriately costumed, she first identified herself as 'Queene to Brutes noble Companion *Corineus*' (41), thus linking this occasion to the long-standing Trojan myth of British history. Corinea adds that she comes 'in honor of this generall rejoicing day, and to expresse the endeared affections of Londons Lord Maior, his Bretheren the Aldermen, and all these worthie Cittizens'. At Whitehall, the seat of royal power, Henry arrived, there to be greeted by Amphion, who insists that he represents Wales. He joins Corinea in expressing the devotion of London's citizens. With great noise, the river pageant ended. Henry had thus travelled from Richmond, a place long identified with his ancestor Henry VII, met with ancient figures, and landed safely at Whitehall, with the full blessing of the City's authorities. Their commitment to this event can be underscored by Munday's choice of the renowned actor Richard Burbage to present Amphion and John Rice to represent Corinea; both served as members of the King's Men, Shakespeare's acting company.

Sunday 3 June focused on worship and the elaborate ceremony of the installation of Knights of the Bath. Monday 4 June featured the actual investiture ceremony in the presence of assembled members of Parliament, nobility, and royalty in the Court of Requests. A contemporary letter describes the scene in which King James arrived in his royal robes; then 'After a good space of time the Prince entred at the lower end of the Great-chamber, having a surcote of purple velvet close girt unto him'.[26] Henry approached his father, who delivered the crown, staff, and patent 'with the King's own hands. Which done, and the Prince with a low reverence offering to depart, the King stept to him, and, as it were by the way of welcome into that degree of greatness, took him by the hand, and then kissed him.' Henry received the patent that created him Prince of Wales, which had been read aloud by Cecil. Munday reports that Henry 'had his creation ... with all the due ceremonies and vestures therto belonging, his Majestie himselfe girding on his Sworde' (43).[27] On Tuesday night 5 June royalty and aristocrats gathered in the Banqueting House in Whitehall to watch and participate in Samuel Daniel's masque, *Tethys' Festival*, an opulent court entertainment that involved Inigo Jones's artistry as well.

Daniel represented several rivers, beginning with Tethys, Queen of the Ocean and wife of Neptune, attended by thirteen nymphs of the rivers. Aristocratic and royal women impersonated the rivers, such as Queen Anne as Tethys, Princess Elizabeth as Thames, and Lady Arbella Stuart as the river Trent. These women as rivers controlled the masque, presiding and participating. Elizabeth as Thames may have reminded spectators of the recent river pageant. Prince Henry and King James served as the principal spectators, surrounded by a court of noblemen and women, including Lennox. The enclosed space of the court unleashed Jones's creative imagination, offering a fair return on his payment of £400. The opening scene, for example, contains an elaborate painted device of Neptune and Nereus. Daniel writes: 'On the Travers which served as a curtaine for the first Scene, was figured a darke cloude, interior with certaine sparkling stares, which, at the sound of a loud musick, being instantly drawne, the scene was discovered'.[28] This merely began the elaborate and convoluted display that Daniel and Jones arranged: painted scenes, replicas of classical figures or gods, devices inside of devices. This first scene itself represented a port or haven, by which Daniel had in mind Milford Haven in Wales, crucial to Henry VII's success.

Prince Charles, dressed 'in a short robe of greene satin imbrodered with golden flowers' (311), appeared as Zephyrus, celebrated in song. This song also refers to 'Meliades', the name for Henry in Jonson's *Barriers* six months earlier. On behalf of Tethys, a Triton gives to Henry a scarf, 'the zone of Love and Amitie, / T'ingird the "same" and a sword' (314). Henry had with him a sword during the investiture ceremony, and the masque recalls that detail. The ladies, as the rivers, 'descended out of their Cavernes one after another, and so marched up with winding meanders like a River, till they came to the Tree of victory; which was a Bay erected at the right side of the state' (319). Soft music from twelve lutes and twelve voices identified this tree as Apollo's Tree, the tree of victory; it celebrates the 'Ocean King', that is, King James. Additional spectacular scenes, paintings, and dancing followed, closing finally with Zephyrus, who conducted the queen and her ladies out of a 'most pleasant and artificiall Grove … from thence they march up to the King conducted by the Duke of Yorke' (323). This dazzling masque, commissioned by Queen Anne, celebrates Henry's life and looks forward to great achievements from him, dramatically realised in the court's private space, even as the open-air river pageant gave voice to Henry's connection to gods and goddesses, summoned by the good will of London's guilds and citizens. One last gasp of entertainment on Wednesday: an afternoon of tilting, in which Lennox participated, and an evening of a sea battle on the Thames, closing with blazing fireworks. Thus Henry's creation as Prince of Wales ended with a bang, a rousing close to this chapter and keen anticipation for the future. All the world seemed to open ever more brightly for his future. Lennox certainly thought so.

Already fêted by city and court, Prince Henry commissioned his own masque and employed Jonson and Jones to produce *Oberon, the Fairy Prince,* performed on the first day of 1611; the euphoria of six months earlier continued. The court spared no expense, and the elaborate quality of the performance gains confirmation both from court records and from the marvellous drawings by Jones that survive.[29] Lennox, among many others, gathered at the Whitehall Banqueting House, as they had twice in the past year for entertainments that honoured the prince. Members of the King's Men participated in performing the antimasque. Out of the hall's stillness a scene opened displaying a rock and wilderness, from which emerged a Satyr; and just as suddenly ten more Satyrs appeared, '*running forth severally from divers parts of the rock, leaping and making antic action and gestures'* (160), according to Jonson. When 3rd Satyr asks, 'Shall we see young Oberon?', Silenus responds: 'Satyrs, he doth fill with grace / Every season, every place; / Beauty dwells but [only] in his face: / He's the height of all our race' (161). The conversation continued in this vein until another scene opened, revealing a *'glorious palace whose gates and walls were transparent'* (163). Silenus greets the two Sylvans who lie before the gates; he speaks of the 'Fairly Land' in which Oberon and his Knights live.

Out of songs and antic dancing, the scene dissolved into a stunning spectacle: *'Then the whole palace opened, and the nation of fays were discovered, some with instruments, some bearing lights, others singing; and within, afar off in perspective, the knights masquers sitting in their several sieges* [seats]' (167). This moment afforded the first glimpse of Oberon, danced by Prince Henry: *'At the further end of all, Oberon, in a chariot, which to a loud triumphant music began to move forward, drawn by two white bears, and on either side guarded by three sylvans'* (167–8). It had taken over two hundred lines of speech and song to get to this moment; but everyone in the hall rejoiced to see Oberon in splendid costume, looking like an antique Roman, moving through the hall in a chariot drawn by white bears. Beauty resided in his face and in this glorious scene. The satyrs leapt for joy; and then the 'foremost Sylvan' began to speak:

This is a night of greatness and of state,
Not to be mixed with light and skipping sport;
A night of homage to the British court,
And ceremony due to Arthur's chair,
From our bright master, Oberon the fair.

(168–9)

Oberon surrounds himself with his knights as Silenus praises them and the royal family. Then *'Oberon and the knights dance out the first masque dance'* (171). After several more dances and songs, Phosphorus, the day star, appeared and summoned the dancers to depart. *'After this they danced their last dance into the work; and with a full song, the star vanished, and the whole machine closed'* (173). This insubstantial pageant faded; but memories continued to resonate about this prince, 'Oberon the fair', who brings credit and emerging renown to the royal family and honour to Arthur's chair.

This vivid image lingered in Lennox's thoughts, seeming all the brighter in the darker days to come when a shining Oberon would be no more. The brightness of 1610–11 cannot be doubted as Henry seemed indeed to 'fill with grace / Every season, every place'.

The eighteen-year-old Henry cut a rather dashing and imposing figure (see Figure 4). He exuded confidence and engendered hope. One contemporary described him: 'He was of a comely tall middle stature, about five foot and eight inches high, of a strong, straight well-made body (as if Nature in him had shewed all her cunning) with somewhat broad shoulders, and a small waste, of an amiable Majesticke Countenance, his haire of an Aborne [auburn] collour, long faced, and broad forehead, a piercing grave eye, a most gracious smile, with a terrible frowne.'[30] Daniel Price, who entered Henry's service in 1608 as one of his chaplains, and who in 1610 preached the sermon on the day before the prince's investiture as Prince of Wales, refers to the prince's 'piercing *eye*, gratious *smile*, grave *frowne*, and divine *face* composed of *modesty* and *majestie*'.[31] Price also comments on Henry as being slow to anger, quick to apprehend, and eager to pardon. Francis Bacon writes succinctly: 'In body he was strong and erect, of middle height, his limbs gracefully put together, his gait kinglike, his face long and somewhat lean, his habit rather full, his countenance composed, and the motion of his eyes rather sedate than powerful. His forehead bore marks of severity, his mouth had a touch of pride.'[32] Bacon adds that 'both arms and military men were in honour with him; nor was he himself without something of a warlike spirit' (328). And yet, something slightly inscrutable lingered in Henry; or, as Bacon says, 'Many points there were indeed in this prince's nature which were obscure, and could not be discovered by any man's judgment' (329). Henry's reticence, in contrast to his father's garrulous qualities, and modesty created mystery.

As Lennox knew first-hand, the prince was a dutiful son, obedient to his father and attentive to his mother. Since he was but 'two yeares old, he both knew and respected the King his father above all others, and never was wearie to be in his companie: albeit his Majestie with the tokens of his love to him would sometimes interlace sharpe speeches, and other demonstrations of fatherlie severitie'.[33] This same respect he showed to his mother, even when she was busy and unable to see him; he waited patiently for her attention. Henry showed affection and concern for Prince Charles.

But, as Bacon notes, 'his sister he especially loved; whom also he resembled in countenance, as far as a man's face can be compared with that of a very beautiful girl'.[34] Their surviving letters reveal a close relationship between brother and sister. When Elizabeth finally arrived at court in 1608 from the Harrington household in Warwickshire, their love for each other deepened; and Henry exhibited great care for her well-being, writing to her at one point: 'There is nothing I wish more then that we might be in one companie.'[35]

A competent student, especially under the tutelage of Adam Newton, Henry did not incline toward scholarship; in this he resembled Lennox. Nicolo Molin, the Venetian Ambassador in 1607, posted an astute analysis of the royal family, including a portrait of the young Henry in which he notes the prince's response to studying. Molin writes: 'He studies, but not with much delight, and chiefly under his father's spur, not of his own desire, and for this he is often admonished and set down.'[36] In fact, the king admonished him on one particular occasion by suggesting that the crown might be left to Prince Charles, the earnest and careful student. Henry's tutor continued in this vein, prompting the prince to cry out: '"I know what becomes a Prince. It is not necessary for me to be a professor, but a soldier and a man of the world. If my brother is as learned as they say, we'll make him Archbishop of Canterbury".'[37] Such a response did not amuse James.

But Henry did exhibit an interest in history. Cornwallis states that he 'read Histories, the knowledge of things passed conducing much to resolution in things present, and to prevention of those to come'.[38] In the epistle dedicatory to his *The Lives of the III. Normans*, published in 1613, John Hayward records an extraordinary conversation with Prince Henry about history in late summer 1612. In a second interview, which took place at St James's Palace, Henry began with a complaint about the quality of the published histories of England compared to other nations: 'the English Nation, which is inferiour to none in Honourable actions, should be surpassed by all, in leaving the memorie of them to posteritie'.[39] Hayward acknowledged that the subject has been 'so soiled heretofore by some unworthie writers' (A2v). To this Henry responded fully:

> And is not this (said he) an errour in us, to permite every man to be a writer of Historie? Is it not an errour to be so curious in other matters, and so carelesse in this? We make choise of the most skilfull

> workmen to draw or carve the portraiture of our faces, and shall
> every artlesse Pensell delineate the disposition of our minds? ... and
> shall our conditions be described by every bungling hand? ... Shall
> our Honour be basely buried in the drosse of rude and absurd writ-
> ings? (A2v)

Despite the attention given to erecting monuments, the greatest monument to the past, Henry insisted, can be found in that which 'is framed by a fortunate penne'.

The prince further explained this focus on history as deriving from an interest in his ancestors: 'he desired nothing more then [than] to know the actions of his Ancestours; because hee did so farre esteeme his descent from them, as he approached neere them in honourable endeavours' (A3). 'Hereupon', Hayward writes, 'beautifying his face with a sober smile, he desired mee, that against his returne from the progresse then at hand, I would perfect some-what of both sorts for him, which he promised amply to requite'. Hayward's history of the Norman kings became the finished product of this exceptional conversation, and Hayward also pre-sented a version of Queen Elizabeth's history when Henry returned from the progress. John Holles, of the prince's household, reports that Henry 'stipended Doctor Heyward at 200l. per annum to write the universal history of this kingdom'.[40] The prince's curiosity and genuine interest come through readily in the discussion with Hayward: Henry manifested more than some passing knowledge about writing history.

Henry obviously led the active life expected of and desired by him. 'Hee used in a manner daily to ride and manage great horses, with which hee had his stables most excellently furnished, oftimes to runne at the Ring and sometimes at Tilt', becoming in these activ-ities 'second to no Prince in Christendome, and to many that prac-ticed with him much superiour'.[41] His performance at the *Barriers* in 1610 certainly bears out this assessment. 'His other exercises were dancing, leaping, and in times of yeare fit for it learning to swimme, at sometimes walking fast and farre' (16). Henry became devoted to playing tennis, in which he did not observe his usual moderation, sometimes playing three and four hours at a stretch. Indeed, praise of Henry as a warrior governs a number of contem-porary accounts. George Marcelline, for example, writing in 1610, says boldly: 'This young Prince is a warrior already, both in gesture and countenance, so that in looking on him, he seemeth unto us, that in him we do yet see *Ajax* before *Troy*, crowding among the armed Troops, calling unto them, that he may joyne body to body with *Hector*.'[42] Marcelline speaks darkly of Henry's waiting for the right opportunity to spring into action. Many people anticipated and desired the prince's military prowess, which they saw in contrast to James's pacifist policies.

But the prince also supported the arts generously, doubtless inspired by the example of his mother. Henry Peacham acknowledges in the dedication to his 1612 emblem book, *Minerva Britanna*, the prince's patronage: 'Having by more then ordinarie signes, tasted heeretofore of your gratious favour ... I am emboldened once againe, to offer up at the Altar of your gratious acceptance these mine *Emblemes*.'[43] Henry also served as patron to George Chapman, Ben Jonson, Michael Drayton, and Inigo Jones, among others. Like Lennox, Henry had numerous books dedicated to him.

Jonson dedicated *The Masque of Queens* (1609) to the prince, underscoring the playwright's connections to the court. In a handwritten statement in the British Library presentation copy, Jonson first offers the text to Queen Anne, 'her Sacred Majesty'.[44] Jonson writes: 'I chose him [Henry] that is next your sacred person, and might the worthiest of mankind give it proper and natural defence' (302). In the epistle dedicatory to Henry, Jonson makes clear that the prince has asked him to provide annotations to the holograph copy of the text, which the poet readily did, giving him a chance to demonstrate his scholarship. Not surprisingly, the dedication begins with praise of Henry: 'When it hath been my happiness ... but to see your face, and, as passing to consider you, I have with as much joy as I am now far from flattery in professing it, called to mind the doctrine of some great inquisitors in nature who hold every royal and heroic form to partake and draw much to it of the heavenly virtue' (303). In Jonson's view, Henry was both 'born a Prince' and 'became' a prince. Jonson makes clear a sign of the prince's special importance: 'Amongst the rest, your favour to letters and these gentler studies that go under the title of humanity is not the least honour of your wreath' (304). Jonson continues: 'it is now my minute [appropriate time] to thank your Highness, who not only honour her [Poetry] with your ear, but are curious to examine her with your eye, and inquire into her beauties and strengths' (304). The playwright thus provides great praise for Henry's involvement with the arts, and he hopes to 'write at nights the deeds of your days'.

The prince also began to build an impressive collection of paintings that eventually passed to Prince Charles. The Venetian Ambassador, Marc Antonio Correr, reported in June 1610 that the Dutch ambassadors 'before leaving presented to the Prince some very finished paintings on canvas. They were painted on purpose to adorn one wall of his gallery.'[45] Increasingly, aristocrats and other foreign ambassadors presented Henry with art works for both Richmond Palace and St James's Palace.[46]

These households Henry seemed to have managed reasonably well. Cornwallis, his Treasurer, writes: 'Plenty and magnificence were the things that in his house he especially affected, but not without such a temper as might agree with the rules of frugality and moderation; he caused to bee set downe in writing unto him the several heads of al his annuall charges, the ordinary expence of his house and his stables.'[47] Cornwallis creates the image of Henry poring over the account books. Certainly compared to the functioning of James's household, Henry's looked like the model of order. The prince excluded Catholics from his household and surrounded himself with Protestant men of action. He even severely fined those who indulged in swearing, reinforcing the moderate tone that Henry had established.

With this assessment the prince's chaplain Daniel Price concurs, noting his frugality in managing the estate.[48] Not surprisingly, Price has much to say about Henry's religious practice and devotion, which forms part of the character that the chaplain describes: 'he stood like a *Center*, unmoved. ... how hee lived without the *compasse* of an *adversarie*, his Person being as a *Saint*, his Court as a *Temple*' (4). In him, Price insists, there 'never was *divorce* between devotion and patience' (16). Even in his fourteenth year, Price reports, 'he approved himselfe to be a *religious hearer, judicious* observer, and *obsequious* obeyer of the word of his *maker*'. Henry commanded that daily prayers should be observed in his closet, and, of course, he regularly attended sermons. Such religious constancy provided him with what Price calls 'holy patience' (13) in his suffering in October 1612.

Cornwallis captures the prince's regard for the noblemen who regularly accompanied him and served him: 'Of the titular Nobility of this Kingdome upon occasion offered, he would expresse himselfe best to love and esteeme such as were most anciently descended, and most nobly and honestly disposed, when sometimes also he would not forbeare by name to particulate.'[49] Henry surely had in mind the Duke of Lennox, who had faithfully supported and nurtured him from his earliest days, even as Lennox occupied a special place in the king's confidence.

With those who worked for him Henry could be exceptionally kind; the case of Phineas Pett, the builder of a royal ship for Henry, illustrates the point. Pett had been accused of all kinds of misdeeds in his shipbuilding activities; this led to a 'trial' in 1609 with James and Henry present. The prince had great faith in Pett and made a public display of it. As Pett reported, Henry summoned him to St James's, 'where his Highness vouchsafing to lead me in his hand through the park to Whitehall, in the public view and hearing of many people there attending to see him pass to the King, ... did in such loving manner counsel me with such comfortable, wise, and grave advice touching my carriage and resolution in my trial',[50] as testified to Henry's care of Pett. The trial exonerated the shipbuilder, who later recalled his last meeting with Henry in August 1612: Henry 'gave me a farewell in these words: "Go on cheerfully" saith he "in that which I entrust you with, and let not the care for your posterity incumber you any ways, for you shall leave the care both of yourself and others to me"' (98). Moved to tears as he kissed Henry's hand, Pett 'little thought ... that had been the last time I should have seen him alive'.

In the early months of 1612, the prince engaged in several festive activities. On Shrove Tuesday, for example, he with five others 'ran a match at the ring for a supper, against the Duke of Lennox' and his supporters.[51] Henry won, 'and the Supper and Plays were made at the Marquesse of Winchester's house on the Tuesday after'. During the summer, he went on progress to, among other places, Coventry and Kenilworth Castle. He accompanied King James for part of this journey. Finally arriving at Woodstock on 26 August, he hosted a sumptuous feast for his father, mother, and sister. According to Cornwallis, Henry 'had given order to his Officers to provide a most magnifique Feast against their comming to the foresaid house; withal having ordained a great Summer-house of greene boughes to bee built in the parke wherein the great supper should bee'.[52] Cornwallis adds that the King and Queen sat at a table by themselves at the upper end of the room, 'his Highnesse with his Sister accompanied with the Lords and Ladies sitting at another Table of thirty yards long and more, by themselves, there was to bee seene one of the greatest and best ordered feasts as ever was seene' (27). Admiring the whole scene and occasion and seeing the splendour, the king 'was forced to say, that he had never seen the like before all his lifetime, and that he could never doe so much in his owne house'.[53] The royal family would have much occasion to recall this convivial moment and all the good will that prevailed as they revelled in Henry's gracious hospitality: a fitting end to summer even as an uncertain future lay ahead.

One subject of conversation that August would have been a potential marriage for Henry. Having arrived at a marriageable age, Henry endured in fact considerable speculation about his future as husband. The court pursued various candidates, especially during the 1610–12 period, including Princess Christine, the nine-year-old second daughter of Marie de Medici, and Maria, third daughter of the Duke of Savoy. About marriage Henry himself can best be described as willing but reticent, not unlike his father earlier. On the subject of marriage, Lennox could not offer much advice: he struggled in a most unpleasant marriage. Francis Bacon observes of Henry: 'For of love matters there was wonderfully little talk, considering his age: insomuch that he passed that extremely slippery time of his early manhood, in so great a fortune and in very good health, without being particularly noted for any affairs of that kind'.[54] Cornwallis reports: 'It is true, that to take a wife though hee shewed no vehement desire, yet he demonstrated a good inclination.'[55] Cornwallis adds that he had been present during several feasts hosted by the prince to which the most beautiful ladies had been invited: he 'could neither then discover by his behaviour, his eyes or his countenance, any shew of singular or especiall fancy to any, or at any other time such loosenesse either in words or action, as whereupon in justice or reason to ground any such opinion of him'.[56] On another occasion, 'Mention being made of the mariage of some of his young Gentlemen, his Highnes said, I would not be so soone maried, and yet I wish to see my Father a grandfather'.[57] In a letter to James written from Richmond on 5 October 1612, Henry wished his father to resolve the marriage issue, to determine 'my part to play, which is to be in love with any of them'.[58] If not 'vehement desire', the prince at least registered a dutiful willingness to marry – inclined but not eager.

No marriage took place; instead, an ominous rainbow hung in the dark October sky.

Shortly after the feast at Woodstock and the return from progress in late summer 1612, Henry began to show symptoms of some discomfort. Increasingly, he slept restlessly, he often felt listless and devoid of his usual energy, and occasionally he ran a fever. Just as often he would bounce back and engage in strenuous rounds of swimming and tennis. No one had any reason to be alarmed or worried about his health. By October, however, that changed, as his symptoms became more pronounced and persistent. Lennox and members of the prince's household began to notice. 'At the beginning of *October*', Cornwallis writes, 'his continuall Head-ach, Lazinesse, and indisposition increasing (which … he strove mightily to conceale) … he did lye a bed, almost every morning untill nine of the clocke, complayning of his lazinesse'.[59] Every morning he would ask the grooms of his bedchamber: 'How doe I looke this morning? and at other times the same question againe; which they, fearing no danger, to make his Highnesse laugh, would put off with one jest or other'. By mid-October his condition worsened, and, looking pale, he moved from Richmond Palace to St James's Palace. Dr Hammond, his physician, began treatment by giving him a 'softening Glister [clyster, enema], which had its owne good effects, stirring the humors' (31). No one suspected anything serious – possibly a fit of 'ague', a fever, a cold of some kind.

Henry alternated between being difficult in disposition and having a blank stare, to taking charge of matters regarding his sister's forthcoming marriage and even entertaining Frederick, Elector Palatine. On 24 October, paying no heed to his diminished health, Henry, in fact, played tennis with Frederick, 'as though his body had been of brasse'; he even played 'in his shirt, as if it had been in the heate of Summer' (33). Even so, he looked pale, and everyone noticed. He later went to bed, complaining of laziness and a headache. But on Sunday, 25 October, he emerged and readied himself to hear the sermon in his chapel, which he heard attentively, and then later went to Whitehall and heard another sermon with his father. Afterwards, he and his father dined, 'his Highnesse in outward appearance eating with a reasonable good stomack, yet looking exceeding ill and pale, with hollow ghastly dead eyes perceived of a great many' (37). By three o'clock that afternoon, Henry became violently ill and made his way back to St James's Palace and took to his bed: 'This night hee rested ill' (38). And so he would for the remainder of his days, never leaving the palace again.

On 29 October, the fifth day of Henry's confinement, Cornwallis reports: 'his Highnesse now being forced to keepe his bed continually, his head being so giddy, that he could not stand upright, his eyes also so dimme, that he could not indure the candle light' (46). And yet the doctors, who had begun to increase in number if not skill, kept hope and also greatly feared a wrong diagnosis or treatment and the consequences for them. Their treatments became more extreme, clear signs of desperation. Small wonder that the strange rainbow that appeared that evening could only be interpreted as ominous. Occasionally Henry felt good enough to put on his clothes, and he did respond to visitors. Cornwallis writes: 'the whole World did almost every houre send unto Saint *Jameses* for newes; the better sort who were admitted to visit him; or acquainted with those neere unto him, knowing the danger' (51). Among the 'better sort' the Duke of Lennox came to visit Henry and sensed the impending disaster. On Sunday 1 November, the regular course of bleeding had momentary beneficial effects; and that afternoon 'hee was visited by his Royall Father, Mother, Brother, Sister, the Palsgrave, with divers others of the Court' (53). All departed, Cornwallis says, 'reasonably cheerefull. Yet that night … hee passed unquietly'.

On Tuesday 3 November, 'he became worse then before, all his former accidents encreasing exceedingly, his boundings, being turned into Convulsions, his raving and benumming, becomming greater, the Feaver more violent' (56). Cordials and administered clysters provided temporary relief. But for the extreme pain in his head, the doctors decided to shave his hair, 'and Pigeons and cupping Glasses applyed to lessen and draw away the humour, and that superfluous blood from the Head' (57). Such treatments Henry endured with patience, but they had little positive effect. Hopes of recovery had largely disappeared by Wednesday 4 November. The various physicians, surgeons, and apothecaries decided on a radical new treatment: 'This day a Cocke was cloven by the backe, and applyed unto the soles of his feet, but in vaine; the Cordials also were redoubled in number and quantitie, but without any profit' (59). That afternoon King James came to see Henry; but, sensing the imminent danger, he left without visiting his son and gave an order that no one should see him except those who needed to tend upon him.

In desperation the doctors on 5 November doubled and tripled the cordials, opting not to bleed Henry more. Clearly the end was in sight; therefore, the Archbishop of Canterbury, George Abbot, came hurriedly and began his ministry of comfort and reassurance and prayers, even succeeding in getting Henry to repeat his confession of faith word by word after him. Finally, at last the archbishop confronted Henry frankly about his situation and sought to prepare him for death. Cornwallis reports that this day Henry in his state of confusion began 'many times [to] call upon Sir *David Murray*, Knight (the onely man in whom hee had put choise trust) by his name *David, David, David*' (67); he came immediately; but Henry could not articulate what he wanted to say. But later that same day Henry did manage to make a request of Murray 'for the burning of a number of *Letters* in a certaine cabinet in his closet, which presently after his death was done' (69).

Finally, on Friday 6 November, Henry lay between life and death, experiencing extraordinary convulsions and loss of his senses. He did rally slightly when the archbishop called upon him to acknowledge his abiding faith by raising his fingers or hands, which Henry succeeded in doing. Daniel Price reports: Henry '*lifted up* his holy *hands* united, and afterwards his *eies bent* to *heaven*, from whence not long after appeared, in his deliverance, his *salvation*'.[60] Shortly after, Cornwallis writes, the archbishop left, having 'with streames of teares, powred out at his bed side, a most exceeding powerfull passionate prayer' (73). From three o'clock that morning until Henry's death, 'there was continuall prayer in the house, and in every place where the danger was knowne'. At last, the cloudy night revealed the impending doom, as Henry surrendered life around eight o'clock that evening. The shipwright Phineas Pett had arrived shortly before Henry's death and reported: 'I came to St James about four of the clock, where I found a house turned to the very map of true sorrow, every man with the character of grief written in his dejected countenance, all places flowing with tears and bitter lamentations.'[61] Pett felt his death as a loss to all Christendom. John Hackett likened the experience to a light being extinguished so that 'a Thick Darkness, next to that of Hell, is upon our Land at this day'.[62] The corpse 'shortly after (as the Custome is) was laide along upon a Table on the floore, being the fairest, clearest, and best proportioned, without any kinde of spot or blemish', Cornwallis reports (75). But this once vibrant, active body could not fend off death. By the rivers of Thames, Trent, Avon, and Humber people sat down and wept when they remembered Oberon, the fairy prince.

On the next day, by order of King James, members of the Privy Council, including Lennox, came 'to give order for the opening of his Body' (75), which began at five o'clock that evening in the presence of all the physicians who had been involved in the prince's care, including the Elector Palatine's physician. Thus began the official autopsy, in part to determine if Henry might have had some contagious disease. Cornwallis provides all the intricate details of this analysis. In all likelihood, Henry died 'in the rage of a malicious and extraordinary burning Feaver, wherein his vitals and senses were from the beginning so over-pressed, stupefied, and amazed, chiefely the heart and head' (82) that they could not be relieved. Modern medical science suggests that Henry died of typhoid fever, thus ruling out the possibility of poison.

On Monday 9 November, the lords of the Privy Council returned to St James's Palace to offer directions about what needed to be done, starting with draping all the various chambers in black. Attendants brought in a coffin; 'Threescore and tenne Gentlemen of his Servants … being appointed night and day to attend the same, tenne at a time' (83). As the funeral day had been set for Monday 7 December, the prince's servants moved the coffin into various chambers of the palace, finally taking it to the chapel, where it lay until the funeral, placed under a canopy set with the great arms of union. Servants had disembowelled, embalmed, and enclosed Henry's body in lead. John Holles, the comptroller of the prince's household, reports in a letter to Sir Robert Mansfield, written shortly after the death: 'Since 12 of the clock of Saturday night that I attended my dear master's bowels to the grave, I have kept my chamber, was entering a hot ague for which I purged and let blood; but no mortal hand can cure the everlasting comfortless sickness of my soul.'[63]

On Sunday night, 6 December, 'his representation was brought (made in so short warning, as like him as could be) and appareled with cloathes, having his creation robes above the same, his cap and crowne upon his head'.[64] In brief, this 'representation' appeared clothed in the same manner as he was at the time of his creation (1610). This effigy 'was laid on the back on the Coffin, and fast bound to the same' (85). So it would remain as the coffin moved through the streets for the funeral. The garments of creation now served the purposes of death. The Lord Chamberlain's Records illustrate the procedure of creating the effigy: the figure was to be jointed so that it could be moved 'to sundrie actions first for the Carriage in the Chariot and then for the standinge and for setting uppe the same in the Abbye'.[65] The same records indicate a payment of £10 to 'Abraham Vanderdort for the face and hands of the Princes representation being very curiouslie wrought'. The coffin contained the actual body of the prince; but above a 'representation' could remind everyone of his physical likeness, a faint image of the one who in 1611 had seemed to 'fill with grace / Every season, every place'. Cyril Tourneur wrote a poem, 'On the Representation of the Prince at His Funeralls', to commemorate and react to this object, concluding, 'His aptnesse fluently appeares, / In ev'rie *Souldiers* griefe, and *Schollars* teares'.[66] Sorrowfully Lennox surrendered to the recognition that the world's straying streets indeed lead to death's marketplace.

Of the royal family's sorrow John Chamberlain writes on 12 November that the prince's death 'was exceeding grievous to them both [king and queen], but specially to the King who takes yt with more impatience then was expected'.[67] On Tuesday 10 November, the family gathered in London to share their grief. Chamberlain notes particularly Princess Elizabeth's reaction: 'The Lady Elizabeth is much afflicted with this losse, and not without goode cause, for he did extraordinarilie affect her, and during his sickness inquired still after her, and the last wordes he spake in good sense (they say) were, Where is my deare sister?' (390). Antonio Foscarini, the Venetian Ambassador, reported to the Doge and Venetian Senate: 'The King received the news of the Prince's death at Theobalds; it affected him greatly and made of the happiest the saddest father in the world.'[68] He adds: 'The Queen's life has been in the greatest danger owing to her grief. She will receive no visits nor allow anyone in her room, from which she does not stir, nor does she cease crying.' Elizabeth 'has gone two days without food and cries incessantly'. Equally poignant, 'The Elector Palatine does not know what to do; he is quite upset at finding himself here at such an unpropitious and lamentable juncture'. Unlike Hamlet who left Germany to go to Denmark for his father's funeral, only to encounter his mother's wedding to Claudius, Frederick has come from Germany for a wedding but has found a funeral.

On 23 December, the English Ambassador, speaking to the Venetian cabinet, astutely analysed the situation: 'The King was at the very summit of felicity: all his affairs were prospering; his king-doms were united and at peace, his royal house fairly based upon a progeny not so numerous as to cause confusion. ... the entire country was rejoicing, when lo! in a moment, all is turned to grief and mourning.'[69] Henry's death had shattered the royal family's tranquillity and certainty. All that seemed so bright and promis-ing now lay in disarray. As Phosphorus, the day star, at the end of *Oberon* vanishes and the machine closes, so here.

And then the funeral. On 7 December, 'the representation was layd upon the Corps, and both together put into an open Chariot, and so proceeded'[70] (see Figure 5). Spectators and participants saw Henry's closed coffin with the lifelike effigy on top, this idealised representation seeming to blot out the death that rested below, the 'creation' garments serving death's reality. The whole number reached about two thousand persons in the procession, which took hours to move to Westminster Abbey from St James's Palace. Untold thousands lined the streets. Cornwallis writes: 'As it passed along, the whole World ... seemed to mourne, and have compassion. ... There was to bee seene an innumerable multitude of all sorts of ages and degrees of men, women, and children.'[71]

The procession began with 140 poor men in gowns, followed by three hundred servants of knights, barons, and earls' sons. Sir John Win bore Henry's standard, which contained his motto, *Fax mentis honestae gloria* (Glory is the light of a noble mind). Henry's household servants numbered 306, accompanied by the Duke of Lennox's servants. Then followed eighty servants of the Archbishop of Canterbury, Prince Palatine, and Prince Charles. The gentlemen and knights of Henry's Privy Chamber and Bedchamber processed, along with his Treasurer, Charles Cornwallis, and Sir Thomas Chaloner, the Chamberlain, who carried the white staff of office. The archbishop, the preacher for the funeral, followed. Soon came 'the Corps of the Prince, lying in an open Chariot, with the Princes representation thereon, invested with his Robes of estate'; at the foot of the chariot sat Sir David Murray, Henry's close friend and Master of the Wardrobe.[72] The chariot, drawn by six horses, was covered with black velvet and plumes of black feathers; 'a Canopy of blacke Velvet borne over the representation by sixe Baronets' (B4v). Finally came '*Prince Charles* chiefe *Mourner*, supported by the Lord Privy-Seale, and the Duke of *Lenox*. His *Highnesse* Traine was borne by the Lord *Dawbney* [Esmé Stuart], Brother to

5 Engraving of the funeral procession of Prince Henry from title page of
George Wither, *Prince Henries Obsequies* (1612)

the Duke of *Lenox*' (C1). Twelve earls served as assistants to the chief mourner. Prince Elector Palatine also moved in the procession, attended by noblemen from his own country. Out of the hundreds in the procession Lennox had a prominent position as supporter to Prince Charles, a certain sign of his long devotion to Henry and his status as confidant of the king.

After several hours the procession finally all gathered in Westminster Abbey. After the opening music, which included anthems by Thomas Tomkins ('Know Ye Not') and an elegy by William Byrd ('Fair Britain'), the coffin, with Prince Charles and Lennox following, 'was set under a great stately Herse built *Quadrangle* wise with eight Pillars, shewing three to the view on each side foure square, Cannopy like, rising small on the top' and trimmed throughout with emblems associated with Henry, including the Order of the Garter and his personal motto[73] (see Figure 6). As the crowd silenced, the Archbishop of Canterbury entered the pulpit to preach the sermon, using as his text Psalm 82: 6–7: 'I have said, Ye are gods; and all of you are children of the most High: But ye shall die like men, and fall like one of the princes.' The archbishop began by situating the text in terms of its occasion, scope and meaning. On the matter of princes dying, the bishop 'for ocular proofe and use of all, invit[ed] their eyes to the present dolefull spectacle of their late ever renowned *Prince*, who, not long agoe, was as fresh, brave, and gallant as the best of them' (88–9). The preacher offered consolation by referring to the 'exceeding measure of felicity, his Highnesse had attained unto by death'. Finally 'with exceeding great passion and many teares, hee ended' (90). The sermon took two hours.

The great officers of Henry's household, such as Thomas Chaloner, Charles Cornwallis, and John Holles, after the sounding of a trumpet, approached the coffin and broke their white staffs and rods across the coffin, 'thereby resigning their places' (92). And the service ended. The coffin, however, with its representation remained under the hearse, 'to be seene of all, until the 19. of the said Moneth of *December*' (92–3). For three days after this service prayers, chants, and psalms fulfilled the offices of the dead.

Eventually, Henry's 'representation' took its place among others in a chapel in Westminster. As he left the great Abbey church, the Duke of Lennox looked back at the hearse and its coffin and effigy and the spent candles and the now empty church and felt the pang

6 Engraving of Prince Henry's 'hearse' showing his effigy atop the coffin, from George Chapman's *Epicede or funerall song* (1612)

of loss intensely. A mere two years earlier, he recalled, all the court had rejoiced in Henry's 'creation' as Prince of Wales and all the promise that he showed. And now uncertainty and grief gripped the land.

On 12 November, John Holles wrote a letter to Lennox, responding to their loss. Holles writes: 'But he is gone, the glory of Christendom, the sole hope of this age, and the comfort of all virtues and worthy actions and men, is gone!'[74] Holles had served the king for eight years and, in the past two years, Henry. During this time Holles's service focused on the prince, 'save those whom I knew he inwardly favoured, among whom your lordship was and deserved to be a principal' (33–4). He closes: 'be pleased to accept this testimony of my devotion to your service, which, while I live, the memory of my most worthy master shall cause me to be your's ever at commandment' (34). In this time of great distress, John Holles reaches out to the Duke of Lennox, one of Prince Henry's 'principal' favourites, seeking mutual consolation. Scores of others responded similarly through letters, poetry, and prose as each tried to capture and expunge the shared grief.[75] Indeed, England had probably never experienced such a response in terms of published material.

A sampling would include the effort of John Donne, well known to Lennox and the court. Donne's 'Elegie on the Untimely Death of the Incomparable Prince, Henry' frames the matter of loss in terms of disturbed centres that no longer hold: 'Look to Me, *Faith*; and look to my *Faith*, God: / For, both my *Centres* feel This Period.'[76] These distracted centres challenge both knowledge and faith. The poet refers to Henry as his father's 'greatest Instrument' and one whose activist spirit might have brought peace throughout Christianity (258). In a familiar rumination on death, Donne writes: 'Therfore, Wee / May safelier say, that Wee are dead, then *Hee*. / ... *Hee* is not *dead*, Wee are', no longer nourished by the Henry who 'embrac't the *Fires of Love* with us' (259). Instead, his death brings a 'period'.

Perhaps recalling the prefatory poem in King James's *Phoenix*, the playwright John Webster in 1613 wrote '*A Monumental Columne, Erected to the Living Memory of the Ever-glorious Henry, late Prince of Wales*'. James had begun his poem in honour of Esmé Stuart and by extension Ludovic (Lennox) with a 'Colomne of 18 lynes serving for a Preface to the Tragedie ensuying'; this poem assumes a shape that resembles a rather squat column. Webster dedicates his elegiac poem of rhyming couplets to Robert Carr, Earl of Somerset, in which the poet pursues a different metaphor: 'Were my whole life turned into leasure, and that leasure accompanied with all the Muses, it were not able to draw a Map large enough of him [Henry]: for his praise is an high-going sea, that wants both shore and bottome.'[77] In the elegy itself, Webster imagines Henry as a 'perfect Diamond' from which his glories broke forth (275); he also sees him holding 'in his right hand ... / A *Caduceus*; in th'other *Pallas'* shield'. Men drawn to his court 'Thought that by day *Mars* held his launce, by night / *Minerva* bore a torch to give him light' (276). Webster also creates a fantasy that Prince Henry wished to have lived before the valorous Edward the Black Prince so that he might have served as a model to Edward. In a developed allegory Webster imagines a conflict between Pleasure and Sorrow, who takes on Pleasure's garments in order to deceive. And 'Death lay in ambush for His glorious *Youth*' (279). Returning to the diamond image, Webster instructs readers: 'go view / *Henry* the sevenths Chappell, and you'le find it true, / The dust of a rich Diamond's there inshrin'd' (282). 'When all the cost / Of guilded Monuments shall fall to dust' (283), Webster writes, muse-inspired elegiac verse shall remain, thereby constructing the monumental column in Henry's honour.

The busy dramatist Thomas Heywood also contributed 'A Funerall Elegie' in the same volume in which Webster's first appeared: *Three Elegies on the most lamented Death of Prince Henrie*. Heywood's poem has fifty-three stanzas of eight lines each, invariably touching on some of the same images and ideas that Webster had articulated, such as the conflict between Pleasure and Grief. Heywood develops an explicit theatre image, asserting that no tragedy could have drawn from its spectators more tears than Henry's death. Heywood adds: 'This Universe imagine a Theater, / Nations spectators, and this land a stage, / Was ever Actor, made by the Creator, / That better scean'd his part unto his Age?'[78] Having explored the various possible things to blame for Henry's death and coming up with nothing convincing, having connected Henry to the Trojan myth of England, and having singled out the members of the royal family for consolation, Heywood returns near the end of the elegy to the theatre metaphor: 'He that will act the wonders of his praise, / Shall finde the world a Theater too small' (C3v).

In the real world of London's theatres members of the Common Council sent a letter to the Lord Mayor on 8 November announcing Henry's death. Also, 'They had addressed letters to the Justices of the Peace of Middlesex and Surrey for the suppressing of all plays or shows within those counties, and required them to prohibit all plays, shows, bearbaiting, or other such sights within the City and Liberties'.[79] Henry's part has ended, and the theatres have closed. Heywood writes further: '*Fame* with her Trumpet shall his glories blaze; / Yet (ere to their full height) grow hoarse withall.' Such a reference to Fame compels Lennox and others to recall that empty space in the House of Fame that had been reserved for Henry in the Lord Mayor's Show of 29 October. Henry instead lay ill in St James's Palace where that night the rainbow hung in the sky, mocking any celebration and adding chill to that night.

Finishing his *Britannia's Pastorals*, William Browne paused to pen an elegy also, brought together in a book collected by Christopher Brooke.[80] Browne constructs a twelve-stanza elegy, each stanza having twelve lines, as if underscoring the year of Henry's death. Browne embraces a theatre metaphor, much as Heywood had, when he begins the poem: 'What time the World, clad in a mourning robe / A Stage made, for a woefull TRAGEDIE, / When showres of Teares from the celestial globe, / Bewailed the Fate of Sea-lou'd BRITTANIE' (sig. D3). The Muses have sung a sad strain, 'A Text of woe for grief to comment on'. When Henry sickened, 'then we first began / To tread the LABORINTH of *Woe*' (sig. E2). The poet remains incredulous in the face of the young prince's death.

Elegies can also be found in the year's published music, tapping into a well-established rich heritage of lively and sophisticated music in England, inspired, for example, by the compositions of Thomas Tallis, who had achieved great distinction with his sacred vocal music and motets, and his student William Byrd, renowned for his sacred music and keyboard music. Thomas Morley had created the market for madrigals in England, reinforced by the music of Thomas Weelkes, who wrote original and daring madrigals. Great achievement had occurred in lute music and solo ayres, distinguished especially by the brilliance of John Dowland. Thanks to publication of many musical texts, this music could be performed in many different venues.

Several important musical texts emerged from London's printers in 1613. For example, John Ward published his *The First Set of*

English Madrigals, arranged for three, four, five, and six parts. The collection opens with 'My true love hath my heart', presented from the perspective of the female, who sings: 'His hart in me keepes me and him in one, My hart in him his thoughts and senses guides.'[81] The songs for five parts adopt a pastoral setting. At the end of the volume Ward includes an elegy in memory of Prince Henry; its moving lyrics and mournful tune cry out: 'Let dolorous lamenting still be spread, through all the earth'; 'Oh, oh had he liv'd, our hopes had still encreased … but he is dead and all our joyes deceased' (sig. E3).[82]

Thomas Campion composed and published 119 lute songs and many ayres, being especially busy and productive in 1613. Physician, poet, composer, theorist, and masque-writer, Campion first distinguished himself for Lennox and the court this year with his *Lords' Masque*, performed on the day of Princess Elizabeth's wedding. He also wrote the entertainment offered to Queen Anne at Caversham on her progress in the spring of the year. And Campion published *Two Bookes of Ayres*, a mixture of sacred and secular songs, to be sung to the lute and viols, for which he wrote the music and the lyrics. Book One contains the first collection of sacred ayres in England.

The sacred songs provide considerable variety, including 'paraphrases of psalms, moral verse in the Horatian manner, a thanksgiving ode, elegy, allegorical vision, and several pieces in the "witty" tradition of mediaeval Latin hymnody'.[83] Campion begins elegantly in the first song: 'Author of light, revive my dying spright, / Redeeme it from the snares of all-confounding night' (59). Song XIV offers a moving rendition of Psalm 137; and it begins hauntingly, capturing the desperation of the Israelites: 'As by the streames of *Babilon*, / Farre from our native soyle we sat, / Sweet *Sion*, thee we thought upon, / And ev'ry thought a teare begat' (74). How can one sing in a foreign land? Song XV seems almost an answer: 'Sing a song of joy, / Prayse our God with mirth', an echo of Psalm 104 (75). These sacred songs conclude with an elegy about Prince Henry, which focuses on the prince's physical beauty: 'His Iv'ry skin, his comely hayre, / His Rosie cheekes' (81). The song adds: 'Now in him all want their place.' All that beauty, love, and power have vanished: 'Quencht is all his flame.'

Campion's *Songs of Mourning* commemorates Henry's death and builds on an earlier elegy. The seven songs, each with a slightly different verse form, work various changes on this death by focusing on a particular person who feels the loss intimately. Campion collaborated with Giovanni Coperario, who wrote the music, even as he had written some of the songs for the *Lords' Masque*. Coperario, although an Englishman named John Cooper, changed his name after spending time in Italy; he served as music tutor to all the royal children and thus knew Henry well. In the dedication of the book to Prince Frederick, Campion suggests that the seven songs function to 'soften excessive grief by all our art, and then hope will give us better things' (116). He frames the songs with another elegy on Henry's death wherein he sees himself as 'Priest', prepared to lead the readers and listeners through grief. He writes of Henry's practical talents and skills, closing: 'wee offer now / Guifts which hee lov'd, and fed: Musicks that flow / Out of a sowre and melancholike vayne, / Which best sort with the sorrowes wee sustaine' (119).

'The seven songs that follow are to use this understanding as the basis of a cathartic act involving the emotions, at first indirectly by leading the audience to identify itself with those most deeply affected, then directly by addressing the people of England and Europe themselves as those most broadly affected by Henry's death' (115). Thus Campion works his way through the members of the royal family, beginning with King James, in which the poet refers to Henry as 'Heav'ns hostage, which you bredd / And nurst with such choyce care, / Is ravisht now' (120). For Queen Anne, Campion writes most poignantly: ''Tis now dead night, and not a light on earth / Or starre in heaven doth shine: / Let now a mother mourne the noblest birth / That ever was both mortall and divine' (121) (see Figure 7). He says of the relationship of Henry and Elizabeth: 'But you each other / On earth embrac't in a celestiall chaine' (123). Campion's music compellingy reinforces the dolorous poetry but without over-sentimentalising Henry's life and death.

In his *Monumental Columne* Webster connects Henry's death to the weather: 'What a darke night-peece of tempestious weather, / Have the inraged clouds summon'd together, / As if our loftiest Pallaces should grow / To ruine' (282). Various reports confirm the harsh weather of the final months of 1612, making Webster's observation as literal as metaphoric. Edmund Howes, for example, in his continuation of Stow's *Annales*, notes: 'In the months of October, November and December, this yeere 1612, there hapned many great Winds, violent Stormes, and Tempests, as well by land as sea,

7 Portrait of Queen Anne in mourning (1613), artist unknown

which did exceeding great damage.'[84] The anonymous author of *The Wonders of This Windie Winter* goes to great lengths to document the 'tempestuous weather' that Webster and Howes allude to. This writer sees God's hand and anger working through such weather, calling citizens to repentance: 'we shall finde that the heavy hand of heaven is layd violently upon us, as wel in taking away our great hope, and earthly joy (Henry our Royall Prince) as these our late lamentable mischances by winde and waters'.[85] The writer focuses on the last months of 1612 as being particularly stormy, resulting in numerous deaths throughout the kingdom and considerable destruction in London itself; for example: 'it is reported and knowne for truth, that in the month of October last, a fleet of fourteene sayle' moving from Newcastle towards London encountered destruction (A4v). The writer adds that 'betwixt Michaelmas and Christmas last, the seas have bereaved 7000. … people of their lives' (B1v) throughout the land. For this writer all of these events underscore God's wrath and condemn sinful people. The imagination also projects Henry's death as another kind of storm afflicting the people, a violence that shakes belief and the centres of being.

On this imagined stage of Henry's lamented departure, other writers appropriated an image long associated with Lennox and King James: the phoenix. James Maxwell, for example, in *The Laudable Life* characterises Henry as 'Faire Europes *Phoenix*, and great Britaines blisse, / The Soldiers solace, and the Schollars joy, / Both *Mars* and *Muses* minion, he it is / Whose timeless death doth young and old annoy'.[86] In the expanded version of Joshua Sylvester's *Lachrymae Lachrymaram*, a certain 'G. G.' (possibly Donne's friend George Gerrard) refers to 'This *Phoenix*, that is lately fled / To Life from hence, where all that live are dead'; therefore, 'Onely pronounce, but with a voyce of Thunder, / *Prince Henry's* gon'.[87] In his collection of forty-five elegies in sonnet form, George Wither writes of Henry in Elegie 8: 'Thy Father both a Sunne, and *Phoenix* is, / Prince *Henry* was a Sunne and *Phoenix* too; / And if his Orbe had bene as high as his, / His beames had shone as bright's his fathers doe.'[88] Death has dimmed the rare beauty and accomplishment of this Phoenix (Henry).

Reading, pondering, and absorbing some of this elegiac outpouring, Lennox could relive the events of late 1612. He knew first-hand Prince Henry's virtues and could join in the poets' songs to his memory. Nothing, however, could erase his grief. Several images especially burned in Lennox's memory. He recalled that moment in mid-October as he walked with Henry into the chamber in Whitehall, following Frederick, Elector Palatine. who made his first entry in the English royal court. He also remembered the House of Fame device in Dekker's Lord Mayor's Show of 29 October and the 'representation' of Henry there – and his absence because of illness.

A few weeks later Lennox walked with Prince Charles in Henry's funeral procession, as he accompanied this chief mourner. Lennox thus walked in the city streets that end in the marketplace of death. On that December day, Lennox followed behind the coffin that bore Henry's body and the 'representation' that lay on top. This representation might be very like Henry, as Gertrude in *Hamlet* would say, but it lacked the prince's vitality and life. Death had brought a 'period' to life, as Donne notes. Day-star, fairy prince, and phoenix – now all shrouded in death and embraced by the quiet place of the grave – a noble kinsman dead.

Notes

1 Charles Cornwallis, *The Life and Death of ... Henry Prince of Wales* (London, 1641), p. 47. Cornwallis had served as Treasurer of Prince Henry's household.
2 Information comes from Alan Stewart, *The Cradle King: The Life of James VI and I* (New York: St Martins, 2003), pp. 246–7.
3 *Calendar of State Papers Venetian, 1610–1613* (London: HMSO, 1905), 12: 439.
4 *Calendar of State Papers Venetian*, 12: 443.
5 *The Letters of John Chamberlain*, ed. Norman E. McClure, 2 vols (Philadelphia: American Philosophical Society, 1939), 1: 381.
6 *Calendar of State Papers Venetian*, 12: 443.
7 *The Letters of John Chamberlain*, 1: 384.
8 *The Letters of John Chamberlain*, 1: 384.
9 Reported by Edmund Howes in his continuation of John Stow, *The Annales or Generall Chronicle of England* (London, 1615), p. 915.
10 Howes, *The Annales or Generall Chronicle of England*, p. 915.
11 *The Dramatic Works of Thomas Dekker*, ed. Fredson Bowers (Cambridge: Cambridge University Press, 1958), 3: 230. All quotations from the pageant come from this edition.
12 See my discussion, 'Creating Entertainments for Prince Henry's Creation (1610)', *Comparative Drama* 42 (2008–9): 433–49. In this I draw on the excellent research of Pauline Croft, 'The Parliamentary Installation of Henry, Prince of Wales', *Historical Research: Bulletin of the Institute of Historical Research* 65 (1992): 177–93. For an analysis of the entertainments offered to Henry, see Martin Butler, *The Stuart Masque and Political Culture* (Cambridge: Cambridge University Press, 2008), pp. 183–93.
13 W. H., *The True Picture and Relation of Prince Henry* (Leyden, 1634), p. 17.

14 W. H., *True Picture*, p. 28.

15 *Calendar of State Papers Venetian*, 11: 410.

16 Stow, *The Annales*, p. 897.

17 W. H., *True Picture*, p. 28.

18 For a reproduction of these drawings and discussion, see Stephen Orgel and Roy Strong, *Inigo Jones: The Theatre of the Stuart Court* (Berkeley: University of California Press, 1973), 1: 158–67.

19 *Ben Jonson: The Complete Masques*, ed. Stephen Orgel (New Haven: Yale University Press, 1969), p. 144. All quotations for this and *Oberon* come from Orgel's edition.

20 *The Autobiography of Phineas Pett*, ed. W. G. Perrin (London: Navy Records Society, 1928), p. 76.

21 *Chesters Triumph in Honor of Her Prince* (London, 1610), sig. A3v. Quotations will come from this edition. For a discussion of this pageant, see my *English Civic Pageantry 1558–1642*, revised edition (Tempe: Arizona State University, 2003), pp. 91–2. Susan Anderson is the most recent to discuss this pageant: 'Sound, Vision, and Representation: Pageantry in 1610 Chester', *Early Theatre* 17.1 (2014): 137–57.

22 *Calendar of State Papers Venetian*, 11: 507.

23 *Calendar of State Papers Venetian*, 11: 516.

24 *London's Love to the Royal Prince Henry*, found in my edition, *Pageants and Entertainments of Anthony Munday: A Critical Edition* (New York: Garland, 1985), p. 39. All quotations will be from this edition.

25 Cornwallis, *Life and Death*, pp. 16–17.

26 Quoted in John Nichols, *The Progresses of King James the First* (London, 1828), 2: 359. Nichols includes all the pertinent texts for the 'creation'.

27 For a fuller account see *The Order and Solemnitie of the Creation of … Prince Henrie* (London, 1610). Nichols reprints this text, 2: 324–41.

28 Samuel Daniel, *The Complete Works in Verse and Prose*, ed. Alexander B. Grosart, 5 vols (rpt New York: Russell & Russell, 1963), 3: 310. All quotations come from this edition.

29 See the drawings reproduced in Orgel and Strong, *Inigo Jones*, 1: 204–28. These drawings and many more concerning Prince Henry are reproduced in Catharine MacLeod's *The Lost Prince: The Life and Death of Henry Stuart* (London: National Portrait Gallery, 2012). This beautifully illustrated book served as the catalogue for the exhibition on Prince Henry at the National Portrait Gallery, London, that ran from 18 October 2012 to 13 January 2013, an exhibition that commemorated the four-hundredth anniversary of Henry's death.

30 Cornwallis, *Life and Death*, p. 93.

31 Daniel Price, *Prince Henry His First Anniversary* (Oxford, 1613), p. 5. This recollection of Henry, which Strong mistakenly refers to

as a 'sermon' (p. 54), Price published on the anniversary of Henry's funeral. Price did preach a series of sermons about Henry immediately following his death and throughout 1613. His superb recollections of the prince have largely been ignored. The sermons preached on 10 and 15 November 1612 Price published as *Lamentations for the Death of the Late Illustrious Prince Henry* (London, 1613). The four sermons of 1613 were published as *Spiritual Odours to the Memory of Prince Henry* (Oxford, 1613). Price returned to the topic with his *Prince Henry His Second Anniversary* (Oxford, 1614).

32 Francis Bacon, 'Memorial of Henry Prince of Wales', translated from the Latin, *In Henricum Principem Walliae Elogium*, in *The Works of Francis Bacon*, eds James Spedding, Robert Ellis, and Douglas Heath (London: Longmans, 1878), 6: 327. Bacon's brief description and characterisation of Henry is one of the best of the contemporary accounts.

33 W. H., *The True Picture*, p. 3.

34 Bacon, 'Memorial', p. 328.

35 British Library, Harleian MS 7007, f. 21.

36 *Calendar of State Papers Venetian*, 10: 513.

37 *Calendar of State Papers Venetian*, 10: 513.

38 Charles Cornwallis, *A Discourse of the Most Illustrious Prince, Henry* (London, 1641), p. 15.

39 John Hayward, *The Lives of the III. Normans, Kings of England* (London, 1613), sig. A2. Quotations come from this text. This is probably the most extensive conversation with Prince Henry that has been preserved.

40 John Holles letter to Lord Gray, 27 February 1613, *Report of the Manuscripts of His Grace the Duke of Portland*, Historical Manuscripts Commission (London: HMSO, 1923), 9: 10.

41 Cornwallis, *Discourse*, p. 16. Cornwallis, Henry's Treasurer, actually wrote this tract in 1626, according to the title page.

42 George Marcelline, *The Triumphs of King James the First* (London, 1610), p. 66.

43 Henry Peacham, *Minerva Britanna* (London, 1612), sig. A2.

44 Quotations come from the text edited by David Lindley in *The Cambridge Edition of the Works of Ben Jonson*, gen. eds David Bevington, Martin Butler, and Ian Donaldson (Cambridge: Cambridge University Press, 2012), 3: 302.

45 *Calendar of State Papers Venetian*, 11: 500.

46 See Roy Strong, *Henry, Prince of Wales England's Lost Renaissance* (London: Thames & Hudson, 1986), especially the chapter, 'The Prince's Collections', pp. 184–219.

47 Cornwallis, *Discourse*, p. 10. This favourable view of management gets challenged in 'A Collection of Several Speeches and Treatises of the

late Lord Treasurer Cecil, and of several observations of the lords of
the Council given to King James concerning his estate and revenue in
the years 1608, 1609, and 1610', edited by Pauline Croft in *Camden
Miscellany* 29, Camden 4th series (London: Royal Historical Society,
1987), 34: 245–317. Croft concludes that Henry apparently managed
his household no better than his father, in terms of finances.

48 Price, *Prince Henry*, p. 5.
49 Cornwallis, *Discourse*, p. 23.
50 *Autobiography of Phineas Pett*, p. 50.
51 John Nichols, *Progresses of James*, 2:438.
52 Cornwallis, *Life and Death*, p. 26.
53 W. H., *True Picture*, p. 9.
54 Bacon, 'Memorial', p. 328.
55 Cornwallis, *Discourse*, p. 19.
56 Cornwallis, *Discourse*, p. 19.
57 W. H., *True Picture*, p. 24.
58 British Library, Harleian MS 6986, f. 180b. I have slightly modernised
    the quotation. Cited in my *Royal Family, Royal Lovers: King James of
    England and Scotland* (Columbia: University of Missouri Press, 1991),
    p. 106. In this book I discuss all the members of James's family.
59 Cornwallis, *Life and Death*, p. 30. Quotations come from Cornwallis's
    report. This account is by far the fullest version about Henry's illness
    and death, offering specific and sometimes gruesome information. I
    depend on Cornwallis considerably. W. H., *True Life*, offers a similar
    account but much abbreviated. See also the modern account by J. W.
    Williamson, *The Myth of the Conqueror: Prince Henry Stuart, a Study
    in 17th Century Personation* (New York: AMS Press, 1978), pp. 152–66.
    For additional information about Henry's death and funeral, as well as
    several other subjects, see the collection of essays edited by Timoth
    Wilks: *Prince Henry Revived: Image and Exemplarity in Early Modern
    England* (Southampton: Southampton Solent University, 2007).
60 Price, *Prince Henry*, p. 27.
61 *Autobiography of Phineas Pett*, p. 100.
62 John Hackett, *Scrinia Reserata* (London, 1692), p. 27.
63 *Report of the Manuscripts of the Duke of Portland* (London: HMSO,
    1923), 9: 35.
64 Cornwallis, *Life and Death*, p. 85.
65 Quoted in W. H. St John Hope, 'On the Funeral Effigies of the Kings
    and Queens of England, with Special Reference to Those in the Abbey
    Church of Westminster', *Archaeologia* 60. 2 (1907): 555.
66 Cyril Tourneur, *Three Elegies on the most lamentable Death of Prince
    Henrie* (London, 1613), sig. C2.
67 *Letters of John Chamberlain*, 1: 390.

68 *Calendar of State Papers Venetian*, 12: 449.

69 *Calendar of State Papers Venetian*, 12: 464.

70 *The Funerals of the High and Mightie Prince Henry* (London, 1612), sig. A4. Details about the procession come from this edition, which itself rather resembles a procession as it lists the hundreds of participants. Nichols, *Progresses of James*, reprints this tract, 2: 493–99.

71 Cornwallis, *Life and Death*, p. 86.

72 *The Funerals*, sig. B4v.

73 Cornwallis, *Life and Death*, pp. 86–7. Quotations are from this account. A drawing of this 'hearse', or catafalque accompanies the text of George Chapman's *An Epicede* (London, 1613) in some copies.

74 *Report of the Manuscripts of the Duke of Portland*, 9: 33.

75 For a survey of the elegiac material, see J. W. Williamson, *The Myth of the Conqueror*, pp. 171–92. See also Ruth Wallerstein, *Studies in Seventeenth-Century Poetic* (Madison: University of Wisconsin Press, 1950), chapter 3, 'The Death of Prince Henry', pp. 59–95, for an analysis of this material. More recently Michael Ullyot has explored much of this material in his 'The Fall of Troynovant: Exemplarity after the Death of Henry, Prince of Wales', in *Fantasies of Troy: Classical Tales and the Social Imaginary in Medieval and Early Modern Europe*, eds Alan Shepard and Stephen D. Powell (Toronto: Centre for Reformation and Renaissance Studies, 2004), pp. 269–90. Ullyot says succinctly and accurately: 'The literary impact of Henry's death was both immediate and unprecedented' (p. 279). Even after Henry's death, Jonathan Lamb argues, Jonson's 1616 Folio responds to his death: 'Ben Jonson's Dead Body: Henry, Prince of Wales, and the 1616 Folio', *Huntington Library Quarterly* 79.1 (2016): 63–92.

76 *The Complete Poetry of John Donne*, ed. John T. Shawcross (New York: Doubleday, 1967), p. 257. All quotations come from this edition.

77 *The Complete Works of John Webster*, ed. F. L. Lucas (London: Chatto & Windus, 1927), 3: 273. All quotations will be from this edition.

78 *A Funerall Elegie, upon the Death of the Late Most Hopefull and Illustrious Prince, Henry, Prince of Wales* (London, 1613), sig. B1. Heywood's poem joins those of Webster and Cyril Tourneur in the *Three Elegies*.

79 *Analytical Index of the Series of Records Known as the Remembrancia … of the City of London* (London, 1878), p. 410.

80 *Two Elegies, Consecrated to the Never-dying Memorie of … Henry* (London, 1613). Brooke includes his elegy along with Browne's.

81 John Ward, *The First Set of Madrigals* (London, 1613), sig. B1.

82 Henry Lichfild also published his only known music in 1613: *The First Set of Madrigals of 5. Parts*. He chooses pastoral settings for the most part, and he dwells on love's difficulty.

83 *The Works of Thomas Campion: Complete Songs, Masques, and Treatises*, ed. Walter R. Davis (Garden City, NY: Doubleday, 1967), p. 52. All quotations come from Davis's edition.
84 Howes, Stow's *Annales*, p. 913.
85 *The Wonders of This Windie Winter* (London, 1613), sig. A3.
86 James Maxwell, *The Laudable Life* (London, 1612), sig. C3.
87 Joshua Sylvester, *Lachrymae Lachrymaram, or The Spirit of Teares* … (London, 1613), sig. D1. Several editions of this appeared in 1612. The text of 1613 is about twice as long because it includes many elegies that Sylvester had gathered from other writers.
88 George Wither, *Prince Henries Obsequies* (London, 1612), sig. B2. The stunning title page (Figure 5) shows Henry's hearse with the coffin and 'representation', being drawn by several horses.

3

A queen's translation

Darkness fell early on an October evening in London as a chill gripped the air. In the same month that Prince Henry became fatally ill in 1612, a strange procession of torches slowly moved from the north to Clerkenwell where the Archbishop of Canterbury, George Abbot, and other clergymen and noblemen waited on 8 October. The entourage stopped around 6 p.m. before continuing its journey to Westminster Abbey. The Duke of Lennox, and others scattered throughout the streets, saw a coffin carrying the exhumed body of Mary, Queen of Scots, King James's mother. With ample torches, the procession, which had begun 70 miles away at Peterborough Cathedral, wound its way to the abbey. Henry Howard, Earl of Northampton, captured the event in a private letter:

> We in this place acordinge to direction have laied up the body of the most worthy quene that manie ages have beheld. ... Though we brought her in verie late to shunne concurse yet the people in the streetes and out of the windowes caste their eies upon the passage manie noting and with admiration that justice of god and piety of a motherlesse son that brought her into that place with honor from which she had been in former times repulsed with tiranny.[1]

The sympathetic Northampton notes the crowd's curiosity and interest, despite efforts to downplay attention to the event.

A grand monument awaited the queen's body in the Abbey. This opulent tomb rested in the Henry VII Chapel, deliberately and directly opposite the one that James had commissioned for Queen Elizabeth. This torchlight movement, involving Mary's body, eerily recalls a similar procession that began late at night on 30 July 1587 from Fotheringhay Castle to Peterborough Cathedral, where it arrived at 2 a.m., carrying the embalmed, heavy, lead-incased body of the executed queen. This bizarre nighttime procedure attempted to prevent undue interest in her burial. After a stridently Protestant service, with only English men and women attending (apart from Mary's servants), Mary gained her resting place in the cathedral, not to be disturbed until 1612.

To answer the question of 'why now', Lennox would have had to recall James's, at best, problematic relationship with his mother, one that Lennox knew about from his father and from his own observation. In the letter to the Scottish people, the one that complemented the other document that established Lennox as President of the Privy Council while James went to Denmark to marry Anne in 1589, James had tellingly characterised his delay in marrying: 'The reasons were that I was alone, without father or mother, brother or sister, king of this realm and heir apparent of England.'[2] At the age of thirteen months, James in 1567 had become King of Scotland, his father having been murdered in February of that year, and his mother driven into exile by the Scottish nobles and Kirk after her disastrous and ill-advised marriage to the Earl of Bothwell.

In fact, James never consciously knew his parents. This vulnerability governed many of his actions and offers a psychological base for understanding his search for family. James's knowledge of his mother he gained exclusively through her letters and reports from emissaries. Numerous Scots believed that Lennox's father, Esmé Stuart, had arrived in Scotland in 1579 to do the bidding of the Guise faction in France and to help Mary gain release from imprisonment. Esmé certainly participated in numerous attempts to resolve conflict and even to create an 'Association' by which James and Mary would share joint rule. Not long after the young Ludovic Stuart arrived in Scotland that idea died. By 1584, James had effectively given up on his mother; he saw a more promising potential future awaiting him in England.[3] Indeed, by 1586 he and Elizabeth reached an agreement that she would subsidise him with an annual gift of £4,000 (he had hoped for £5,000).

Two letters from 1584 reveal much about James and his mother. During that summer, James, Lennox, and other Scottish lords played host to the Frenchman M. de Fontenay, one of Mary's supporters and emissaries. Fontenay wrote a long letter to Mary, appending his most trenchant analysis in a secret note to his brother-in-law Claude Nau, who served as Mary's secretary. The document, dating from 15 August 1584, incisively assesses James's strengths and liabilities and reveals much about the mother–son relationship. The Frenchman duly noted the king's knowledge and skill in languages but also commented on his awkwardness in manners; and Fontenay faulted James for his lack of self-knowledge and over-reliance on the Scottish nobles. Only one thing, however, truly astonished this French emissary: 'He [James] has never inquired anything of the Queen [Mary] or of her health, or of her treatment, her servants, her living and eating, her recreation, or anything similar.'[4] In this extended conversation with an official representative of his mother, James had nothing to say or ask about her.

After this visit, the king wrote to Mary, thanking her for sending Fontenay to him. In this disingenuous letter, James writes: 'I do not know how to express the extreme consolation that I have received from it, having heard from him several particularities of your estate, and especially the incomprehensible maternal affection that it pleases you to continue in my respect'.[5] He adds, in this letter written in French code: 'shortly I will send with Fontenay some of mine to receive your holy benediction and to inform you of divers of my intentions, as also to require of the Queen of England your deliverance, for which I wish above all the happiness of this world' (56). And he promises his mother that 'you will receive from me all the contentment that a good mother can hope for from a very humble and obedient son' (56). Humble and obedient do not immediately come to mind in trying to describe James's response to his mother. But they both kept trying for a while to sustain a fiction about their mutual love.

Mary's approval of the 'Babington Plot', a plan by insistent Catholics to assassinate Elizabeth and free Mary, determined her final destiny. On 3 August 1586, English forces arrested Mary for plotting against Elizabeth's life, and a month later they moved her from Chartley to Fotheringhay Castle, 20 miles south-west of Peterborough in Northamptonshire. Mary had become accustomed to being moved to various places: for example, from the relatively pleasant and benign care of George Talbot, Earl of Shrewsbury, at Tutbury Castle and Chatsworth, to the harsh control of Sir Amyas Paulet at Chartley and then Fotheringhay. By 15 October, she stood trial in the great hall at Fotheringhay Castle where a jury easily and readily found her guilty. James sent emissaries, such as Patrick Gray and William Keith, to intervene in her behalf; but he also sent conflicting signals, essentially letting Elizabeth and her government understand that he would take no serious action against England, should Mary be executed. James wrote to the Earl of Leicester twice in December 1586, seeking his assistance. In the letter of 15 December, James laid bare his concern: to protect his claim to the English throne by denying any knowledge of his mother's complicity in foreign plots. James breathtakingly adds: 'how fond [foolish] and inconstant I were if I should prefer my mother to the title let all men judge'.[6]

James wrote to Queen Elizabeth one last time, 26 January 1587, in an attempt to have her spare his mother's life, a letter, however, striking in its dispassionate tone. The letter scores debater's points in urging Elizabeth to be a merciful ruler; James reminds her of the moral and legal precedent that would be set if she executed another sovereign. He writes pointedly: 'What monstrous thing is it that sovereign princes themselves should be the example-givers of their own sacred diadems' profaning!'[7] Should anyone misrepresent his wishes and desire, 'I pray you not to take me to be a chameleon, but, by the contrary, [take them] to be malicious imposters as surely they are' (83). Mary had another thought, assuring all who would listen to her that her son and all those who fulfil his desires are 'open leyarris [liars] and dowble dealarris'.[8]

Nothing could now prevent Mary's execution. In a scene full of theatrical spectacle, Mary, dressed in black and carrying a crucifix and prayer book and wearing two rosaries on her waist, on the morning of 8 February 1587, made her way to the appointed scaffold (an elevated 'stage') and executioner's block in Fotheringhay Castle.[9] The Countess of Bedford as Queen Elizabeth's personal representative attended, as did the Earl of Shrewsbury, who came to honour this woman whom he had guarded and protected and whose company he enjoyed. All the procedures and arrangements had been established by Sir Francis Walsingham, Elizabeth's secretary of state and spymaster. After speeches and prayers, some led by Richard Fletcher, Dean of Peterborough Cathedral and father of John Fletcher, Shakespeare's fellow playwright and collaborator, the assistants stripped Mary's outer garment revealing a red petticoat. Blindfolded by her faithful servant Jane Kennedy, Mary then lowered her head on the block; and the blade fell against her with two blows, severing her head from the body. Bereft, the body lay still on the floor, as Mary's servants wept bitterly – and so did more than one Englishman. Soon, authorities swept up her remains and secreted them in the castle until an autopsy and then the embalming and encasing with lead. Following Walsingham's orders, servants burned all of Mary's clothes and the executioner's block, doing everything to make impossible the likelihood that something of hers could become a relic. Her imposing casket lay unattended and unburied in a secret place, underscoring her end and her isolation.

Finally, some five months later Mary's body made the journey in early morning darkness to Peterborough Cathedral, where Dean Fletcher welcomed it; and he presided over a service, ordered by Elizabeth, that should give due respect to a monarch, a staunchly Protestant service that Mary would have abhorred. The heavy coffin, bearing on its top her lifelike effigy befitting a royal funeral, moved slowly into the beautiful and majestic Norman cathedral, sweeping up the grand nave towards its final resting place in the south aisle of the choir. Mary would find her resting place in an obscure, unmarked grave, directly across from Katherine of Aragon, Henry VIII's first wife, who had lain in the north aisle since January 1536: two foreign queens in an English cathedral. Legend insists that Robert Scarlett, the sexton of the cathedral, prepared the grave for both queens. When he finished the work for Mary's burial, the cathedral grew dark and abandoned, as the limited crowd scattered, some to a festive celebration in the bishop's house.

Meanwhile, in Scotland, James gave out conflicting signals, threatening revenge, weeping, and yet inwardly rejoicing, attested by numerous documents. Bonfires of joy, however, filled London's streets. James, of course, could not go that far, but he surely understood that the way to the English throne now lay more clearly open than ever. His mother's death removed a major obstacle but left for James a residue of simmering guilt.

As with his response to Esmé Stuart's death, which included bringing Ludovic to Scotland, James, consciously or unconsciously, found various ways to respond to Mary's death. These events Lennox watched unfold. In 1596, for example, James took exception to part of Edmund Spenser's *The Faerie Queene*. Books 4 to 6 of this epic poem appeared that year, and James thought that an episode in Book 5 insulted his mother. The English Ambassador to Scotland Robert Bowes reported to Burghley on 12 November 1596:

The King has conceived great offense against Edward [*sic*] Spenser (Spencer) publishing in print in the second part of the Fairy Queen and 9th chapter some dishonourable effects (as the King deems thereof) against himself and his mother deceased. He alleged that this book was passed with privilege of her Majesty's Commissioners. ... But therein I have (I think) satisfied him that it is not given out with such privilege. Yet he still desires that Edward Spenser for this fault may be duly tried and punished.[10]

This remarkable report lets us know, if nothing else, that James as a reader of poetic texts fancied himself an interpreter of literature. It also indicates James's vigilance in looking for slights to Mary's memory. His reaction also casts a suspicious eye toward Elizabeth, the Fairy Queen of the poem.

Since Spenser has cloaked his poem in the dark conceit of allegory, one cannot be surprised to find all kinds of connections to actual persons and events. The 'offending' passage comes in Book 5, canto 9, stanzas 25–50, the trial of Duessa (presumably Mary), presided over by Mercilla (Elizabeth). Zeal presents the charges against Duessa and notes her many heinous crimes, especially her attempt to deprive Mercilla of her crown. That charge, of course, lay at the heart of the ones levelled against Mary ten years earlier at Fotheringhay Castle. In canto 10 Spenser's poem contains the decision to execute Duessa. James's plausible response to this section of the poem nevertheless reflects an attempt to deflect his own guilt and shame and place it on Spenser. He would rewrite history by punishing the poet. Elizabeth did not honour this request.

James took a tangible step of remembering and honouring his mother in 1603, shortly after becoming King of England. He sent a rich velvet pall to Peterborough Cathedral to adorn Mary's gravesite. James never visited the cathedral, but being on English soil apparently prompted him to make the gesture of honouring her grave. He thereby resembled the dutiful son, an idea that could supplant less flattering ones regarding his concern for Mary. Having secured the title of King of England, James might now attempt to refashion and burnish his image as one full of filial piety.

In a sense this process continued in naming his first daughter born on English soil Mary. Her birth on 8 April 1605 at Greenwich triggered universal rejoicing with bonfires and bell ringing. James, of course, had three surviving children, whom he brought to England; but to have an English child only seemed to solidify his standing. James wrote to his brother-in-law, Christian IV of

Denmark, expressing his joy in this birth and observing: 'although this is not our first child, it may nevertheless seem to be the first since it is the first to have occurred for us after the most happy union of our kingdoms'.[11] This Mary was the first royal child born in England since Jane Seymour gave birth in 1537 to the child who became Edward VI. Probably no one still alive could recall this early sixteenth-century birth.

Indeed, much scurrying about and perusing of records took place as the authorities tried to reconstruct the ceremony for a royal baptism. Mary's baptism took place on 5 May 1605 at Greenwich, the first royal baptism that followed the Protestant rites of the by now firmly established Church of England. With Lennox and other noblemen and noblewomen present, this ceremony captured every-one's attention; Lennox in fact served as one of Mary's godparents. No comparable religious ceremony had occurred in the Stuart royal family since the opulence of Henry's baptism in 1594. The chapel at Greenwich shimmered with jewels and a stately font of silver and gold. James's possible dream of this daughter supplanting his mother's memory shattered, however, with Mary's unexpected death on 16 September 1607.[12] This young child could not therefore bring about Queen Mary's 'translation'.

In 1606, James ordered the construction of a marble tomb monument for his mother to be erected in Westminster Abbey, as he had done for Elizabeth. Cornelius and William Cure, superb stone carvers and master masons, carried out the project. In September 1612, they neared completion; and thus James sent a letter to the Dean of Peterborough Cathedral requesting the exhuming of Mary's body. James wrote on 28 September:

> For that we remember it appertains to the duty we owe to our dearest mother that like honour should be done to her body and like monument be extant of her as to others her and our progenitors have been used to be done, and ourselves have already performed to our dear sister, the late Queen Elizabeth, we commanded a memorial of her to be made in our Church of Westminster, the place where the kings and queens of this realm are usually interred. And for that we think it inconvenient that the monument and her body should be in several [separate] places, we have ordered that her said body, remaining now interred in that our Cathedral Church of Peterborough, shall be removed to Westminster to her said monument, and have committed the care and charge of said translation of her body from

Peterborough to Westminster to the reverend father in God, our right trusty and well-beloved servant, the Bishop of Coventry and Lichfield, bearer hereof, to whom we require you, or such as ye shall assign, to deliver the corpse of our said dearest mother, the same being taken up in as decent and respectful manner as is fitting. And for that there is a pall now upon the hearse over her grave, which will be requisite to be used to cover her said body in the removing thereof, which may perhaps be deemed as a fee that should belong to the church, we have appointed the said reverend father to pay you a reasonable redemption for the same.[13]

This letter, submitted 'under the sign manual', presumably written by someone other than the king, nevertheless conveyed his desire that the appropriate care be taken for his mother's remains and that she be 'translated' to London.

The letter emphasises her 'body' and that the king intends to honour that body, of which he had little conscious awareness. James finds it 'inconvenient' that her body should remain in Peterborough and the monument be in Westminster; he intends, rather, to reconcile body and tomb. For this purpose, he has appointed Richard Neile, Bishop of Coventry and Lichfield, 'a right trusty and well-beloved servant', to carry out the task. Later in 1613, James will appoint Neile to the committee that sat in judgement in the divorce proceedings of Frances Howard and the Earl of Essex. Rather pointedly, James does not include the Bishop of Peterborough, Thomas Dove, in these arrangements, probably because James did not much care for him. They had had an unpleasant encounter in the Hampton Court Conference of 1604. In his letter to the Dean of the cathedral, James notes that monarchs 'of this realm are usually interred' in the Abbey church. Mary, of course, derives from another realm, but he will make her central in England's recollection and commemoration. In a moment of unusual frugality, James also insisted that the velvet pall be sent along with the coffin.

Three things will bring about Mary's 'translation': the actual movement of the body, the velvet pall, and the monument. In a little over a week, Mary's remains had been 'translated' from Peterborough to the outer precincts of London where Archbishop Abbot met the procession on that October night in 1612 on its way to the Abbey. She will have been released from the obscure grave in Peterborough in order to take her place in a magnificent tomb in the symbolic heart of English political and religious life.

The translation of Mary also underscored a translation of James, a kind of expiation of whatever lingering guilt he felt about his mother. Her remains now moved to the Henry VII chapel where her corpse will occupy the largest and grandest monument. For the first time in English history a Scottish monarch would reside in the great Westminster church, a monarch executed by order of James's English predecessor. Now Elizabeth and Mary would lie across from each other in the chapel, seemingly equal, creating an unmistakable irony. Not exactly 'equal', since Mary's tomb 'is about twice the size of Elizabeth's, and … took much longer to complete and was much more expensive'.[14] James placed his mother's tomb 'in line with Henry VII's mother Margaret Beaufort' (524), thereby linking her and eventually himself with the Tudors, underscoring Mary's claim to the *English* throne.

The 1618 edition of John Stow's *Survey of London*, prepared by Anthony Munday, includes the lengthy Latin inscription, written by the Earl of Northampton, on Mary Stuart's tomb in the Abbey.[15] The text begins with an outline of Mary's lineage, emphasising that she was daughter of James V of Scotland and 'sole heir and great granddaughter of Henry VII King of England'.[16] 'She was descended from truly regal and ancient lineage, connected to all the greatest princes of Europe'; yet she suffered the 'mistrust of the cowardly, and the plots of her mortal enemies, [and] she was at last struck by the axe.' Latin verses praise her qualities, adding: 'The Queen finished the course which the heavens bestowed: God gave happy times and hard times.' But, 'Fate being quick, she gave birth to the extraordinary James, whom Pallas, the muses, and Delia, and the fates honour'. And the text closes with a kind of benediction: 'God grant that her children and those descended from her may henceforth look on eternal days without clouds.'

In various senses Mary and James got whatever revenge they desired. James had made an everlasting and self-satisfying revisionist statement about his official role as loving son, which, not incidentally, managed also to comment favourably on himself, whom the Muses love. Mary's magnificent white marble statue, lying in repose, her hands clasped in prayer, and a Scottish lion at her feet, now exuded a serenity that life had denied her.

As in the darkness that surrounded her initial stealthy burial in Peterborough, the body in October 1612 moved through dim London streets to the cold Westminster church where Lennox and others could pay their respects and confirm her 'translation', forever etched in their collective memory. Arthur Wilson, writing in the 1650s, describes the scene in the Abbey: 'The Tapers placed by the Tomb and the Altar, in the *Cathedral*, smoaking with them like an *Offertory*, with all the *Ceremonies*, and *Voices*, their *Quires* and *Copes* could express, attended by many Prelates and Nobles, who payd this last Tribute to her *memory*.'[17] Mary thereby contributed to the cultural context of 1613. In a few weeks her grandson Prince Henry would sadly join her in death and become the focus of a service in this same abbey church, underscoring autumnal chill.[18]

Notes

1 Quoted in John Watkins, *Representing Elizabeth in Stuart England: Literature, History, Sovereignty* (Cambridge: Cambridge University Press, 2002), pp. 31–2. For a brief account see Edmund Howes's continuation of John Stow's *Annales* (London, 1615), p. 913. The *Calendar of State Papers Domestic, 1603–1625* (London, 1857–72), 9: 152, contains a brief reference to Northampton's letter.

2 *Letters of King James VI & I*, ed. G. P. V. Akrigg (Berkeley: University of California Press, 1984), p. 98. The letter dates from 29 October 1589.

3 For a discussion of the relationship of James and Mary, see my *Royal Family, Royal Lovers* (Columbia: University of Missouri Press, 1991), pp. 35–46.

4 *Calendar of State Papers Relating to Scotland*, 13 vols (Edinburgh: HM General Register House, 1898–1969), 7: 274.

5 *Letters of King James*, p. 55.

6 *Letters of King James*, p. 78.

7 *Letters of King James*, p. 82.

8 *Calendar of State Papers Relating to Scotland*, 9: 250.

9 Antonia Fraser offers a superb account of the final moments in Mary's life: *Mary Queen of Scots* (New York: Delacorte Press, 1969), pp. 531–42.

10 *Calendar of State Papers Relating to Scotland*, 12: 359–60.

11 *The Letters of King James I to King Christian IV, 1603–1625*, ed. Ronald M. Meldrum (Brighton: Harvester Press, 1977), p. 44. This microfiche edition contains translations of James's Latin letters to Christian IV.

12 Another English daughter was born to James and Anne on 22 June 1606. This child, named Sophia after Anne's mother, lived only a few hours.

13 *Letters of King James*, pp. 326–7.

14 Julia M. Walker, 'Reading the Tombs of Elizabeth I', *English Literary Renaissance* 26.3 (1996): 523.
15 John Stow, *Survey of London* (London, 1618), pp. 880–1. I am indebted to Professor Jonathan Lamb for his help with an English translation of this inscription.
16 I quote from Lamb's translation.
17 Arthur Wilson, *History of Great Britain* (London, 1653), p. 61.
18 Antonia Fraser points out that a nineteenth-century survey of the tombs in the Henry VII chapel discovered that Mary shared her space with her grandson Henry and her granddaughter Princess Elizabeth, pp. 554–5.

4

'Death be not proud': drama's solace

When Hamlet emerges from his first wrenching soliloquy in 1.2, he encounters his friend Horatio, who, like Hamlet, has come from Wittenberg to Denmark. Hamlet asks him why he has come; and they have the following exchange:

> HORATIO. My lord, I came to see your father's funeral.
> HAMLET. I prithee do not mock me, fellow student.
>   I think it was to see my mother's wedding.
> HORATIO. Indeed, my lord, it followed hard upon.
> HAMLET. Thrift, thrift, Horatio. The funeral baked meats
>   Did coldly furnish forth the marriage tables.
>
> (1.2.176–81)

Frederick, Elector Palatine, had, of course, come to the Jacobean court from Germany for a wedding, only to encounter an unexpected funeral. Antonio Foscarini, the Venetian Ambassador, reported back to his colleagues in mid-November 1612: 'And so the nuptial festivities of this house are turned to mournful trappings.'[1]

In his ironic mode, Hamlet hits upon a fundamental problem: how can one sensitively make the transition between a funeral and a wedding; how much time should elapse between the two? King James, the Duke of Lennox, and other members of the court establishment wrestled with this issue directly as they attempted to move beyond Mary's reburial, Henry's death and funeral, and the political uncertainty caused by this event. Can a royal wedding follow hard upon a state funeral? Can such a wedding erase the pain of a funeral? John Chamberlain, writing to Sir Dudley Carleton on 19 November 1612, refers to Frederick, 'whose mariage by this late accident is retarded, because yt wold be thought absurd that forrain ambassadors comming to condole the Princes death shold find us feasting and dauncing'.[2] Such ambassadors might recall the English Ambassador who arrives in 5.2 of *Hamlet* naively expecting a reward for executing Rosencrantz and Guildenstern only to learn that that had not been Claudius's intention. Expectation founders on the threshold of reality.

Early on, James suggested postponing the wedding until May 1613. That idea did not last long because of economic and political pressures. As Foscarini reported at the end of November: 'The nuptials will be celebrated in great state and at a great cost. They are delayed for that very purpose and to give the Ambassadors time to change their festal robes into mourning for the Prince.'[3] And time to change back again. Foscarini, in early January 1613, noted: 'The request of the Palatine that the marriage should take place at once has proved efficacious with the King, who has given orders that every one is to go out of mourning on March the 14th and to don gala dress' (472). James tried to stand resolute against the desire for the wedding to proceed. Foscarini reports to Venice on 11 January 1613: 'his Majesty stood firm, declaring that mourning should be mourning, and marriage rejoicings rejoicings' (474).

While discussions continued about setting the precise date for the wedding, King James also pursued another kind of marital negotiation. At the time of Prince Henry's death, James was exploring marriage possibilities for him with Princess Christine, the six-year-old second sister of King Louis XII of France. On 14 December 1612, James wrote to his ambassador in France, Sir Thomas Edmondes, suggesting that they might just shift gears and line up the princess for Prince Charles, he but twelve years old. Typical of James, he first admonished Edmondes for having raised this issue at such a sensitive time: 'For it had been a very blunt thing in us that you, our minister, should so soon after such an irreparable loss received by us have begun to talk of marriage, the most contrary thing that could be to death and funerals.'[4] James entertained the view that the matter of marriage would come up anyway, so why not respond appropriately. He cautioned Edmondes to behave such that the French 'may neither apprehend that we are become greedy in urging it [the marriage], nor yet upon the other side to give them any sense of distaste upon apprehension of our slowness and averseness in it' (329): cautiously interested but certainly not indifferent. As monarch, James must keep focus, despite the grief caused by Henry's death. James walked a thin line between being respectful of his son's death and yet moving on with the demands of the kingdom.

Two events began the transformation that led toward Princess Elizabeth's wedding: the official contract between her and Frederick on 27 December, and the outpouring of dramatic performances at court, beginning in the Christmas season and spilling over into 1613. On Christmas Sunday, the Duke of Lennox, the royal family, and others gathered in Whitehall for the official contractual engagement of Elizabeth and Frederick, a sure sign that the wedding plans were advancing. On that morning, according to Antonio Foscarini, Frederick went 'to the Princess's Chamber, gave her his right hand and led her to the King's Chamber, surrounded by her ladies. There they kneeled to receive the blessing which his Majesty gave. They then went to the Great Hall, where all their festivities are held.'[5] In this hall, the couple found Prince Charles and the king. One report adds: 'About two yerdes below the degrees of State was spread a large Turkie carpett, whereon they stode when they were affianced. The Nobilitie and Prince Charles brought him [Frederick] in appaireled in a black velvet cloake caped with gold lace. Then followed she in a black velvet gown seemè of crosletts or quatrefoiles sylver, and a small white feather on her head.'[6] After the ceremony, everyone returned to mourning garments.

Sir Thomas Lake, serving temporarily as Secretary (in place of the deceased Robert Cecil), read the marriage words from the Book of Common Prayer. Foscarini reports: 'Then the Palatine said, "I Frederick, Elector of the Holy Roman Empire, Count Palatine of the Rhine, Duke of both Bavarias, take you Madame Elizabeth, daughter of the most powerful, high and glorious King of Great Britain, for rich or poor, for well or ill, to be my wife while life me lasts"'[7]. Elizabeth responded accordingly with the same promise. The Archbishop of Canterbury gave them his blessing and added a few words. John Chamberlain, writing to Dudley Carleton on 31 December, adds some pertinent details, such as the cumbersome and amusing French translation that Lake had made of the ceremony from the prayer book. Chamberlain writes: 'But they say he [Lake] had translated the wordes of our communion booke into French so badly, and pronounced them worse, that yt moved an unseasonable laughter as well in the contractors as the standers by' (1: 399). The archbishop interposed himself and restored dignity, adding this blessing: 'The God of Abraham, Isaacke and Jacob blesse these nuptials, and make them prosperous to these kingdoms and to his church.'

Chamberlain adds: 'This affiancing was solemnised in the great banketting roome on Sonday before dinner, in the presence of the King and great store of nobilitie; but the Quene was absent, being troubled (as they say) with the gowte' (399). Lennox would have understood Chamberlain's parenthetical statement well, for he knew of Anne's reluctance about this marriage, a reluctance that he did not share, having spent considerable time with Frederick from his arrival in mid-October when Lennox brought him to the royal court. Anne disapproved of Frederick, believing him a minor prince and insufficiently powerful for her daughter; further, Anne truly desired a Catholic prince for Elizabeth. Eventually Anne would come round, accepting Frederick, at least on some level. The Scots had also hoped that Elizabeth would marry one of their nobles, especially in light of Henry's death. But after 27 December, only the official extravagant wedding ceremony remained to secure the political, legal, and religious link between Elizabeth and Frederick and the two countries.

Not only did Hamlet agonise over the close proximity of his father's funeral and his mother's wedding, but also he sought an outlet through drama. Theatre became a means of catching the conscience of the king; it also functioned as a means for Hamlet's understanding of the changed world that he now confronted. He instructs the players who have arrived at the Danish court about how to present drama, underscoring its purpose. Hamlet says that the 'purpose of playing … is, to hold, as 'twere, the mirror up to nature, to show virtue her feature, scorn her own image' (3.2.20–3). The Christmas season of 1612–13 at the Jacobean court offered an exceptional number of play performances, which collectively or individually held up some kind of mirror that bounced off the court's recent experiences. Hamlet understood drama as both a reflection of life and a transition. Therefore, he can, in Act 2, begin reciting from a play that he had seen that focused on the slaughter of Priam, based on the account of the Trojan experience in Virgil's *Aeneid*. This drama had lingered in his memory and had profoundly shaped his understanding; it also led him to feel the discrepancy between the passion of the actor reciting the death of Priam and Hamlet's own greater cause of passion, reeling from his father's murder by Claudius. Drama leads to drama.

Drama at the Jacobean court stood between Henry's funeral and Elizabeth's impending wedding; it constructed a bridge, a translation, a confrontation with raw feelings. These performances underscored the efficacy of art, which provides an aesthetic distancing, making it possible to experience fictional death, comedy, and history in the plays performed by the King's Men and other acting companies. The season of 1612–13, from Christmas through mid-April when Elizabeth and Frederick left England, saw twenty court performances by the King's Men alone. This exceptional number reflected the court's need to shift from mourning garments to festive wedding clothes.

On 1 January 1604, the new Jacobean court had seen a performance of Shakespeare's *A Midsummer Night's Dream*, which, when the play's love problems have been resolved, ends by the characters coming to the Athenian court to see a play in anticipation of multiple weddings. Theatre before a wedding seems logical. The course of true love has not run smoothly, but the lovers have been correctly paired off; thus, the court has much reason to celebrate. The opening moments of 5.1 anticipate some kind of entertainment to complete the transfiguration, the 'translation', of the lovers. The Athenian ruler Theseus asks: 'Is there no play / To ease the anguish of a torturing hour?' (5.1.36–7). Did not the Jacobean court in late 1612 ask a similar question? Philostrate, the equivalent of the Master of the Revels, steps forth with a list of possible drama topics, which Theseus reads over. They include: '"The battle with the Centaurs, to be sung / By an Athenian eunuch to the harp"; "The riot of the tipsy Bacchanals, / Tearing the Thracian singer in their rage"; and finally, "A tedious brief scene of young Pyramus / And his love Thisby; very tragical mirth"' (44–57). Theseus asks a probing question: 'How shall we find the concord of this discord?' (60), even as he selects the Pyramus and Thisby story, which on its face would seem inappropriate for a wedding celebration. What can 'tragical mirth' mean? The performance by the Athenian 'rude mechanicals' answers that question. The experience in the fictional Athenian court might well linger in the memories of Lennox and others as they confronted the plays selected for performance in 1612–13. Theseus seems to have anticipated the later actual court productions: 'A fortnight hold we this solemnity / In nightly revels and new jollity' (358–9).

Thinking back over the ten years since he and the king had arrived in England, Lennox could marvel at the extravagance and quantity of dramatic performances at court, beginning at Christmas in the 1612 season. What brought about the court's connection to professional adult acting companies starting in 1603? Scotland did not have well-established acting companies; indeed, Lennox had lamented the relative lack of art in Scotland. And he remembered the extraordinary action of King James on 19 May 1603, just weeks after their arrival in London, by which the king took the major companies under royal patronage. Shakespeare's company, the Lord Chamberlain's Men, would henceforth be known as the King's Men, servants of the royal household. As such, they lined the route for James's official royal entry into London on 15 March 1604, an exceptional civic pageant, authored by Ben Jonson and Thomas Dekker, with a speech written by Thomas Middleton, all major dramatists at this point.

On that date in May, the king issued a proclamation to all office-holders throughout the kingdom, announcing his action:

> Wee of our speciall grace certeine knowledge & mere motion have licensed and authorized and by theise presentes doe license and auc-thorize these our Servauntes [here follows a list of the actors, includ-ing Shakespeare] … and the rest of their Associates freely to use and exercise the Arte and faculty of playinge Comedies Tragedies histories Enterludes morralls pastorals Stageplaies, and Suche others like as theie have already studied or hereafter shall use or studie aswell for the recreation of our lovinge Subjectes, as for our Solace and pleasure when wee shall thincke good to see them duringe our pleasure.[8]

This singular and unexpected action provided the actors unusual protection and patronage and assured their preferred position for court performances. Nothing in James's background quite antici-pates this action, although Scotland enjoyed some dramatic perfor-mances, including visiting English players.[9] Certainly the king might have seen this move as an expression of royal power, whatever else motivated him. Beyond self-interest, the king solidified the status of the King's Men and protected them against attack. These actors can move about the country secure in the king's support, 'authorized' by him and the royal patent; they provide 'recreation' for the country's citizens. But they also noticeably offer something quite different: what James refers to as 'Solace and pleasure'. Clearly solace must have been one of the primary effects of the drama presented at court in 1612–13. The worlds of the Guildhall enter Whitehall through drama, both patronage and performance.

James's document of May 1603 offers evidence of an exceptional genre range, beginning with the obvious comedies, tragedies, and histories, in a formulation that echoes Polonius's description of the actors arriving at the Danish court: 'The best actors in the world, either for tragedy, comedy, history, pastoral, pastoral-comical, historical-pastoral' (2.2.339–41). Both James and Polonius uncannily anticipate the types of plays offered in 1612–13. In the royal patent, the king also took note of the virulent outbreak of the plague, which had forced a closure of the theatres and delayed the official royal entry of James into London until the following year.

But royal support for acting companies did not stop with the King's Men. 'By the end of the first year of the new reign, not only had the Chamberlain's men become the King's men but the Admiral's men had become Prince Henry's men, Worcester's men had become Queen Anne's men, and the boys' company at Blackfriars had become the Children of the Queen's Revels.'[10] On 30 March 1610, the Duke of York's men became Prince Charles's Men; in the following year on 27 April, Lady Elizabeth's Men received a royal patent. Prince Henry's Men became Elector Palatine's Men or Palsgrave's Men after Henry's death. The royal family thus developed a far-reaching apparatus for support of drama. These acting companies performed in various public theatre buildings in greater London and at court. The King's Men also began to perform in the private theatre known as Blackfriars after they acquired this property in 1608. Thus, a substantial part of the court's cultural energy from 1603 onward focused on theatre in various ways, including the sponsorship of elaborate masques. Lennox well understood the dynamic intermingling and interchange of the court and theatre, creating a circulation of cultural energy.

For years, the Duke of Lennox had actively been involved in a number of theatrical events, starting in Edinburgh and Anne's royal entry pageant in 1590, extending through the baptismal festivities for Prince Henry in 1594, and moving into numerous masques in the early Jacobean years in England. He regularly participated in Accession Day Tilts, appearing stunningly arrayed with feathers in the 1610 event, and he attended street pageants, such as the 1612 Lord Mayor's Show. He also for a while had his own acting company, Duke of Lennox's Men. Lennox intervened to help prevent George Chapman's arrest for his play *The Conspiracy and Tragedy of Byron*, performed in spring 1608; the play had stirred the antipathy and anger of the French Ambassador, de la Broderie, who convinced Robert Cecil to issue a warrant for Chapman's arrest. A letter survives from Chapman in which he thanks Lennox for the 'Shelter' he has been accorded during the 'Austeritie of the offended time'.[11] In a more indirect way, Lennox had connections to the Office of the Revels through his brother because 'King James granted the part of St John's Priory in which the Revels Office was housed to his cousin Esmé Stuart for his own use as a residence'.[12] And, of course, Lennox would have known Ben Jonson through his brother, who served as one of Jonson's major patrons and in whose home Jonson lived during one of his several separations from his wife. Such explicit and wide-ranging experience equipped Lennox to confront the 'tragical mirth' of the court productions, which helped transform the court's atmosphere from the tragedy of Henry's death to the comic anticipation of Elizabeth's wedding.[13]

The court depended on the Master of the Revels to arrange for dramatic performances. This office George Buc now filled, having in 1610 finally succeeded the long-serving Edmund Tilney.[14] The position had been created under Henry VIII with the express purpose of providing entertainment for the court; but over the years the Master's functions expanded, including regulation of the professional acting companies and oversight of publication of plays, sometimes involving censorship of various kinds. Like Philostrate in *A Midsummer Night's Dream*, George Buc had the task of choosing the plays for the 1612–13 court season. The Revels Accounts contain a payment of £75 for this purpose, entered for Buc and four of his men 'for rehersalls and makeinge choice of plaies and Comodies and reformeing them as for other his attendaunces for maskes and devices presented at the Courte against the maryadge of the Lady Elizabeth to the Prince Palatine'.[15] Not surprisingly, Buc turned to the King's Men for most of the plays, tapping into their repertory of current and past plays, some of which had been performed at court earlier in the decade. Beyond that, what prompted Buc's choices or who might have influenced him remain a mystery. The hundreds who attended performances at Whitehall may have puzzled over the generic stew that greeted them nightly in that extraordinary season.

Buc chose some nineteen different plays to be performed from Christmas 1612 to Shrovetide 1613, not counting the masques performed for the wedding of Elizabeth and Frederick. Information about their titles – the most extensive of any group of plays performed at court during the Jacobean court's first ten years – comes from payments recorded in the Revels Accounts and in the Chamber Accounts.[16] Several entries spell out the names of the plays and cite the payments, most of them coming in summer 1613. The King's Men performed eight plays by Shakespeare: *Much Ado about Nothing* (comedy, performed twice), *1 and 2 Henry IV* (history), *The Winter's Tale* (tragicomedy), *Othello* (tragedy), *Julius Caesar* (tragedy), *The Tempest* (tragicomedy), and the lost *Cardenio*, presumably written with the assistance of John Fletcher. Francis Beaumont and Fletcher had five plays presented: *The Captain* (comedy), *The Maid's Tragedy* (tragedy), *A King and No King* (tragicomedy), *Philaster* (tragicomedy, performed twice), all acted by the King's Men; and *Cupid's Revenge* (tragedy), performed by the Children of the Queen's Revels twice, on 1 and 9 January. Buc chose Jonson's *The Alchemist* (comedy), *The Twins' Tragedy* by Niccols (lost), *The Nobleman* by Tourneur (lost), *The Merry Devil of Edmonton* by Dekker and others (comedy), plus two anonymous plays: *A Bad Beginning Makes a Good Ending* (lost) and *The Knot of Fools* (lost).[17] Buc's apparent criterion was his familiarity with the plays. For example, *Cupid's Revenge, The Winter's Tale, The Tempest, A King and No King*, and *The Twins' Tragedy* had all been performed at court within the previous year or so (others may have been, but the records are silent).[18]

What did Lennox and the crowds of courtiers who gathered in Whitehall experience in these plays that spread over several weeks, beginning at Christmas? What subject matter, what ideas and images emerged from the activity of watching the performances day after day in this heady time of transformation from funeral to wedding? A glimpse into the likely experience can be found in the fictional version of entertainment captured by the playwrights who collaborated on the late Elizabethan play *Sir Thomas More*, including Anthony Munday, Henry Chettle, Thomas Dekker, Thomas Heywood, and Shakespeare. In Act 3, scene 2, More at his house in Cheapside awaits the arrival of the Lord Mayor and Aldermen of London and their wives, who will be coming for a feast. More's wife interrupts him with the announcement that a Player has arrived, who claims: 'M'y lord, my fellows and myself / Are come to tender ye our willing service'.[19] These actors, servants of the Cardinal, have come to present a play.

Understandably, More asks the Player what plays they might have ready to perform. The Player responds:

Diverse my lord: *The Cradle of Security,*
Hit Nail o'th' Head, Impatient Poverty,
The Play of Four P's, Dives and Lazarus,
Lusty Juventus, and *The Marriage of Wit and Wisdom.*

(143)

More opts for the last-named play. Unlike the list that Philostrate offers in *A Midsummer Night's Dream*, the Player here lists titles of actual plays, much as George Buc would have done in deciding on the plays for the Christmas season. Somehow the actors, with only four men and a boy, will present the entire play. More says in anticipation: 'Wife, hope the best, I am sure they'll do their best, / ... My good lord Cardinal's players, I thank them for it, / Play us a play, to lengthen out your welcome' (147). The Prologue finally arrives and says: 'We therefore intend, good gentle audience, / A pretty short interlude to play at this present, / Desiring your leave and quiet silence' (149). The performance encounters a number of problems so that by the time Luggins arrives with a 'beard', More is ready to move on to the banquet: 'My lord and ladies, we will taste that first / And then they shall begin their play again' (155). But More himself has been summoned to an unexpected meeting of the Council and leaves. The play and feast have nevertheless roused More from his dispirited state, overcoming his regret at the earlier departure of Erasmus. Drama can indeed bring about transformation.

Arriving at Whitehall out of the chill and snow of a late December night, Lennox came with anticipation and some knowledge of the plays that had received performances at court in the recent past. Expectation and excitement hung in the air as hundreds of courtiers gathered in the Banqueting House, each spectator attempting to build on the joy of Elizabeth and Frederick's betrothal on 27 December. A hush began to overtake the hall as King James, Queen Anne, Prince Charles, Princess Elizabeth, and Frederick assumed their places. The stage glowed with lights, and the King's Men readied themselves for performing. Variations of this procedure took place over the next few weeks as the play performances continued, seemingly unabated with revels unending. John Donne in his verse epistle 'To Sir Henry Wotton' may have captured the scene in the Jacobean court: 'Believe me Sir, in my youth's giddies and days,

/ When to be like the Court, was a play's praise, / Plays were not so like Courts, as Courts are like plays.'[20] Theatre in Whitehall took place on several different levels, as the whole scene at court resembled and replicated drama.

During the performances and later on reflection, Lennox thought about the subjects, images, ideas, and spectacle of the plays of this exceptionally rich Christmas season. From the frivolous high jinks of, say, *The Merry Devil of Edmonton* to the tragic consequences of *Othello*, spectators could seize on the multiple variations on marriage, which, at least theoretically, would have been a particularly suitable subject at court. Royal children, as in *The Winter's Tale* and some of the Beaumont and Fletcher plays, highlight the current situation in the Jacobean court and the importance of these children for the kingdom's future, in part because they raise the question of succession. A recurrent theme focuses on politics, the nature of kingship, power, and the need for loyalty, as in the *Henry IV* plays. Betrayal may come in matters of love or in politics, witness *Much Ado* and *Julius Caesar*. Mystical, supernatural power emerges in *The Tempest* and in a parodic form in *The Alchemist*. The subject of magical power would certainly have interested King James. The gods manifest another dimension of power, particularly and cruelly compelling in *Cupid's Revenge*. This partial list reveals the infinite variety of these plays and suggests the likely impact they would have had on spectators. The court indeed resembled a play, tragical mirth and all.

The Prologue speaker in *The Merry Devil* may serendipitously offer a kind of motto for the plays at court: 'Sit with a pleased eye, until you know / The comic end of our sad tragic show.'[21] Tragedy, in other words, may not be the final word. Although *Merry Devil* has some romantic mishaps, it never comes close to tragedy, in part because of the intervention of Peter Fabell, necromancer, who in the Induction successfully receives seven more years of life, having formerly bargained away life for magical power, reminiscent of Faustus. Fabell intervenes on behalf of his friend Raymond Mounchensey, who desires Millicent Clare, daughter of Sir Arthur Clare, who unwisely decides that the Mounchensey fortune is insufficient and seeks to break the betrothal between Raymond and Millicent in favour of a marriage of his daughter with Frank Jerningham, son of the wealthy Sir Ralph Jerningham. Sir Arthur proposes to ship his daughter to the Cheston Nunnery for at least a year. Millicent has overheard her father rail against the Mounchensey lack of fortune; and she rightly concludes: 'Treason to my heart's truest sovereign! / How soon is love smothered in foggy gain!' (1.1.79–80).

Such love cannot remain 'smothered' – not in this play at least. In the pattern of many comedies, the lovers must overcome recalcitrant parental will. This they can do, thanks in part to Fabell, who announces his assistance in a soliloquy that opens 1.3. If necessary, he will 'hang Enfield in such rings of mist / As never rose from any dampish fen' (21–2) and cause the sea to rise to Ware and drive the deer from Waltham forest. Being able to do these things, Fabell remains undaunted about helping his fellow student from Cambridge. In fact, he will send spirits into the nunnery, there to create mischief. Further, he will disguise Raymond as a Friar, who will successfully rescue Millicent from the nunnery, which he does in 3.2. Millicent recounts a dream that she has had in which a spirit came to her while she was praying, 'And by his strong persuasions tempted me / To leave this nunnery' (3.2.93–4). The spirit seemed a 'glorious angel', which Millicent now recognises as her lover Raymond, who whisks her away.

Act 4 includes the wandering about in the dark woods of Waltham by Sir Arthur, Sir Ralph, and most of the other characters – an apt image of the machinations of magic, the triumph of love, and the confusion of the fathers. With some uncertainty Sir Ralph says in Act 5: 'We have been in the forest all night almost' (5.2.23). The Host interrupts their reverie with an announcement: 'there's a good breakfast provided for a marriage that's in my house this morning' (30–2). Puzzled, Sir Arthur asks about this marriage; and the Host explains: 'A conjunction copulative; a gallant match between your daughter and master Raymond Mounchensey, young Juventus' (34–6). After much clarification, Fabell enters and asserts, 'No law can curb the lover's rash attempt' (136), and concludes: 'Smile, then, upon your daughter and kind son, / And let our toil to future ages prove, / The Devil of Edmonton did good in love' (138–40). Overcome and chastened, Sir Arthur accepts Raymond as his son-in-law and forgives his daughter, achieving the 'comic end' of this show.

Closer to the site of the court performances, Jonson's *The Alchemist* takes place in the Blackfriars section of the City of London, well known to Lennox, Shakespeare, and Jonson, who moves away from the countryside setting of Hertfordshire of *The*

Merry Devil. The magic and love pursuit of that play Jonson turns upside down, offering instead a satiric foray into the realm of greed and desire, manifested in the presumed supernatural power of alchemy, practised by the charlatan Subtle and his companions Dol Common and Face, in whose master's house they reside and practise their con game. *The Alchemist*, first produced at the Globe by the King's Men in 1610 and first published in 1612, takes place during plague time; therefore, Lovewit, the master, has vacated London and waits for the death toll to subside before returning. The play's first production itself came at the end of an extended period of virulent plague that had shut the theatres in the city. As the theatres had closed, so Lovewit's house has presumably been shuttered, except that the enterprising 'venture tripartite' manages to open it to all those who would know the pleasure and wealth that alchemy can offer. Paradoxically, the confinement of plague and limitation of the house and a single day of action nevertheless provide Jonson an expansive outlet as the allure of alchemical charms attracts would-be beneficiaries to this house like a magnetic force. Unlike the rambling *Merry Devil*, spread over a few days, Jonson's play zeroes in on a precise, limited moment. Out of this restricted time and place, the audience would have perceived Jonson's trenchant satire, focused in part on religion, especially Puritans, such as Tribulation Wholesome and Ananias, and the whole apparatus of seeming science and its seductive, enticing appeal. Subtle, the alchemist, offers a veritable motto for the play when he tells the newly arrived Kastril: 'Welcome; I know thy lusts and thy desires, / And I will serve and satisfy 'em' (4.2.15–6).[22]

Nowhere does Jonson make Subtle's idea more transparent and valid than in the case of Sir Epicure Mammon, who arrives at the beginning of Act 2, accompanied by the sceptical (and appropriately named) Surly. Subtle, Face, and Dol have already dispensed with the first two seekers: Dapper, the law clerk, and Drugger, the tobacconist – decidedly small-fry, compared to Mammon and the Puritans. Already spying him coming, Subtle admits that this day Mammon expects the 'magisterium' to be completed. And Subtle captures Mammon's grandiose vision: 'He will make / Nature ashamed of her long sleep; when art, / Who's but a step-dame, shall do more than she' (1.4.25–7). Subtle concludes: 'If his dream last, he'll turn the age to gold' (29). Stepping into Lovewit's house, Mammon asserts to an incredulous Surly: 'This is the day wherein, to all my friends, / I will pronounce the happy word, "Be rich!"' (2.1.6–7). The golden age, the triumph of art, wealth: these ideas constitute a partial list of Mammon's desires in what becomes an ever expanding and romantic vision.

Mammon is a believer with faith in alchemy and in himself and certainly in Subtle, who has already fed his desires. By contrast, Surly has no faith, little hope, and less charity; in a word, a wonderful counter to Mammon. Mammon believes and therefore he knows. In this play world, alchemy comes wrapped in religious language, as well as in the cant of alchemical terms, the mumbo-jumbo that Subtle utters that sounds mysterious and therefore credible. Face presents Subtle as a man of faith, who wears out his knees in prayer. Mammon moves back and forth along an exotic–erotic axis. He intends, he says, to 'have a list of wives and concubines / Equal with Solomon, … / and I will make me a back / With the elixir, that shall be as tough / As Hercules, to encounter fifty a night' (2.2.34–8). The house in Blackfriars will satisfy his lusts and desires. The play skilfully sets Mammon aside once he has had a glimpse of Dol and seeks to have a 'conference' with this 'rare scholar'.

Tribulation Wholesome reminds Ananias: 'The children of perdition are oft-times / Made instruments even of the greatest works' (3.1.16–17). This viewpoint rationalises the Puritans' involvement with the con artists in Lovewit's house. Like everyone else, the Puritans, their religious views aside, want money – the easy way – presumably for more good works. In a sense, they offer another variation of Mammon's greed. Subtle promises success within fifteen days with the derivation of the 'Stone'; and he defines alchemy's appeal: 'The art of angels, nature's miracle, / The divine secret that doth fly in clouds' (3.2.103–4). In a word, alchemy offers *transformation*.

But the change that Mammon provokes in Act 4 comes unexpectedly. First, he boasts to Dol: 'I am lord of the Philosopher's Stone, / And thou the lady' (4.1.120–1). But his lustful pursuit of Dol leads to her supposed fit of madness, which then causes the explosion of the alchemical laboratory, even though Mammon insists sheepishly to Subtle: 'dear father, / There was no unchaste purpose' (4.5.37–8). When Mammon learns that all has been lost, he cries out: 'O, my voluptuous mind! I am justly punished' (74). 'Punishment' becomes the order of the day, as all the seekers return in Act 5 to press their claims. Alas, for them, Lovewit has returned, apparently sent for by Face, and an 'implosion' occurs. Lovewit tells this rowdy bunch: 'If you can bring certificate that you were gulled of 'em, / Or any formal writ out of a court, / That you did cozen yourself, I will not hold them' (5.5.68–70). His golden age lost, his dreams sullied, his wealth gone, his desires unrequited, Mammon announces: 'I will go mount a turnip-cart, and preach / The end o' the world within these two months' (81–2). Through the machinations of Face, Lovewit obtains the widow Dame Pliant, having his desires satisfied; and Face survives the scheme. But many false hopes, based on a misguided faith, go up in smoke, literally and figuratively, in a late afternoon in Blackfriars, no bulwark against Jonson's satiric vision.

'For all mens eyes, / Ears, faiths, and judgements, are not of one size'; so says the Prologue to Beaumont and Fletcher's *The Captain*.[23] Had the *Merry Devil* or *The Alchemist* somehow not suited the spectators, they needed only wait for the performances of Beaumont and Fletcher's plays. *The Captain*, for example, opens the issue of love and marriage in ways radically different from the naive *Merry Devil* without the greed that dominates Jonson's play. The blocking parental will of Sir Arthur to the marriage of Millicent and her lover Raymond gives way to another parent, the unnamed Father, who confronts his widowed daughter Lelia, noted for her lustful activities that redound to her shame. To her sullied reputation her father arrives to impose moral judgement, which Lelia resists. In this strange play, fitting no single size of comedy, Jacamo, the soldier and woman-hater, comes under assault by Franck, a woman who inexplicably and passionately loves him. Beaumont and Fletcher interweave these love strands into the exotic setting of Venice and Spain, according to the note found in the 1679 Beaumont and Fletcher folio, although not a single reference to setting occurs in the text, apart from some Italianate names. In any event, the spectators at the Jacobean court knew that they weren't in England any more.

Hoping that Lelia would know his lusts and desires and seek to satisfy them, Julio arrives at her house in 1.3, shortly after her Father has denounced her. Lelia feigns shock at Julio's advances and sends him packing, although she admits to her Waiting Woman: 'Fortune I pre'thee / Give me this man but once more in my armes, / And if I loose him, women have no charmes' (280–2). In their encounter in 3.4, Lelia once again uses her wiles to frustrate Julio's desire. He cries: 'Y'ave conquer'd me: / I did not thinke to yield'

(3.4.155–6). She toys with his affections but does not satisfy him. In the rhetoric and on the surface this looks like a love pursuit, but it is not. In fact, in a perverse twist, Lelia attempts to seduce her Father in 4.4: 'I have turn'd the reverence of a childe / Into the hot affection of a Lover', she says to him (4.4.167–8). This response appears through the prism of his soliloquy (69–84), a speech that morally condemns Lelia. With the help of Angilo, the Father drags the daughter away until tears of repentance shall 'flow all o're thy body foul'd with sin' (282).

The course of true love does not run very smoothly in the other plot either. But little by little Franck breaks down Jacamo's resistance, this man who has hated all women and instead loves the soldierly life. As Franck tells her female companion Clora: 'He's to be made more tractable I doubt not' (3.3.166). Tractable he becomes; only his misguided masculinity has stood in the way. His friends forcibly bring him in 5.4 to Franck's house where he finally breaks down and admits his love for her. Through the deceitful machinations of the Father, Piso agrees to marry Lelia, not knowing that he would be marrying the lusty widow. But she now insists that she has a pure heart. All these marriages lead Angilo to observe: 'If a marriage should be thus slubberd up in a play, er'e almost any body had taken notice you were in love, the Spectators would take it to be but ridiculous' (5.5.32–5). This self-conscious response implies the question: it may be marriage, but is it love?

For spectators at court three additional plays by Beaumont and Fletcher pointedly confront political issues, the matter of succession, and the intersection of love. These plays, *Philaster*, *A King and No King*, and *The Maid's Tragedy*, wrestle with the problem of intemperate princes who raise disturbing questions about monarchy and the power of the sovereign. These issues surely resonate with the Jacobean court whose king jealously guarded his power and prerogatives. *Philaster* opens with a conversation between Dion and Cleremont, trusted noblemen at the Sicilian court, presided over by an unnamed King, who has actually usurped his power from the rightful heir Philaster. Dion announces that a Spanish prince, Pharamond, has arrived at court in order to marry the King's daughter, Arethusa, who actually loves Philaster. Like the Jacobean court, this court readies itself for a royal wedding. Cleremont observes: 'it is thought, with her he shall enjoy both these kingdoms of Sicily and Calabria' (1.1.20–1).[24] Dion notes the looming controversy because

Philaster's father 'was by our late King of Calabria unrighteously deposed from his fruitful Sicily' (29–31). In this play the politics of a royal wedding and the subsequent matter of succession remain clouded by the prior political problem of usurpation. The play keeps asking: what constitutes legitimate rule and truthful love?

The King, who arrives with Arethusa and Pharamond, proclaims in open court his intention that Pharamond marry Arethusa and become his heir. The grateful Pharamond clearly has his own political agenda. This seemingly happy moment gets interrupted by Philaster, who recalls his father and presses his claim to the kingdom. Pharamond and the King decide that Philaster must be mad. He admits that he is possessed 'with my father's spirit' (287). Arethusa departs with her father at line 300, having spoken not a word since her arrival at line 97. Such silence underscores her limited position in the negotiations for a royal marriage and her tenuous position regarding her love of Philaster. On the surface, this opening scene looks orderly and hopeful for a smooth succession to the reign of Pharamond. But a major tension of politics and love punctures this happy illusion. In 1.2, Arethusa makes clear to Philaster her love without which, she says, 'all the land / Discovered yet will serve me for no use / But to be buried in' (1.2.83–5). Amazed, Philaster accepts and reciprocates her love and offers his page Bellario to serve as a go-between.

Unintentionally, Pharamond lets Arethusa off the hook by having a sexual encounter in Act 2 with the wily Megra, one of the court ladies. Arethusa had rebuffed his earlier advances to her. The King and others in 2.4 confront Megra and Pharamond, who do not deny their experience. When the King speaks sternly to Megra, accusing her of the loss of honour and many other things, she responds by saying, 'I cannot choose but laugh to see you merry' (2.4.150). Then she moves maliciously to accuse Arethusa and Bellario of having an illicit relationship. Unfortunately, everyone at court apparently finds this outrageous claim quite plausible, and this seeming truth governs almost everything else that happens in the play. Philaster accepts the likelihood and in 3.1 confronts Bellario, who has to respond to Philaster's jealous outburst.

Like the characters in the *Merry Devil of Edmonton* who spend Act 4 wandering about in the woods, so here in *Philaster*, except that the issues and actions become perilous and sinister. Instead of wounding animals in the hunt, as might be expected, the characters succeed in wounding each other, literally as well as figuratively. The King desperately seeks his daughter and commands Dion to find her, as he grows more insistent: 'am I not your King? / If aye, then am I not to be obeyed?' (4.2.115–16). But Dion counters: 'Yes, if you command things possible and honest' (117). In this rapid exchange, the play highlights the question of royal authority, which the King thinks challenged just because Dion cannot locate Arethusa. These country woods, which Philaster has found momentarily nourishing and offering a tranquil life that he now desires (4.2.40–50), turn out to be not so much lovely as dark and deep.

The darkness deepens for the love problems as Philaster, several times threatening to take his own life, succeeds only in wounding first Arethusa (4.3) and then Bellario (4.4) in a bizarre set of developments in which Beaumont and Fletcher skirt close to the ridiculous and absurd. The woods appear to heighten the possibility of satire. Meanwhile, the country folk are the only ones who seem to have any good sense, such as the Country Fellow who interrupts Philaster's wounding of Arethusa; but she, ordinarily level-headed, turns on this Fellow: 'What ill-bred man art thou, to intrude thyself / Upon our private sports, our recreations?' (4.3.92–3). Incredulous, this Fellow says that he does not understand them – a view that the audience might readily share – and he fights Philaster and wounds him. Staggering in the woods, Philaster comes upon the sleeping Bellario and promptly stabs him. Nobly, Bellario urges him to hide in the bushes, which he does, only to emerge later: 'Philaster creeps out of the bush' (4.4.83 SD). And so the satire of courtly romance continues. At least Philaster accepts responsibility and owns up to what he has done, which leads the King to send him off to prison.

But prison becomes a liberating place for Philaster and Arethusa, who succeed in getting married there, while the citizens of Messina have rioted against Pharamond and captured him. At court Bellario offers a spoken epithalamium in praise of the lovers. Philaster directly challenges the King, should he deign to harm Arethusa. Mutiny in the streets and the cries to make Philaster king compel the King to ask his forgiveness and eventually to restore him to the throne. Pharamond will be put on a speedy boat back to Spain. Only one thing remains to be resolved: the identity of Bellario, who reveals that he is actually Euphrasia, daughter of Dion. To this happy revelation, Philaster cries: 'The gods are just' (5.5.136). The play thus ends with a royal wedding, just not the one anticipated at the play's opening. Orderly and proper succession will occur, a goal common to royal marriages. The Jacobean court might have fastened on to the King's final words: 'Let princes learn / By this to rule the passions of their blood' (5.5.214–15). The King might have made the same point about lovers, of course.

Whatever the audience at Whitehall might have thought about Philaster wandering in the woods stabbing people, they encountered a moral problem of a greater magnitude in the person of Arbaces, King of Iberia in *A King and No King*. (The very title would surely have puzzled King James.) No one disputes Arbaces' rule; indeed, everyone defers to him, acknowledging his power. His military prowess draws major attention in the play's opening, for he has defeated Tigranes, King of Armenia. But Arbaces undercuts his own authority by his intemperance, a quality countered by the moral rectitude of Mardonius and even Tigranes. Exercising his royal prerogative, Arbaces determines to take Tigranes with him back to Iberia as a potential marriage partner for Panthea, his sister, whom he has not seen in years. Arbaces calls this act 'Fit for a god to do upon his foe' (1.1.145).[25] Regularly he makes unchecked assumptions about his power as king, even insisting that he has patience 'Above a god' (242). When Arbaces arrives in Iberia, he reminds the grateful citizens: 'Now you may live securely in your towns' (2.2.93), an echo of James's own words about the stability, peace, and benefits that they had brought to England in 1603.

Arbaces meets his sister in 3.1 and immediately experiences strange urges for her. His subsequent bizarre behaviour confirms these incestuous longings. Arbaces fully understands the moral problem but seems powerless to yield to its wisdom. Thus he concludes: 'Incest is in me / Dwelling already, and it must be holy / That pulls it thence' (334–6). This statement comes after he has kissed Panthea and ordered her to prison, just as he also dispatches Tigranes to prison in a violation of kingly obligation to another sovereign. Arbaces seeks to resolve his problems by imposing his political will, which action only exposes his moral weakness and the infirmity of will. But he does honestly admit to the noble Mardonius: 'I would desire her love / Lasciviously, lewdly, incestuously, / To do a sin that needs must damn us both' (3.3.79–81). Meanwhile, the genuine love of Tigranes and Spaconia, who has shrewdly and cleverly followed him to Iberia, counterpoints (seen especially in 4.2) the increasingly lurid, if compelling, story of Arbaces and Panthea, whose expression of love reaches its zenith in 4.4, a dramatically and rhetorically powerful encounter between brother and sister.

For the first time they can give free rein to their illicit passions, acknowledging their love and struggling with its moral implications. Arbaces speaks in an aside, wanting 'To quench these rising flames that harbor here' (4.4.8). The 'rising flames' of passion engulf them both. Panthea does not recoil when Arbaces says: 'I have beheld thee with a lustful eye. / My heart is set on wickedness' (71–2). Only the words 'brother' and 'sister' can stop them; and Panthea agrees: 'There is nothing else, / But these, alas, will separate us' (114–15) – two little words yet more powerful than twenty worlds. Arbaces asks plaintively: 'Panthea, / What shall we do? Shall we stand firmly here / And gaze our eyes out?' (128–30). No easy answer emerges. They kiss, a tangible sign of the unfulfilled passion that rages inside. Arbaces senses that they have reached a flashpoint, a dangerous moment: 'away. / Sin grows upon us more by this delay' (162–3). Departure momentarily quenches the rising flames.

How can Beaumont and Fletcher resolve this conundrum? They choose an answer from romance: mistaken identity, which can settle the battle between infirm will and moral restraints. The playwrights thus blunt the narrative trajectory that moves towards tragedy. Arbaces' opening soliloquy in 5.4 encapsulates the difficulty and his determination: 'Hell, open all thy gates, / And I will through them' (5.4.2–3). The dramatists bring in the noble Mardonius and Gobrius as counters to Arbaces' purpose; and they eventually include Arane, Arbaces' presumed mother. Gobrius startles Arbaces when he responds to the king's threat: 'Know / You kill your father' (117). The speeches by Gobrius, starting at line 200, reveal Arbaces' identity as his son, and not the queen's child, the result of her own strategy to provide the king a son. Meanwhile, unexpectedly, Arane had produced a child by the king, namely Panthea. Arbaces asks excitedly: 'Panthea, then, is not my sister?' (256). Because she is not, Arbaces loses legitimacy as king: 'I am found no king!' (264). What in other circumstances might cause considerable dismay and danger turns out to be a moment of unusual joy for Arbaces and for Panthea also, who readily accepts his proposal of marriage. The play closes with Arbaces' invitation to everyone to sing 'Loud thanks for me, that I am proved no King' (353). The rising flames of passion can now enclose Arbaces and Panthea, the new queen, in a refining embrace of legitimate love.

No such joy greeted the court spectators who watched in mounting horror *The Maid's Tragedy*, which includes adultery, jealousy, regicide, suicide, murder, and, for good measure, an intemperate King of Rhodes who insists on his absolute authority. They did get to see a formal masque in 1.2, such as they had experienced in *Oberon*, *The Masque of Queens*, or *Tethys' Festival*. Strato's definition of a masque's function would have sounded most familiar to Lennox: 'They must commend their king and speak / In praise of the assembly, bless the bride / And bridegroom in person of some god. / They're tied to rules of flattery' (1.1.8–11).[26] Beaumont readies himself to present his own masque for the wedding in a few weeks of Princess Elizabeth and Frederick, a masque textually shorter than the one in this play. Perhaps he tries out the genre here in preparation for the actual royal wedding. The idea of commending the king in the masque certainly pervades the Jacobean court, as does Lysippus's assertion: 'The breath of kings is like the breath of gods' (16).

But the masque, full of Night, Cynthia, Neptune, Aeolus, Proteus, music and dancing, obscures the reality of this wedding celebration. Amintor explains to his dear friend Melantius: 'She [Aspatia] had my promise, but the King forbade it, / And made me make this worthy change' (1.1.138–9). Instead of marrying his loved one, Aspatia, Amintor will have to marry Evadne, Melantius's sister. Imposition of royal will produces dismay and a tearful Aspatia, who 'carries with her an infectious grief / That strikes all her beholders' (1.1.97–8). Night in the masque may say more than she intends in her opening line: 'Our reign is come' (1.2.117). Even as the gods come to honour this nuptial, the scene cannot shake the presence of darkness, a blackness that will soon begin to permeate the play. An uneasy solution of tragical mirth governs the masque.

That mood continues into 2.1 where Aspatia appears near Evadne's bedchamber on the wedding night as a haunting presence and cries out that this should have been her marriage celebration. A tension between the festive wedding and the funereal presence of Aspatia dominates the opening moments. She greets the arriving Amintor: 'Thus I wind myself / Into this willow garland' (119–20). Amintor acknowledges that he has wronged Aspatia but insists: 'It was the King first moved me to't' (130). He then turns his attention to Evadne cheerfully: 'To bed, my love! Hymen will punish us / For being slack performers of his rites' (143–4). But Evadne adamantly refuses, leading Amintor to think that this is but the 'coyness of a bride' (159); but she removes all doubt, saying: 'I hate thee. / Thou shouldst have killed thyself' (183–4). Surely Amintor experiences some kind of dream, he thinks; instead, he endures the darkness of a nightmare, now intensified when she reveals that she has a lover, who is the King (304). Evadne has agreed to this marriage that is no marriage so 'that my sin may be / More honorable' (318–19). Worried about his own shame, Amintor suggests to Evadne: 'Come, let us practice; and, as wantonly / As ever loving bride and bridegroom met, / Let's laugh and enter here' (357–9). To which Evadne responds: 'I am content'. But no contentment can come of this 'practice', at best an artful fiction.

The morning after brings its lies as when Amintor claims, 'We ventured for a boy' (3.1.23); then he and Evadne engage in playful banter. The King enters and wants to know how the night went. The practised responses from Amintor and Evadne stir the King's jealousy. Evadne assures him that she has sworn never to love 'A man of lower place' (184); in fact, she claims: 'I love with my ambition, / Not with my eyes' (187–8). She regards all men as potentially useful to her, no more, no less. Amintor challenges the king and calls him a 'tyrant' (235) but hesitates to go beyond that because of the 'divinity' that surrounds the king. Evadne parts from Amintor by saying: 'I am gone. / I love my life well' (293–4); to which he can only respond: 'I hate mine as much' (294). In 3.2 Amintor encounters Melantius and finally tells him the truth that his sister 'to the King has given her honor up, / And lives in whoredom with him' (3.2.126–7). After some resistance, Melantius accepts this new reality, and the word 'revenge' enters the play. Not only a dear friend, Melantius serves as a strong moral compass for Amintor as they set out to find some way to kill the King.

But first Melantius confronts Evadne, the business of 4.1. She eventually admits her fault and cries out: 'Oh, I am miserable' (114), the beginning of her repentance, which immediately manifests itself when Amintor enters. Understandably, he thinks that she mocks him, but she convinces him otherwise; and he extends forgiveness also. The desire for revenge punctures the banquet celebration of 4.2, offered by the King in honour of the bride and bridegroom. Irony saturates the conversations in this scene, and talk turns openly to revenge once the King exits.

Revenge Evadne embraces in 5.1 in a gripping and gruesome scene in the King's bedchamber. Echoing the masque of 1.2, Evadne says: 'The night grows horrible, and all about me, / Like my black purpose' (5.1.13–14). She draws the bed curtains and reveals the sleeping King, whose arms she immediately ties to the bed. When he awakens, he thinks that Evadne has indulged in some 'pretty new device' (47), perhaps to heighten their sexual pleasure. But she announces starkly: 'I am come to kill thee' (83). When he insists that 'I am thy king', she responds, 'Thou art my shame' (97, 98). Evadne stabs the King repeatedly, concluding: 'This for my lord Amintor, / This for my noble brother, and this stroke / For the most wronged of women' (110–12). Having fulfilled her black purpose, Evadne exits.

Night continues 'her reign', and death seems to have an insatiable appetite. Aspatia returns to the play in 5.3, disguised as a man, and announces: 'This is my fatal hour' (5.3.1), echoing Evadne. Aspatia confronts Amintor and pretends to be Aspatia's 'brother' come to right the wrongs that he has done to her and accuses him of base 'injury' that he has done. She draws a sword and strikes Amintor, who has tried to ignore her bellicose remarks. In self-defence, he responds and wounds her. At that moment Evadne enters, *'her hands bloody, with a knife'* (105 SD). She cries: 'Joy to Amintor, for the King is dead' (126); and she presses the cause of her love for Amintor, prompting him to respond: 'Thou monster of cruelty, forbear!' (156). Rebuffed, Evadne takes her own life. Perplexed by what is unfolding, Amintor turns his attention to Aspatia, who confesses her true identity and her love for him and then dies. Attempts to revive her fail, and Amintor kills himself. Lysippus, now king, interprets the events: 'For on lustful kings / Unlooked-for sudden deaths from God are sent; / But curst is he that is their instrument' (293–5). While possibly true, that statement seems reductive and inadequate to encompass the experience of this powerful tragedy whose narrative trajectory has moved past a wedding celebration and spectacular masque to the undercurrents of adultery and revenge, a night world that encompasses Rhodes.

Many of the qualities in the Beaumont and Fletcher plays appear also in *Cupid's Revenge*, which the court had seen a couple of years earlier and which it saw twice in early 1613: on 1 January, performed by the Children of the Queen's Revels and sponsored by King James; and a few days later on 9 January, performed by the same group and sponsored by Prince Charles. (Of all the plays performed during this season, only this one offers evidence of the dates of performance, thanks to the records in the Chamber Accounts.)[27]

In *Cupid's Revenge*, Leontius, the ageing and decrepit King of Lycia, an Arcadian kingdom, has a son Leucippus and a daughter Hidaspes, who would seem to assure an orderly succession. But Leontius articulates a kind of motto for the play when in frustration he says 'The greatest curse the Gods lay on our frailties, / Is will and disobedience in our Issues' (1.5.115–16).[28] Lennox and others would recognise this theme from the other Beaumont and Fletcher plays. In addition, this play includes the active intervention of the god Cupid, who appears several times and imposes his malign will on the kingdom.

On the occasion of his daughter's birthday, Leontius allows her to make whatever request she desires. With the concurrence of Leucippus, Hidaspes asks 'That these erected obsceane Images [of Cupid] / May be pluckt downe and burnt: and every man / That offers to 'em any sacrifice, / May lose his life' (1.1.74–7). The worship and veneration of Cupid has had a deleterious effect on the kingdom, Hidaspes thinks, justifying all kinds of immoral behaviour. Worried about the possible reaction of the god, Leontius nevertheless honours the request; and from this decision all follows. By 1.2 the authorities send away a Priest of Cupid and destroy the temple, leading to Cupid's first appearance in 1.3. Cupid promises revenge that will leave 'this a most wretched Land' (1.3.20). Can the kingdom survive the profaning of the gods?

The royal children exhibit poor judgement, witness Hidaspes' righteous request. In addition, she perversely decides to marry Zoylus, an ugly dwarf. Such action outrages the king, who banishes Zoylus and has him beheaded. Hidaspes languishes and dies (2.5). Leucippus meanwhile carries on an affair with the lusty widow Bacha (2.2). In her naked ambition and sexual activity she would remind spectators of Evadne. But Leontius finds himself smitten by Bacha and unexpectedly decides to marry her. The king justifies his decision in terms of marriage rejuvenating him, and this includes the ironic scene (2.4) in which he remains preoccupied with his appearance and his athletic skill. But, of course, Bacha will only use him for her purposes. Cupid begins to work through her.

The moral Leucippus rebuffs Bacha's advances in 3.2; and Bacha plans her revenge (3.2.247–52). No longer merely concerned about sex, she now focuses on political ambition, the future of the kingdom itself. Her strategies include extensively praising Leucippus's virtues, thereby triggering Leontius's jealousy. By 4.2,

Bacha asserts that the son has sought Leontius's death (4.2.42). When guards drag Leucippus into the court, Leontius lashes out at him: 'shame of Nature, / Bastard to Honour, Traytor, Murderer' (95–6). And the king wonders as they take Leucippus to prison, 'Are these the comforts of my Age?' (91). The king's earlier statement about 'disobedience in our Issues' has certainly come true. The 'disobedience' of numerous Citizens, however, frees Leucippus from prison (4.3).

Cupid makes one last appearance and claims: 'The time now of my Revenge drawes neere' (5.3.1). The following scene makes clear the completion of this revenge. Urania, Bacha's daughter, appears disguised as a male (reminiscent of Bellario in *Philaster* and Aspatia in *The Maid's Tragedy*) and in fact saves Leucippus from certain death by Timantus who runs at him with a sword as she steps in front of Leucippus. As a result of this encounter, Urania dies; and so does Timantus, who has subsequently been wounded by Leucippus. When Ismenus, Leucippus's faithful friend, brings in the enraged Bacha, she lashes out at them, cursing them and hoping that 'your base issues may be ever Monsters' (5.4.164); and she acknowledges: 'I am at the worst of evils' (187). Then she proceeds to stab Leucippus and herself, bringing about their deaths. In his dying breath, Leucippus urges that 'the broken Image of *Cupid* be reedified, / I know all this is done by him' (216–17). Ismenus, the new ruler, has the final judgement: to honour Leucippus's body, 'But dragge her [Bacha] to a ditch, where let her lye / Accurst, whilst one man has a memory' (232–3). True to his word, Cupid has left this kingdom 'a most wretched land'.

What an extraordinary dramatic and fictional journey Beaumont and Fletcher have provided the Jacobean court, from simple love stories to desperate tragic events to challenges to the political status and stability of the kingdom. Tragical mirth indeed! As another avenue to the court's transition and transformation from funeral to wedding, Shakespeare offered the court several plays, performed by his company. These plays, of various genres, intersect and illustrate the words of the Prologue in *Merry Devil*: 'Sit with a pleased eye, until you know / The comic end of our sad tragic show.' Far removed from the Mediterranean and Arcadian setting of the Beaumont and Fletcher plays, Shakespeare's *1 and 2 Henry IV* examine the political and military history of early fifteenth-century England.[29] Part 1 focuses on the events following Richard II's deposition and the coronation of Henry IV up through the successful battle at Shrewsbury in 1403; Part 2 moves from 1403 to 1413 and includes the coronation of Prince Hal as Henry V, which occurred in early April 1413.

Thus, the Jacobean court, gathered in January 1613, could easily be celebrating the two-hundredth anniversary of the rise of Henry V, a precursor for the now deceased Prince Henry – hence a possible reason for selecting these two plays for performance. In the enthusiastic response to James's son, many people clearly saw him in martial and militaristic terms and held out hope that he would engage in some kind of as yet undefined exploit, all of this in contrast to his pacifist father. What better model than Henry V, the paragon of military accomplishment, especially the defeat of the French at Agincourt in 1415. The character Merlin in Jonson's *Prince Henry's Barriers*, performed at court in early 1610, speaks at length of Henry V and makes the link to Prince Henry:

> Yet rests the other thunderbolt of war,
> Harry the fifth, to whom in face you are
> So like, as Fate would have you so in worth,
> Illustrious prince! This virtue ne'er came forth
> But Fame flew greater for him than she did
> For other mortals.[30]

Not only does Henry look like Henry V, his presence continues to daunt the French. The *Henry IV* plays thus compel the Jacobean court to confront their great loss, still burning in their memories.

The narrative arc of these plays, which date from the 1590s, traces Prince Hal's seeming transformation from profligate and irresponsible son to self-confident and sagacious new king. All of this occurs in the mix of serious rebellion from the Percy faction and the comic and frivolous high jinks with Hal's boon companion, the ahistorical Falstaff, who might well feel at home in Jonson's *The Alchemist*. But Hal's self-conscious theatricality comes through clearly in his soliloquy in 1.2 of *1 Henry IV*, in which Hal refers to 'My reformation glitt'ring o'er my fault, / Shall show more goodly and attract more eyes / Than that which hath no foil to set it off' (206–8).[31] Hal's understanding Shakespeare sets in opposition not only to Falstaff but also to the rebellious Hotspur, son of the Earl of Northumberland, who rallies the Percys against Henry IV. Hotspur's impatience, hotheadedness, and delight in battle define him throughout. Shakespeare encapsulates and demonstrates these qualities in Hotspur's reaction to the anonymous letter that he reads in 1.3. He heaps satiric scorn on this unidentified person who has the gall to resist the idea of rebellion because of its danger. Hotspur dismisses him as a 'dish of skim milk' (1.3.31). On the battlefield at Shrewsbury, Hotspur behaves similarly, unfazed by the lack of adequate troops; courage resembles foolhardiness.

No one would accuse Falstaff of being a 'dish of skim milk'; that seems much too dainty for this large man. Courage also does not reside among his virtues. Indeed, Shakespeare creates this character to challenge political and military assumptions. Falstaff offers a satire of chivalric virtue and honour, creating the space for Hal to occupy between him and Hotspur. The great tavern scene of 2.4 gives full vent to all of these issues. The Eastcheap tavern could fit in Jonson's Blackfriars as a place of chicanery, theatre, satire, deceit, and just plain fun.

Falstaff arrives at the tavern, railing at cowards, believing falsely that he has been abandoned by his companions, Hal and others, as they set upon unwary pilgrims in order to rob them. Hal and Poins have in fact robbed Falstaff. He cries out, 'A plague of all cowards', and asks, 'Is there no virtue extant?' (2.4.108, 112). That rhetorical question courses through the play, as does Falstaff's later, 'Is not the truth the truth?' (220–1). Virtue and truth seem more like alien concepts for Falstaff, whose veracity Hal has successfully challenged. Like Face in *The Alchemist*, Falstaff manages to divert attention from his situation by raising the prospect of a play-within-the-play, lines 360–465. First, Falstaff pretends to be King Henry IV and chides Hal for being an unacceptable son; second, Hal acts as the king, and Falstaff, Hal. In this role Falstaff insists: 'Banish plump Jack, and banish all the world'; and Hal responds, 'I do, I will' (465). A knocking at the door interrupts this playfulness, which has turned in a serious direction. Hal's pregnant and disturbing statement looks to the future, which finds its culmination at the end of *2 Henry IV*.

From this London setting, Shakespeare shifts the play to Wales and Owen Glendower's castle where the rebellious forces have gathered to map strategy. With this move Shakespeare opens the play to magic and mystery, which certainly seems at odds with the rebels, especially Hotspur who has no use for Glendower and his mystical understanding of the world. Glendower may take the Jacobean court back to the world of *Merry Devil* and Fabell's magical skills, or, conversely, remind spectators of the bogus magic of *The Alchemist*. Glendower insists that 'I can call spirits from the vasty deep' (53); to which Hotspur curtly responds, 'Why so can I ... / But will they come when you do call for them?' (54–5). Glendower's interest in poetry further grates on Hotspur, whose understanding of the world cannot accommodate mystery and the supernatural.

In 3.2, Shakespeare shifts again, this time to the royal palace of Henry IV, where the king anxiously awaits the arrival of Hal, the son who seems to the king less desirable than Hotspur. The mock interviews of the tavern scene now become realised in the actual conversation between king and son. Henry IV thinks that Hal serves as some kind of punishment of him; he even worries that perhaps Hal has allied himself with the Percys, and he calls Hal 'the shadow of succession' (3.2.99). The king echoes another king, Leontius in *Cupid's Revenge*, who observed that the 'greatest curse the Gods lay on our frailties, / Is will and disobedience in our Issues' (1.5.115–,6). But Hal counters: 'I will redeem all this on Percy's head' (132). With these ringing promises, Henry and Hal set forth to meet the rebels at Shrewsbury, the focus of the remainder of the play.

Heroic attitudes and chivalric behaviour govern part of what happens on the battlefield as Hotspur urges on his outnumbered troops and as the king and his representatives try to negotiate with the rebels. But one voice hovers over the battlefield: Falstaff's, which casts a biting and different light on heroic efforts. Along the road to Coventry, Falstaff has gathered his troops, which even Falstaff admits: 'No eye hath seen such scarecrows' (4.2.37). They embarrass him sufficiently so that he does not want to march with them through Coventry. And when Hal encounters him and observes, 'I did never see such pitiful rascals' (63), Falstaff quickly retorts: 'Tut, tut! good enough to toss; food for powder, food for powder. They'll fill a pit as well as better' (64–5). Falstaff brings to a head the pervasive issue of the play when he asks and answers: 'What is honor?' (5.1.133). For Falstaff 'honor' has little meaning; and he concludes: 'Therefore I'll none of it. Honor is a mere scutcheon – and so ends my catechism' (138–40). Fortunately, Hal gives the lie to this unduly cynical view by his brave actions in battle and his defeat of Hotspur, leading Henry IV to say of him: 'Thou hast redeemed thy lost opinion' (5.4.47).

2 Henry IV makes abundantly clear the fleeting nature of such victories. In fact, this play opens with Northumberland, who had not been able to go to Shrewsbury, seeking a reliable report of what happened. Morton, who had been present, finally tells Northumberland: 'The sum of all / Is that the king hath won' (1.1.132–3) and that Hal slew Hotspur. This dispiriting setback leads to the poignant encounter in 2.3 with Hotspur's widow and her conversation with Northumberland and his wife in which Lady Percy offers an idealised portrait of her husband, the 'glass / Wherein the noble youth did dress themselves' (2.3.21–2). Various characters try to offer a picture of warfare and valour that can somehow counter Falstaff's grim assessment.

Although Falstaff continues to prowl the halls of power, he seems to have lost some of his lustre, finding himself accused of having promised marriage. Hal meanwhile readies himself to succeed his ill and dying father. Falstaff's last gasp on the battlefield comes in his claim to have vanquished Coleville and boasts of his valour (4.3.37). What, the audience may wonder, does Falstaff know about valour? Hal appears as the new Henry V in 5.2 where he reconciles himself to the Chief Justice, a new surrogate father for him, and assures his brothers. Hal, the voice of reason, will with his father's spirit survive 'To mock the expectation of the world, / To frustrate prophecies and to raze out / Rotten opinion' (5.2.126–8). Truly now he redeems lost opinion; this new confidence enables him to face the last hurdle: getting rid of Falstaff, which is the burden of 5.5. Hal says to the eager Falstaff, who hails him as friend, 'I know thee not, old man' (47); and he sends Falstaff off to prison. However cruel this moment, it does complete Hal's turn away from his former self. To be the true successor of his father and now guardian of the kingdom, he can no longer indulge the Eastcheap tavern companion. History expunges ahistory.

Shakespeare approaches another version of history in *Julius Caesar*, among the first plays performed in the Globe Theatre's opening year, 1599. The ancient history of the first century BCE nevertheless raises the familiar questions of rule, tyranny, and the consequences of action. In fact, Lennox and the court might hear Falstaff's question surging through this play: 'What is honor?' Cassius insists: 'honor is the subject of my story' (1.2.94). The conspirators certainly wrap themselves in the mantle of doing the honourable and noble thing in their assassination of Caesar.

Cassius also says to Brutus, 'thou art noble' (1.2.308), and therein hangs the moral problem for him. The choice of *Julius Caesar* could have resonated in another way, namely King James's identification with Augustus Caesar, the Octavius Caesar of the play. This link between James and Caesar the king enjoyed, and various writers explored that connection, seen obviously in the great royal entry civic pageant in the streets of London on 15 March 1604. Further, the recollection of Roman history forms part of the Trojan foundational myth of British history, the belief that England enjoyed some special relationship to the ancient world of Troy through Brutus, the great-grandson of Aeneas. Virgil in the *Aeneid*, written for Augustus Caesar, had helped create the Roman idea of its inheritance from the remnants of Troy.[32]

Julius Caesar embraces the idea of the supernatural as an adjunct and participant in history, seen in the Soothsayer, the storms, the omens, dreams, and appearance of Caesar's Ghost to Brutus in 4.2. Caesar is famously susceptible to the allures of the supernatural, clearly demonstrated in 2.2, which ironically allow him to ignore warnings about his personal safety. The conspirators proceed in a straightforward way, as they map their rebellious plan. Brutus accepts the idea of Caesar's tyranny, which might enslave them; and he frames the conspiracy in moral terms. Thus, he resists the idea that they should also kill Marc Antony by saying, 'Let's be sacrificers, but not butchers' (2.1.166). And he defines the mission: 'A piece of work that will make sick men whole' (2.1.326). This justification does not sound radically different from that of the Percys in the *Henry IV* plays. Certainly in the assassination scene, 3.1, the conspirators claim that their deed can grant peace, freedom, and liberty. Somewhat smugly, Cassius asserts, as they smear their hands with Caesar's blood: 'How many ages hence / Shall this our lofty scene be acted over, / In states unborn and accents yet unknown!' (3.1.112–14). Sacrifice become theatre history as at the Jacobean court.

In the Forum, Brutus speaks first and explains his action: 'not that I loved Caesar less, but that I loved Rome more' (3.2.21–2). The ethos of this moral man the crowd accepts and supports. But Brutus exits, leaving the space open for Antony, who with a brilliance and eloquence unparalleled in the rhetoric of the play chips away at Brutus's 'honor' and the alleged justness of the conspirators' cause. Skilfully, the more that Antony refers to 'honor', the more it diminishes. Antony even descends from the pulpit, uncovers

Caesar's body, and claims: 'I am no orator as Brutus is' (211) – a moment of intended irony. All that Antony does lifts the crowd into a frenzy; and they rush out to 'fire the traitors' houses' (247), leading to their bizarre encounter with Cinna the Poet, whom they kill for his bad verses (3.3).

Act 4 opens with the triumvirate of Antony, Octavius, and Lepidus, who present themselves as the new rulers of Rome. They busily select which persons should be killed, soliciting Lepidus's consent for the death of his brother. They also make preparations to encounter Brutus and Cassius and their armies at Philippi. After their petty squabble, Brutus tells Cassius: 'There is a tide in the affairs of men / Which, taken at the flood, leads on to fortune' (4.2.270–1). But if one does not seize the opportunity, 'the voyage of their life / Is bound in shallows and in miseries' (272–3) – a possible echo of Hotspur's voice. The remainder of the play throws doubt on Brutus's assumption. Even the bracing and rhetorically ironic encounter of Octavius, Antony, Brutus, and Cassius on the battlefield does not resolve the issue. Instead, Octavius challenges the opponents: 'Defiance, traitors, hurl we in your teeth. / If you dare fight today, come to the field' (5.1.64–5). On the false news that 'Titinius is enclosèd round about' (5.3.28), spoken by Pindarus, Cassius despairs and takes his own life. Arriving too late, Brutus draws this conclusion: 'O Julius Caesar, thou art mighty yet. / Thy spirit walks abroad' (94–5). Thus Brutus also commits suicide (5.5). The play closes with Antony's defence of Brutus, whom he characterises as 'the noblest Roman of them all' (5.5.67); only he had the 'general honest thought / And common good' to become one of the conspirators (70–1). Brutus will, according to Octavius, receive 'all respect and rites of burial' (76). Despite the praise heaped on Brutus, his initial goal of creating a work that will make sick men whole has proved to be seriously flawed and resting on a false moral principle. What indeed is honour?

Unlike the English history plays and *Julius Caesar* with their emphasis on politics, *Othello*, which Lennox and the court would have first seen on 1 November 1604, examines the private life and a marriage between Othello, the Moor and outsider, and Desdemona, daughter of Brabantio of Venice.[33] The natural storm in 2.1, which bangs the Turkish ships and defeats them, can serve as the basis for a recurring metaphor in the play. A series of storms tears apart the fabric of social and private life. The violence that erupts on the island of Cyprus in 2.3 and Cassio's involvement in it leads him to outline his moral trajectory: 'To be now a sensible man, by and by a fool, and presently a beast!' (2.3.293–4). This assessment creates a marker for all those who fail as a result of the diabolical machinations of Iago, who views the world cynically and therefore finds it devoid of reliable love and beauty. He comments in Act 5 on why he wants to kill Cassio: 'If Cassio do remain, / He hath a daily beauty in his life / That makes me ugly' (5.1.18–20). For Iago every noble, heroic, and beautiful action and attitude must be brought low, sullied, and tarnished. His psychological storm of activity brings this to pass, making beasts of people who had been sensible. Dozens of times credulous people in the play refer to Iago as 'honest'; but he offers an accurate view of himself: 'I am not what I am' (1.1.64). This statement becomes the predicate of his behaviour. Iago may share some qualities with Bacha of *Cupid's Revenge* or Evadne of *The Maid's Tragedy*, but mainly he exists in a league of his own. He has a narrative trajectory, but not a moral one.

The play begins with a storm in Venice as Iago and his sidekick Roderigo rouse the sleeping Brabantio into the darkness with cries of 'Thieves! thieves! / Look to your house, your daughter, and your bags!' (1.1.78–9). Startled and alarmed, Brabantio insists, 'This is Venice' (104), as if the city were somehow immune to disturbance. Roderigo claims that Desdemona has rushed 'To the gross clasps of a lascivious Moor' (124), thereby exacerbating Brabantio's fears with racism. The enraged father seeks out the Duke and Senate of Venice for aid and accuses Othello of practising witchcraft. Calm and composed, Othello resists this emerging storm. His powerful defence and definition of himself, 1.3.76–170, wins over everyone, except Brabantio, who merely resigns himself to the loss of his daughter. The Venetian government seeks Othello's services to lead an expedition against the Turks, who seem to be headed to Cyprus. Othello goes out into a potential military storm. He and Desdemona, sailing on separate ships, survive the natural storm and arrive safely in Cyprus. Reunited with her, Othello calls her his 'soul's joy' (2.1.183) and claims: 'If it were now to die, / 'Twere now to be most happy' (188–9). But the psychological storm that awaits them will break down this happiness and love. That becomes the burden of life on Cyprus.

Through his actions in 2.3, Iago gets Cassio drunk and engaged in a fight, which rouses Othello, echoing the play's opening scene.

Othello cannot understand this irrational behaviour; thus he decides: 'Cassio, I love thee, / But never more be officer of mine' (2.3.237–8). The fall of Cassio foreshadows Desdemona's fall, as sensible people give way to fears and seeming proof. Court spectators watch in stunned amazement and mounting fear the powerful scene in which Iago convinces Othello of Desdemona's unfaithfulness (3.3). As Iago offers 'proof' and argument, Othello tries desperately to hang on to his faith in Desdemona, but he has allowed himself to fall into the trap of believing that love can be proved. He loses in turn faith, hope, and love. Othello says at one point about Desdemona: 'Perdition catch my soul / But I do love thee! and when I love thee not, / Chaos is come again' (90–2). Exactly. Othello shifts his love to Iago: 'I greet thy love' (469), as they have knelt together at the scene's end. And Othello says to Iago: 'Now art thou my lieutenant'; and Iago reciprocates: 'I am your own forever' (479–80). But, of course, Iago belongs only to himself. For the moment this storm has subsided, and love has shifted. Desdemona has lost.

Shocked at Othello's striking Desdemona, Lodovico, recently arrived from Venice, asks: 'Is this the noble Moor whom our full Senate / Call all in all sufficient?' (4.1.258–9). A storm opens Act 5 in the darkened streets of Cyprus as Roderigo encounters Cassio, who wounds him, and then in the dark Iago stabs Cassio. Othello believes that Iago has kept his word by killing Cassio. The urban streets of Cyprus shrink into Desdemona's bedchamber in the final scene, site of a storm of passions, death, and revelations. Desdemona's maid Emilia accosts her husband Iago and asks if he has misled Othello about Desdemona's faithfulness; and he responds: 'I told him what I thought, and told no more / Than what he found himself was apt and true' (5.2.177–8). The power of suggestion, implication, and inference has done its work, leading to Desdemona's wrongful death at Othello's hands. But gradually Othello comes to understand his mistake. 'What shall be said to thee', Lodovico asks (293). Ironically, letters found in the dead Roderigo's pockets condemn Iago and confirm Othello's error. In a final speech, before committing suicide, Othello asks for a report to be written down, relating 'these unlucky deeds' (341): 'Speak of me as I am. Nothing extenuate, / Nor set down aught in malice. Then must you speak / Of one that loved not wisely, but too well' (342–4). From a sensible warrior Othello has transformed into a beast, rejecting the love offered him, unable to negotiate between the competing claims of Desdemona and Iago. Clearly, *Othello* might have become a comedy with the ingredients of love, marriage, successful military exploits, and a civilising Venice; instead, it became a tragedy, starting in 3.2, with suggestion leading to proof and then to disaster for one who loved too absolutely, 'too well'.

If assassination, betrayal, murder, and suicide become fit subjects for Shakespeare's tragedies, are they also fit subjects for an impending royal wedding? Whatever governed his choices, George Buc presumably chose these plays on the assumption that they would not give offence. Surely spectators saw them for the fictions they are without drawing any necessary conclusions about their possible commentary on the Jacobean court. Lennox knew from first-hand experience that marriage does not always work out. What if, however, Shakespeare also offered another perspective, one that allowed the court to see the 'comic end of our sad tragic show' (*Merry Devil*)? This Shakespeare does in three comedies: *Much Ado about Nothing*, *The Tempest*, and *The Winter's Tale* – the last two first seen at court in November 1611.

In the late Elizabethan *Much Ado*, located in Messina, Sicily, the playwright constructs multiple marriages. The newly arrived Claudio of Florence immediately falls in love with Hero, the daughter of Leonato, Governor of Messina, assisted by the good offices of Don Pedro, Prince of Aragon, also recently arrived from some kind of warfare. The other principal couple consists of Benedick of Padua and Beatrice, niece of Leonato, whose chief activity seems to be to engage in a civil war of wits, assuring that they will not get married. Don John, the bastard brother of Don Pedro, also appears with a sad, taciturn, malign disposition – a clear foe of love and marriage. He's up to no good. Conrad asks him: 'Can you make no use of your discontent?' (1.3.34); the remainder of his function focuses precisely on creating discontent, the 'heartburn' that Beatrice sees in him (2.1.4). Don John with Borachio's help creates the illusion that Hero has somehow been unfaithful to Claudio by being 'every man's Hero' (3.2.95). Alas, Claudio falls for this ruse.

Don Pedro, on the other hand, first woos Hero for Claudio's sake, which also leads him to distrust Pedro for a while. Claudio has loved Hero right away; in fact, he says to Hero: 'I am yours, I give away myself for you and dote upon the exchange' (2.1.291–2). Perhaps even more important, Leonato offers the daughter to him: 'Count, take of me my daughter, and with her my fortunes' (285–6).

Nothing seems to stand in the way of their satisfactory love – except Don John's machinations. Pedro also sets in motion a plan to assist the potential love of Beatrice and Benedick (2.3 and 3.1). These wonderful scenes, which Benedick and Beatrice, respectively, overhear, convince them of the other's love. Leonato confirms that Beatrice sits up at night attempting to write on a sheet of paper. The reference to 'sheet' leads to the time-worn jest, which Leonato recalls: 'O, when she had writ it, and was reading it over, she found "Benedick" and "Beatrice" between the sheet' (133–5). Startled, Beatrice tore the sheet in a thousand pieces. The play seeks to find a way to bring them between the sheets.

At the wedding of Claudio and Hero, Claudio speaks of 'proof' (perhaps anticipating Othello) as he turns his withering scorn on the 'unfaithful' Hero. Benedick sums up the situation: 'This looks not like a nuptial' (4.1.67). Under the intense charges, Hero 'swoons', and Beatrice cries out that she is 'dead' (112). Three events undo this harm. First, Hero has not truly died; second, the Friar thinks of a strategy to redeem the situation by letting Claudio continue to think that she has died. And third, the unlikely event of Dogberry, Verges, and the Watchmen who unearth the truth of the incriminating scene that Don John had created. But not before Beatrice has demanded of Benedick: 'Kill Claudio' (4.1.288), one of the most chilling and difficult lines in the play.

Although Benedick challenges Claudio to a fight, it does not come about because of the discovery by Dogberry and others, leading Borachio to admit: 'What your wisdoms could not discover, these shallow fools have brought to light' (5.1.224–5). Instead, Leonato thinks of another possible comic solution: the offer of his 'niece' in marriage to Claudio. Thus the play readies itself for another wedding, after Claudio has first paid homage to the 'dead' Hero at her tomb (5.3). In 5.4, Claudio accepts the masked Hero, and she then unmasks, being very much alive. And for good measure, Benedick and Beatrice agree to marry, finally acknowledging their love. *Much Ado* in its own mirthful way shows a transforming path from death to weddings, erasing misunderstanding, chasing away the discontented Don John, and allowing love to flourish – a true comic end.

The final two Shakespeare plays performed at court in 1613, *The Tempest* and *The Winter's Tale*, construct royal weddings with serious political consequences, especially the matter of succession. They take the relatively simple love stories of *Much Ado* and compound them with royal politics that may include usurpation, rebellion, and alleged adultery. *The Tempest* also contains Prospero, exiled Duke of Milan, magic, and a servant Ariel on a strange island somewhere in the Mediterranean. Prospero manages to create the circumstances that bring his enemies to this place for one afternoon of startling action that leads to reconciliation, renouncing of political power, and a planned wedding. Looking forward to Princess Elizabeth's wedding, Lennox might have found this play particularly reassuring, possibly seeing in Ferdinand and Miranda images of the princess and Frederick. The performance certainly had an additional resonance in 1613, given recent events in the royal family and the imminent wedding.[34]

A storm and shipwreck begin the play, a beginning that looks like an ending for Alonso, King of Naples, his son Ferdinand, Gonzalo, Antonio (Prospero's usurping brother of Milan), and others. Not yet having been introduced to other characters, the audience might conclude that they are watching Shakespeare's shortest tragedy. But 1.2 opens with Prospero, creator of the storm, and his daughter Miranda. The scene unfolds with retrospection, history, the strange creature Caliban, and the unexpected appearance of Ferdinand, who has not died in shipwreck. Prospero and Miranda have lived on this island for twelve years, having been expelled from Milan. Only today has Prospero decided to tell the innocent daughter, now fifteen years old, about the usurpation by Antonio, assisted by Alonso. Thus, in one brief day, they relive the past twelve years and beyond; indeed, Miranda cannot fully understand this single day without its contextual history, much as 1613 can best be comprehended through the events of its immediate past. In the correct and former order of things Prospero would be ruler of Milan with Miranda as his successor. But politics and rebellion have disrupted this order. The play determines to set right this situation and add nuptials that will reconcile Milan and Naples. Ferdinand, believing his father dead in the storm, thinks of himself already as King of Naples. In fact, when he first meets Miranda, he holds out this promise: 'I'll make you / The Queen of Naples' (1.2.449–50). This actually pleases Prospero who watches and says simply, 'It works' (494). In 3.1, they explicitly acknowledge their love, so that this potential marriage will not be just a political reckoning.

Not so lucky Claribel, daughter of Alonso, as the audience learns in 2.1, and it also discovers that the rest of the shipwrecked party indeed lives, counting their survival a miracle, at least in Gonzalo's view. Spectators understand for the first time why the Italian group has been travelling in the Mediterranean: they have gone to Tunis for the wedding of Claribel to an African prince and are returning to Naples. Alonso cries out: 'Would I had never / Married my daughter there! for, coming thence, / My son is lost' (2.1.107–9). And in a sense, so is Claribel, 'so far from Italy removed / I ne'er again shall see her', Alonso says (110–11). Sebastian mercilessly chides Alonso for allowing this marriage instead of blessing 'Europe with your daughter / But rather loose her to an African' (124–5). Claribel herself seems to have been reluctant, at least according to Sebastian. The presumed loss of the royal children as heirs to Naples leads Sebastian and Antonio to plot a rebellion by killing Alonso and Gonzalo. This would eerily parallel the removal of Prospero back in Milan, as Sebastian observes: 'You [Antonio] did supplant your brother Prospero' (270). Only Ariel's intervention prevents this murder, yet Sebastian and Antonio continue to think about it and seek an opportunity. A storm of political intrigue lingers over the island, parodied by Caliban's joining Stephano and Trinculo in their misguided and dubious plan to kill Prospero and take over the island.

Act 4 confirms the forthcoming nuptials of Ferdinand and Miranda; it includes a beautiful wedding masque that functions in a radically different way from the problematic one in *The Maid's Tragedy*. The masque may have been either influenced by the ones at the wedding of Princess Elizabeth or anticipated them. In any event, the Jacobean court audience would soon experience such a masque. This product of Prospero's art includes Iris, Juno, Ceres, and others. Iris states their purpose: 'A contract of true love to celebrate / And some donation freely to estate [bestow] / On the blessed lovers' (4.1.84–6). Ferdinand speaks correctly when he says: 'This is a most majestic vision, and / Harmonious charmingly' (118–19). But these revels end when Prospero recalls the looming rebellion of Caliban and his group; this is not a trouble-free, idealised island. The play offers a wedding masque without yet a wedding, which lies in the future.

The remainder of the afternoon involves Prospero's surrendering his magical powers, convinced that 'The rarer action is / In virtue than in vengeance' (5.1.27–8). Thus with Ariel's help he rounds up the island's visitors so that he might extend forgiveness, which Alonso immediately accepts and responds: 'Thy dukedom I resign and do entreat / Thou pardon me my wrongs' (118–19). Prospero's brother Antonio, to whom Prospero also extends forgiveness, gives no overt sign of acceptance. Finally, the group sees Ferdinand and Miranda playing chess; this looks like another miracle. Gonzalo asks the right question: 'Was Milan thrust from Milan that his issue / Should become kings of Naples?' (204–5). In the space of one short afternoon, the political world has been reordered, awaiting only confirmation by the wedding of Ferdinand and Miranda. This recognition causes rejoicing; and Gonzalo sums up the accomplishment:

> in one voyage
> Did Claribel her husband find at Tunis,
> And Ferdinand her brother found a wife
> Where he himself was lost; Prospero his dukedom
> In a poor isle; and all of us ourselves
> When no man was his own.

(208–13)

Even allowing for Gonzalo's possibly idealised view, a spectator might agree with Miranda that this is a brave new world if such reconciliation and forgiveness have occurred, opening a new world of political hope and succession, secured by a royal wedding. In early 1613, that understanding would be hard to resist.

Three key words permeate *The Winter's Tale* with powerful meaning: 'succession', 'issue', and 'nothing'. As in *The Tempest*, an impending wedding of royal children will solidify the kingdoms, after an earlier death and abandonment had disrupted succession in Sicily. The first recorded performance of *Winter's Tale* dates from 15 May 1611 when the notorious Simon Forman saw the play at the Globe and recorded his reaction. The court saw the play on 5 November later that year on Guy Fawkes day. The supernatural takes the form of Apollo, who, although he never appears, has a profound effect on the outcome, seen memorably in the report in 3.1 of Cleon and Diomenes, who have just returned from Delphos (Delphi) and bring with them a sealed document which contains Apollo's judgement. As in *Cupid's Revenge*, the characters here, especially Leontes, learn at their own peril the danger of trying to cross the will of the gods.

The Winter's Tale, unlike *The Tempest*, begins confidently and with assured hope about the future. It begins in the Sicilian court of King Leontes with a conversation between Camillo of Sicily and Archidamus, a lord of Bohemia, ruled by Polixenes. They establish two essential facts for the play: the longevity and solidity of the friendship between Leontes and Polixenes, and the 'unspeakable comfort' that the young prince Mamillius provides for Sicily's future. Camillo responds to Archidamus's comment: 'I very well agree with you in the hopes of him. It is a gallant child' (1.1.36–7). In addition to the prince, the queen, Hermione, appears in 1.2 as pregnant, the birth of another royal child imminent. Succession seems secure. The Jacobean court has itself been working through the presumed certainty of succession, recently disrupted by Henry's death, and its consuming grief.

Complication comes quickly when Leontes tries to persuade the visiting Polixenes to remain longer in Sicily, and he enlists Hermione's help in making the case. As she and Polixenes join hands to walk away, Leontes unexpectedly lashes out: 'Too hot, too hot! / To mingle friendship far is mingling bloods. / I have *tremor cordis* on me. My heart dances / But not for joy, not joy' (1.2.109–12). He even turns to the young prince and asks: 'Art thou my boy?' (121). Jealousy begins to consume him in a destructive and unrelieved vision of faithlessness: Leontes has decided that the child that Hermione carries belongs to her and Polixenes, not him. Increasingly, he begins to act like Othello, the victim of Iago's perverse skill – except that Leontes has no Iago. He is confident in the presumed 'evidence' that he has of Hermione's guilt, crying out: 'My wife is nothing, nor nothing have these nothings, / If this be nothing' (295–6). He even tries to get the faithful Camillo to murder Polixenes; fortunately, Camillo's moral strength instead compels him to tell Polixenes of the danger, and together they escape to Bohemia.

From this moment the narrative accelerates in a downward spiral for Leontes and thus for the kingdom. Even the birth of a daughter does not mitigate his passion. Instead, he accuses Hermione of being an adulteress and banishes Mamillius from her presence. When Paulina brings the new-born baby to him in hopes of softening his heart, he rails at her and the child, denies his paternity, and orders the infant out of the kingdom: 'This brat is none of mine; / It is the issue of Polixenes' (2.3.92–3). Leontes has thereby banished joy. Antigonus, Paulina's husband, tries to curtail such actions as he admonishes the king: 'Be certain what you do, sir, lest your justice / Prove violence, in the which three great ones suffer, / Yourself, your queen, your son' (2.1.127–9). Leontes turns a deaf ear to all such entreaties, thereby becoming a tyrannical king. Instead of burning the baby or bashing its brains out, as he first indicates, Leontes asks Antigonus: 'What will you adventure / To save this brat's life?' (2.3.161–2). Antigonus responds simply: 'Anything, my lord' (63). Against the 'nothingness' that Leontes has been creating, Antigonus counters with 'anything'. It then becomes his task to take the child away from Sicily. What a king Leontes has become in a brief space of time.

But Leontes wants everyone to think that he is not a tyrant; thus, he has dispatched Cleomenes and Dion to Delphos (2.1.180f) to get confirmation of his belief of Hermione's infidelity; and he further intends to place her on trial, fairly judging her case and exonerating him (3.2). The great trial scene masterfully brings together competing claims. Hermione gives a wonderful and moving defence of herself, proving herself to be thoughtful, of good character, and not complicit in any kind of plot. But the trial needs Apollo's judgement; indeed, Hermione cries out: 'Apollo be my judge' (3.2.115). At that moment the two who went to Delphos enter the courtroom with the scroll that carries the oracle's message, which succinctly says: 'Hermione is chaste, Polixenes blameless, Camillo a true subject, Leontes a jealous tyrant, his innocent babe truly begotten; and the king shall live without an heir if that which is lost be not found' (131–4). This judgement from the god undercuts everything that Leontes has allowed himself to believe. But first he lashes out at this oracle: 'There is no truth at all i' th' oracle. / The sessions shall proceed. This is mere falsehood' (138–9). Immediately, Leontes learns that Prince Mamillius has died; at which point, Hermione swoons, and Paulina pronounces her dead. Leontes recognises that 'Apollo's angry' (144), and he has violated the god's will. He seeks to make amends. The remainder of the scene functions as Leontes' 'trial', presided over by Paulina, the agent of Apollo. Chastened, Leontes promises: 'Once a day I'll visit / The chapel where they lie, and tears shed there / Shall be my recreation' (236–8). The winter of tragedy has deepened in Sicilia; the royal family has no heir. If the play ends here, no one could doubt its genre.

But Shakespeare has other ideas in mind. Act 3, scene 3, for example, transports the action to the famous, non-existent 'seacoast of Bohemia'. To this place Antigonus has come in the midst of a storm, bringing the baby, now named Perdita, with him. He has had a vision about Hermione and determines to leave Perdita here. He hears a rumble and starts to flee. Shakespeare provides a famous stage direction: '*Exit, pursued by a bear*' (3.3.58 SD). The bear devours Antigonus, and the Mariners perish at sea. What kind of transition is this? The Shepherd, who comes upon the infant, tells his son Clown, who has found Antigonus's remains: 'thou met'st with things dying, I with things new-born' (109–10). The play starts to answer the question of how life can come out of death, a question vexing Lennox and the royal court. The appearances of the allegorical figure of Time (4.1) and the rogue Autolycus (4.3) signal a new departure; the play moves away from the winter's tale of Sicily to the possible springtime of Bohemia.

The long, sprawling sheep-shearing scene (4.4) contains Florizel, son of Polixenes, and Perdita, now sixteen years old, who believes that the Shepherd is her father. The scene luxuriates in song, dance, and festivities of all sorts as Perdita presides as queen of the festival. Florizel has fallen in love with her, not knowing her true identity, and intends to marry her. Polixenes and Camillo, disguised, watch over the events until Polixenes, hearing of the intended marriage, asks his son: 'Have you a father?' (4.4.391). And Florizel answers with smug adolescent impertinence: 'I have, but what of him?' (391). Polixenes reveals his identity and chastises his son, claiming, 'we'll bar thee from succession' (428). The son tells the startled Perdita: 'From my succession wipe me, father. I / Am heir to my affection' (479–80) – an engaging sentiment but not politically wise. Under Camillo's guidance, Florizel, now wearing Autolycus's garments, and Perdita set out to sea and toward Sicily. The seemingly idyllic world of Bohemia has begun to resemble Sicily in terms of problematic royal succession. Shakespeare is not making this easy.

'The king shall live without an heir if that which is lost be not found', so Apollo said. The lost one, Perdita, returns to her father's kingdom, although she does not yet know that she is his child. When she and Florizel arrive at Leontes' court, Leontes says: 'I lost a couple that 'twixt heaven and earth / Might thus have stood begetting wonder as / You, gracious couple, do' (5.1.132–4). He tells Florizel that because of his 'sin' the heavens 'Have left me issueless' (174). That situation changes in 5.2, which contains the marvellous report of the reunion of Perdita and Leontes, prompted by the opening of the fardel (bundle) that had been left with the infant in Bohemia; these objects identify her as the king's daughter. Bonfires sweep across the kingdom in joy. 'Our king', the Third Gentleman reports, 'being ready to leap out of himself for joy of his found daughter' (5.2.49–50), embraces her repeatedly. 'I never heard of such another encounter', the Gentleman says (56). Curiously, Shakespeare chooses to provide a report, but not a representation of the actual reunion. The whole court group decides to go to Paulina's 'removed house' to see a statue of Hermione, fashioned by the Italian artist Giulio Romano. The First Gentleman says more than he can know: 'Every wink of an eye some new grace will be born' (108–9). The Sicilian court has begun to heal.

But nothing prepares the group – the Jacobean court or later audiences – for the spectacular 5.3, in which, against all expectation, Hermione appears *'like a statue'* (5.3.20 SD), and everyone marvels at the artist's skill. In some ways this statue torments Leontes as it reminds him of his 'sin'. Paulina cautions all to prepare for more amazement. She claims that she can make the statue move; but 'It is required / You do awake your faith' (94–5). Music sounds; and Paulina speaks in halting cadence: 'Music! Awake her; strike! / 'Tis time; descend; be stone no more; approach' (98–9). Faith is indeed the substance of things hoped for. Leontes cries: 'If this be magic, let it be an art / Lawful as eating' (110–11). Hermione embraces Leontes, and she speaks to Perdita, claiming that she has preserved 'Myself to see the issue' (128). All of Leontes' suffering and torment now seem to have been efficacious in ways that he could not have anticipated. While the court recalls the death of the Prince Mamillius, it also has reclaimed its queen, presumed dead, and regained the banished princess, who herself will marry Florizel of Bohemia. Issue and succession erase nothingness. Sicily can rejoice beyond a common joy.

Out of the comfort of Whitehall and the excitement of the performances, Lennox moved into the darkness of London's streets, as the city continued to endure one of the coldest winters in years. He had experienced his own private 'winter's tale', beginning with Prince Henry's death. But these plays, creating a spectacularly diverse and challenging landscape of emotions and experiences, wrenched him away from despair and towards the renewal that certainly characterises *The Winter's Tale*. What a glorious answer to human suffering. Maybe something worthwhile inheres in 'tragical mirth'. A comic end that responds to a tragic beginning prompted Lennox to recall the way in which King James back in Scotland had envisioned that Lennox would be the new phoenix, replacing his father and thus bringing about a comic end. Dramatic performances provide not merely entertainment but solace for the court's dismay and suffering. The plays point to a transformed court, readying itself for the glories of a royal wedding. In light of this new hope, Lennox could anticipate the words of John Donne's Holy Sonnet 6, 'Death be not proud' and its conclusion: 'death shall be no more, Death thou shalt die'. Or, in the simple words of the Shepherd in *The Winter's Tale*: 'thou met'st with things dying, I with things new-born'. Solace.

Notes

1 *Calendar of State Papers Venetian, 1610–1613* (London: HMSO, 1905), 12: 449.
2 *The Letters of John Chamberlain*, ed. Norman E. McClure, 2 vols (Philadelphia: American Philosophical Society, 1939), 1: 391.
3 *Calendar of State Papers Venetian*, 12: 452.
4 *The Letters of King James VI and I*, ed. G. P. V. Akrigg (Berkeley: University of California Press, 1964), p. 329. Akrigg voices the opinion that this letter shows James's 'singular lack of sensitivity' (328), and it can certainly be read that way. A less harsh view says that James was just going about the business of being king and looking out for the future of his only surviving son. No marriage would be imminent because Princess Christine would have to be twelve for a legal marriage.
5 *Calendar of State Papers Venetian*, 12: 473.
6 From an account quoted by John Nichols, *The Progresses of King James the First* (London, 1828), 2: 513.
7 *Calendar of State Papers Venetian*, 12: 474.
8 Quoted from Andrew Gurr, *The Shakespeare Company, 1594–1642* (Cambridge: Cambridge University Press, 2004), p. 254. I draw on this excellent study of Shakespeare's acting troupe and his earlier *The Shakespearian Playing Companies* (Oxford: Clarendon Press, 1996).
9 Jane Rickard has countered the usual idea that Scotland provided few theatrical experiences. In *Writing the Monarch in Jacobean England* (Oxford: Oxford University Press, 2015), Rickard writes: 'It would seem, then, that for James there were important continuities between the activities of English players at his Scottish court and his patronage of the King's Men in England' (p. 50). Taking all the adult acting companies under royal patronage within weeks of arriving in London still seems unexpected. The King's Men obviously attained special

status through the King's patronage. The importance of the court for Shakespeare's career has been skilfully delineated by Richard Dutton in *Shakespeare, Court Dramatist* (Oxford: Oxford University Press, 2016).

10 Roslyn Knutson, *The Repertory of Shakespeare's Company, 1594–1613* (Fayetteville: University of Arkansas Press, 1991), p. 104.

11 Cited by Richard Dutton, *Mastering the Revels: The Regulation and Censorship of English Renaissance Drama* (Iowa City: University of Iowa Press, 1991), p. 185.

12 John Astington, *English Court Theatre 1558–1642* (Cambridge: Cambridge University Press, 1999), p. 24. Astington's study is invaluable in assessing the importance of productions at court.

13 For additional discussion of Lennox's involvement with the theatre, see my 'The Stuart Brothers and English Theater', *Renaissance Papers 2015* (2016): 1–12.

14 For a discussion of Buc's career as Master of the Revels, see Richard Dutton, *Mastering the Revels*, pp. 194–217.

15 *Collections XIII: Jacobean and Caroline Revels Accounts, 1603–1642*, ed. W. R. Streitberger (Oxford: Malone Society, 1986), p. 59.

16 See previous note for the reference to the Revels Accounts. For the Chamber Accounts, see *Collections VI: Dramatic Records in the Declared Accounts of the Treasurer of the Chamber 1558–1642*, ed. David Cook (Oxford: Malone Society, 1961).

17 John Astington, *English Court Theatre*, offers a convenient listing of the court performances, see especially pp. 246–7 for the 1612–13 season. We have no information about the order in which the plays were performed, except for *Cupid's Revenge*. I have thus chosen my own order without any idea that it represents the actual order of performance.

18 Astington writes: 'we can note that comedy predominated among the Christmas performances of 1612–13; perhaps the Lord Chamberlain and the Master of the Revels deliberately chose plays which stayed clear of the sensitive matter of the death of princes' (*English Court Theatre*, p. 203). Given the generic diversity of the plays, one can hardly claim that comedy 'predominated'. And clearly *The Winter's Tale* confronts the matter of the death of a young prince.

19 *Sir Thomas More*, eds Vittorio Gabrieli and Giorgio Melchiori (Manchester: Manchester University Press, 1989), p. 142. All quotations will be from this edition. (I thank Gaywyn Moore for drawing my attention to this example.)

20 *The Complete Poetry of John Donne*, ed. John T. Shawcross (New York: Doubleday, 1967), p. 194. I have slightly modernised Shawcross's text.

21 *The Merry Devil of Edmonton* from *Five Elizabethan Comedies*, ed. A. K. McIlwraith (1934; rpt London: Oxford University Press, 1969),

p. 258, ll. 40–1. All quotations will come from this edition. The play, first published in 1608, had a new edition in 1612 and four more editions before the end of the seventeenth century. The title page says that 'it hath beene sundry times Acted, by his Majestites Servants, at the Globe'.

22 *Ben Jonson: Three Comedies*, ed. Michael Jamieson (Baltimore: Penguin, 1966). All quotations come from this edition.

23 *The Dramatic Works in the Beaumont and Fletcher Canon*, gen. ed. Fredson Bowers (Cambridge: Cambridge University Press, 1966), 1: 551. All quotations from this play derive from the Bowers edition; L. A. Beaurline edited *The Captain*.

24 *Six Plays by Contemporaries of Shakespeare*, ed. C. B. Wheeler (Oxford: Oxford University Press, 1971). All quotations from *Philaster* come from this edition. For an excellent discussion of the play, see Philip J. Finkelpearl, *Court and Country Politics in the Plays of Beaumont and Fletcher* (Princeton: Princeton University Press, 1990), the chapter on *Philaster*, pp. 146–66.

25 For *A King and No King*, I cite the edition in *Drama of the English Renaissance: The Stuart Period*, eds Russell A. Fraser and Norman Rabkin (New York: Macmillan, 1976). For an analysis, see Finkelpearl, *Court and Country Politics*, pp. 167–82.

26 Quotations from *The Maid's Tragedy* come from *English Renaissance Drama*, gen. ed. David Bevington (New York: W. W. Norton, 2002). Again, Finkelpearl has an excellent analysis in *Court and Country Politics*, pp. 183–211.

27 *Collections VI: Dramatic Records*, p. 57, two entries of payments, one for each performance.

28 Quotations from the play are from *The Dramatic Works in the Beaumont and Fletcher Canon*, gen. ed. Fredson Bowers (Cambridge: Cambridge University Press, 1970), 2: 350. The text hopelessly confuses Leontius's title, using both 'king' and 'duke'. Since the playwrights regularly refer to the 'kingdom' and to Leucippus as a 'prince', I have chosen to refer to Leontius as King.

29 I am assuming that the King's Men presented both plays, although the contemporary records do not make that clear. We find references to a play noted as 'Falstaff' and one designated as 'Hotspur'. A safe inference would be that these are the two parts of *Henry IV*. I accept that inference.

30 *Ben Jonson: The Complete Masques*, ed. Stephen Orgel (New Haven: Yale University Press, 1969), p. 153.

31 All quotations of Shakespeare come from *The Complete Pelican Shakespeare*, gen. ed. A. R. Braunmuller and Stephen Orgel (New York: Penguin, 2002). Claire McEachern edited the *Henry IV* plays.

32 For background information, see Robert S. Miola, *Shakespeare's Rome* (Cambridge: Cambridge University Press, 1983).

33 Astington in *English Court Theatre* writes about the 1604 performance: '*Othello* was not presented, however, during the immediate Christmas period, for which its bleak emotional power does not seem particularly suited' (p. 201). He does not, however, say anything about how the play might or might not be appropriate for the Christmas season of 1612–13.

34 For further discussion of Shakespeare's last plays and their connection to the Stuart royal family, see my *Shakespeare's Romances and the Royal Family* (Lawrence: University Press of Kansas, 1985). Possibly Shakespeare revised *The Tempest* and *The Winter's Tale* to respond to the court life of early 1613. The only text that we have of these two plays is the Folio of 1623, and who knows what might have happened to the text in a decade?

5

A Valentine wedding

The path away from the court's dramatic entertainment pointed toward the much-anticipated wedding, the occasion of a new beginning, full of excitement and joy. Even the weather brightened. Lennox took delight in all the festivities, including the installation of Prince Frederick into the Order of the Garter, the group in which Lennox himself, along with Prince Henry, had been inaugurated in summer 1603. The Garter ceremonies for Frederick took place at Windsor on Sunday 7 February 1613, also the final Sunday at which clergy read the wedding banns for Elizabeth and Frederick.

The Order of the Garter, the highest English knightly order, began in 1348 under the aegis of King Edward III with St George as the patron saint. Of French birth and Scottish residence, Lennox knew the exceptional privilege of a non-native being inducted; and now Frederick would join the ranks, a grand compliment and a sign of King James's determination to have the prince fully recognised with an English pedigree. Anthony Nixon responded to this celebration with a dream vision poem, the last item in his *Great Brittaines Generall Joyes*, which captures the order's history and the specific event of Frederick's installation. In the poem Nixon imaginatively sees King Edward and the knights garbed 'In roabes with pretious colours of S. George, / And they had Garters all, buckled with gould'.[1] He also finds a 'golden booke' in which he can read the names of all the knights, including the late Prince Henry, whose 'vertue doth out live th'arrest of death' and whose honour, courage, and vivacity created his renown (sig. C3v). Nixon envisions King James, 'Great Brittaines King, richly attyrde, / Leading with him a sort of goodly Knights' as they emerge from the house of fame. Frederick joins the group; and Nixon offers moral direction: 'Shape thou thy noble course, / As vertue (loadstarre of renowne) directs,

/ That as thy royall Auncestors have donne, / Thine earthly race in honor thou maist ronne' (sig. C4v). Having done that, Frederick will have his name entered in the records where his name 'immortally may shine'.

Nixon captures Frederick's plight early in his stay in England: 'Thou great Prince *Palatine*, and Prince elector, / That didst for our Prince lately with us greeve: / ... Thy welcome first, was a sad Funerall' (sig. A4v). Fortunately, this funeral 'now's transformd to a joyfull Nuptiall'. From the happy October arrival, Frederick has enjoyed the Lord Mayor's Show but without the ill Prince Henry, has experienced Henry's death, leaving him, in the judgement of the Venetian Ambassador, not knowing what to do. But Christmas, the abundance of plays presented at court, the ongoing planning for the wedding, Elizabeth's regard for him, and now the granting of knighthood in the Order of the Garter have indeed transformed Frederick, as these events changed the royal court.

John Chamberlain went to court to meet the wedding couple; and on 4 February 1613, wrote to Alice Carleton, giving his assessment of the teenaged pair:

> On Tewsday I tooke occasion to go to court because I had never seen the Palsgrave, nor the Lady Elizabeth (neere hand) of a long time: I had my full view of them both, but will not tell you all I thincke, but only this, that he owes his mistress nothing yf he were a Kings sonne as she is a Kings daughter. The worst is mee thincks he is much too young and small timbred to undertake such a taske.[2]

Whatever Chamberlain means precisely, and it may be no more than their obvious youth, Queen Anne had been at best lukewarm about this marriage, failing to appear at the official exchange of vows on 27 December, 'beeing troubled (as they say) with the gowte'.[3] She had openly mocked Frederick, but even she had begun to change. Thus, Chamberlain can report on 10 February, 'The Quene growes every day more favorable, and there is hope she will grace yt [wedding] with her presence' (1: 418). As Lennox well knew, some of the residue of resentment or uncertainty grew out of the court's wrestling still with the overwhelming reality of Henry's death. But in the final outburst of wedding festivities Queen Anne participated fully.[4]

John Taylor, the Water Poet, having written an elegy for Prince Henry, now captures effectively what spectators experienced in the wedding celebrations: 'Gunnes, Drums, and Trumpets, Fire-works, Bonfires, Bells, / With acclamations, and applausefull noyse; / Tilts, Turneyes, Barriers, all in mirth excells, / The ayre reverberates our earthly joyes.'[5] Taylor acknowledges how these events respond to or overcome Henry's death: 'And when we all were drench'd in black dispaire, / Joy conquered grief, and comfort vanquish'd care.' So everyone hoped. Having barely had time to catch their breath after all the play performances, the court swung into full gear to ready Whitehall Palace for the wedding and its associated activities. Many noted the stir, expense, and decorations produced by the court staff under the guidance of the Office of the Revels and the Office of the Works, whose Surveyor provided for the stage and seating in the Banqueting House. The Office of the Wardrobe outdid itself in preparing costumes and garments for the royal household. The Treasurer of the Chamber kept a ready, but inadequate, eye on expenses, all of this under the control of the Lord Steward, Master of the Household. All of these officials served, of course, the wishes of the Privy Council. Thus, ushers, grooms, porters, artificers of all kinds flooded the palace's hallways, bustling about to prepare for the most important royal wedding in decades. With both wistfulness and excitement Lennox, leaving the Holbein Gatehouse, wandered further into Whitehall's premises, checking on the arrangements in the Great Hall, the royal chapel, and the somewhat new Banqueting House. He moved silently and sometimes noisily through this space certain that he and the royal family were approaching a monumental occasion of things new-born.

According to John Chamberlain in a letter of 11 February, the authorities had already spent £6,000 for the planned fireworks and sea fights for Thursday and Saturday. He adds: 'I beleve there was never such a fleet seen above the bridge, besides fowre floting castles with fire workes, and the representation of the towne, fort and haven of Argier upon the land.'[6] A few days later Chamberlain had a measured response to the fireworks: 'the fireworks were reasonablie well performed all save the last castle (of five) which bred most expectation and had most devises, but when yt came to execution, had worst successe' (423). Even this slight disappointment cannot dampen the enthusiasm that greeted the evening spectacle. Another source highlights the setting: in the evening the King, Queen, Prince Charles, Prince Frederick, Princess Elizabeth 'with the rest of the nobilitie of England' had gathered 'in the galleries and windowes about his highnes Court of Whitehall, and in the sight of thousands of people, many artisticall conclusions in Fire Workes were upon the *Thames* performed'.[7] This anonymous writer found the displays to be 'pleasurable'.

The performance began with peals of ordnance 'like unto a terrible thunder ratled in the ayer, and seemed as it were to shake the earth'.[8] Immediately followed a burst of fireworks into the sky, which 'mounted so high into the Element that it dazeled the beholders eyes to looke after it'. More explosions followed, 'spredding so strangely with sparkling blazes, that the skie seemed to be filled with fire', striving with nature's stars. Lennox and others could contrast this brightness, prompted by joy, with the ominous rainbow that hung over St James's Palace on 29 October 1612 as Henry lay sick and dying. Perhaps John Taylor inadvertently hinted at the connection when he reported the 'many artificiall balls of fire [shot] into the ayre, which flew up in one whole fierie ball, and in their falling dispersed into divers streams like ranebowes in many innumerable fires'. In the 'Triumphall Verses' section, Taylor had written, 'the ayre reverberates our earthly joyes'.

Incorporating accounts from several individuals who had constructed the fireworks, Taylor in his *Heavens Blessing and Earths Joy* provides considerable information about the spectacle, which included extraordinary feats of romantic, mythic, and allegorical imagination. Not much seemed to be beyond the workers' artistic aspirations. For starters, the imperial and beautiful Lady Lucida, Queen of the Amazons, had repulsed the advances of Mango, the magician. He therefore created a fiery dragon and an invincible giant in a tower. Enter St George, who saw the beautiful Lucida and demanded entertainment and also embraced the task of quelling the 'burning dragon' and conquering 'the big-boned Giant, subvert the inchanted castle, and enfranchise the Queene with her followers'.[9] The fireworks attempted to capture this narrative. From Lucida's 'pavilion' many actions took place, such as a 'Royall hunting of bucks, and hounds, and huntsmen, flying and chasing one another' (B2). One part of the pavilion 'is all in a combustious flame, where rackets, crackers, breakers, and such like, give blowes and reports without number'. Then St George took leave of Lucida and set out towards 'the inchanted Towre of Brumond'.

This Tower 'is in hight forty foote and thirty square, betweene which and the Pavilion of the Amazonian Queene is a long bridge, on the which bridge the valiant and heroicke Champion, Saint George, being mounted on horseback, makes toward the Castle of Brumond' (B3). Carrying a burning lance and wearing a burning feather, St George assailed the Dragon and after some struggle conquered him. Mango's Giant fared no better, as St George thrusts his sword into the Giant's 'greedy throat'. He even captured Mango, binding him to a pillar that 'burned with fire and lights'. Then, 'the maine Castle is fyered', and everything extinguished with fire, 'always rackets flying, and reports thwacking, and lights burning' (B4).

John Tindall reports in Taylor's account of the fireworks what he created and 'performed', which consisted of a 'Castle, old and very ruinous, called the Castle of Envie, scituated and erected on a rock' (C2). The foundation of this allegorical Castle contained numerous 'adders, snakes, toades, serpents, scorpions, and such venomous vermin, from whose throates were belched many fires, with crackers, rackets, blowes, and reports in great numbers'. Three ships, Goodwill, True love, and Assurance, led by appropriate allegorical figures, assaulted Envy's castle, where after a half hour's battle they defeated the vicious creatures and razed and demolished the castle itself. In case the thousands of spectators had not seen enough fireworks, William Fishenden adds in Taylor's book the report of a pyramid 'in the forme of a triangled spire, with a globe fixed on the top thereof', which for a half hour set off countless fireworks, 'to the great delight and contentment of the King, the Queene, the Prince, the Princesse Elizabeth, the Prince Palatine, and divers others, the Nobilitie, the Gentry, and Commons of this Kingdome' (C2v). Who could possibly disagree, even if everything did not work exactly as planned? In one evening of spectacular fireworks along the Thames spectators saw the Amazonian Queen, her nemesis, and her saviour St George (not incidentally patron saint of the Order of the Garter). For good measure they got to witness the destruction of the Castle of Envy and countless fiery explosions, blanketing the sky. The anonymous account adds: 'These are the delights of Princes. ... Where kings commands be, Art is stretcht to the true depth' (sig. A3).

Another kind of artistic stretching took place two days later on the Thames. Again, the royal family gathered at Whitehall near the river between two and three o'clock on the thirteenth in order to witness the sea fight between supposed Christian ships and

Turkish galleys.[10] Great swaths of the river had been cordoned off in order for this show to take place. Sounds of ordnance filled the air. According to Taylor, the warring fleet included sixteen ships, sixteen galleys, and six frigates, all 'artificially rigged and trimmed, well manned and furnished with great ordinance and musquettiers' (A3v). Altogether a flotilla of 250 boats filled the river, stretching from Southwark to Lambeth bridge. The Turkish galleys lay in wait and at anchor near Westminster in a harbour, which 'harbor or haven ... belonging to a supposed Turkish or Barbarian Castle of Tunis, Algiers, or some other Mahometan fortification'. The ship-builder Phineas Pett had been instructed to help prepare ships for the event: 'ships and galleys for a sea-fight to be presented before Whitehall against the marriage of Lady Elizabeth'.[11] The Lord Admiral compelled Pett to serve as captain of the *Spy*, but he did not enjoy the experience: in this 'jesting business I ran more danger than if it had been a sea service in good earnest' (103).

Suddenly 'friendly exchanging of small shot and great ordinance [took place] on both sides, to the great delectation of all the beholders', causing 'reverberating echoes of joy'.[12] The Turkish fleet sounded a warning shot as the Christian ships approached; 'Then all the ships and galleys met in friendly opposition and imaginary hurley-burley battalions'. The curious predication of a battle between Christians and Turks recalls, Taylor insists, 'the manner of the happy and famous battell of Lepanto, fought betwixt the Turks and the Christians in the yeare of grace 1571'. Such a recognition recalls, of course, King James's poem *Lepanto*, which celebrated the great Christian victory. This 1613 theatrical spectacle might also provoke recollection of the 'memorable battaile betwixt us and the invincible (as it was thought) Spanish Armada in the yeare 1588'. The battle lasted some three hours 'to the great contentment of all the beholders' (A4v), Taylor says.

Although Taylor thinks that the battle was inconclusive and dissolved itself into friendly exchanges between the competing warriors, the anonymous *The Magnificent Marriage* presents a slightly different perspective. Here the writer insists that the Christians sacked the Turkish castle 'and tooke prisoner the Turkish Admirall, with divers Bashawes and other great Turkes' (B1). The English Admiral then, 'in a most triumphant manner', escorted the Turkish Admiral, 'attired in a red jacket with blew sleeves, according to the Turkish fashion', to the privy stairs at Whitehall, where Lennox and royal family waited. The English carried the Turkish prisoners to the king, 'as a representation of pleasure, which to his Highnes moved delight, and highly pleased all there present'. Not a good day for the Turks. All of this may vaguely recall what spectators had seen in the performance of *Othello* at court a few weeks earlier, in which Othello set out from Venice to defeat the Turks, only to have nature bang their ships into defeat, leaving Othello and his entourage somewhat without a mission on Cyprus.

Once again, John Chamberlain, in a letter of 18 February to Alice Carleton, took a somewhat contrary view, indicating that the £9,000 spent on the extravaganza was wasteful, just so much powder and noise. He also claims that the 'fight upon the water came short of that shew and bragges had ben made of yt'.[13] And he insists that the king and others 'tooke so litle delight to see no other activitie but shooting and potting of gunnes that yt is quite geven over and the navy unrigged and the castle pulled downe'. Chamberlain adds a grim account of the number of people injured in the spectacle. Perhaps his high artistic standards caused his failure to appreciate art's stretch. John Taylor may be closer to the purpose when he commented on the fireworks and the sea fight as demonstrating the country's military might and skill. Spectators at Whitehall and along the river may simply have been content with the occasion and the celebration, marvelling at the marshalling of such resources in the name of festivity. Or perhaps John Taylor was on to something when he suggested in his verses that the much-desired union of Elizabeth and Frederick 'well in time (I hope) this sacred worke, / Will hunt from Christian lands the faithles *Turke*' (D1).

Sunday morning, the 14th, arrived fresh, cold, and full of hope. After all the noise and stir of the fireworks and sea fight, tranquillity permeated the early hours of Sunday. Or, as Antonio Foscarini, the Venetian Ambassador, wrote to the Doge and Senate: 'For many days we have heard nothing in this City but the noise of a crowd, salvoes of artillery, blare of trumpets, nor seen aught but a crush of nobles and gorgeous dresses and all the signs of rejoicing.'[14] Everything since late December had led to this moment, occasion, and ceremony. At last, a royal child would be marrying; this had not been true in England for decades. In the words of Anthony Nixon, '*England* hath put a face of gladnesse on'; young and old alike celebrate 'This Nuptiall day, wherein we all enjoy / Such perfect comfort throughout *Brutes* new *Troy* [London]'.[15]

Whitehall Palace began to stir in anticipation. Lennox readied himself for the event and his part in the ceremony, remembering with fondness his participation in the baptism of Henry in 1594 and creation as Prince of Wales in 1610, and Princess Elizabeth's baptism in 1596. Memories flooded his mind, as he recalled the many occasions involving the royal family in which he had been key. What a particularly enchanting day this would be, Lennox thought, the culmination of planning and diplomatic negotiation, the results stretching far into the future. Chamberlain rushed from St Paul's to catch a glimpse of the wedding party, the Venetian Ambassador enjoyed a privileged place from which to watch the spectacle unfold, and hundreds of others crowded into Whitehall for a chance to see and be seen. King James made a point of processing from his Privy chamber through the palace so that many could see him, especially those not invited to witness the actual ceremony in the Chapel Royal.

As the great organ sounded, the procession began with Prince Frederick, accompanied by Lennox and Charles Howard, the Earl of Nottingham, and other young courtiers, English, Scottish, and German. Frederick appeared attired in a white suit, 'richly beset with pearle and gold'.[16] Princess Elizabeth followed, preceded by her guardian Lord Harington; she wore a gown of white satin, 'upon her head a crown of refined golde, made Imperiall by the pearles and diamonds thereupon placed, which were so thicke beset that they stood like shining pinnacles upon her amber-coloured haire' (542–3). Pearls, diamonds, and rich stones filled her hair, which she wore hanging down, a sign of virginity; 'many diamonds of inestimable value, embrothered upon her sleeves, which even dazzled and amazed the eies of the beholders' (543). Elizabeth's brother Prince Charles and Henry Howard, Earl of Northampton, led her into the chapel. 'Virgin Bridemaids attended upon the Princess, like a skye of caelestial starres upon faire Phoebe' (544). Members of the king's Privy Council, bishops, and Thomas Howard, Earl of Arundel, the bearer of the king's sword, followed. King James, 'himselfe in a most sumptuous blacke suit, with a diamond in his hatte of a wonderful great value' (544) then appeared, along with Queen Anne, 'attired in white satin, beautified with much enbrothery and many diamonds'. (This account later suggests that the king's jewels were 'esteemed not to be less worth than six hundred thousand pounds', and the queen's jewels were valued at 'four hundred thousand pounds'

(546).) Many others accompanied the royal party. Chamberlain complained of the excess and 'braverie' that did dazzle so that 'I could not observe the tenth part of that I wisht' (423).[17]

Inside the Chapel Royal rich hangings adorned the upper end, depicting the History of the Acts of the Apostles; in the middle stood a stage or scaffold about 5 feet high and about 20 feet long, having several steps to ascend or descend on each end. On this 'stage' sat King James on the right hand, with the Earl of Arundel nearby; below the sword sat Frederick on a stool, and after him Prince Charles on another stool. On the other side sat the Queen 'in a chair most gloriously attired' and near her Princess Elizabeth.[18] Upon a stage for all to see sat the royal performers. This arrangement makes literal James's metaphor in his *Basilicon Doron* that a 'King is as one set on a stage' whom people gazingly behold.

The organ ceased, and the choir of the Chapel Royal sang an anthem. Then the Bishop of Bath and Wells, James Montagu, ascended the pulpit and preached a sermon, based on St John's gospel account in the second chapter of the wedding miracle performed by Jesus at Cana in Galilee.[19] While the choir sang another anthem, the Archbishop of Canterbury, George Abbot, and the Bishop of Bath and Wells withdrew into the vestry and adorned their 'rich copes'. They returned and ascended the stage as the Archbishop led the marriage service. Prince Frederick had learned enough English so that he could respond to the royal wedding ceremony, which for the first time in English history followed the service in the Book of Common Prayer. King James presented the bride. When the marriage vows ended, the choir sang another anthem, and Frederick and Elizabeth knelt before the communion table. The Garter Principal of Arms made the official announcement of the couple's titles, followed by congratulations from all the lords present; then several of the lords brought out of the vestry bowls of wine, hippocras, and wafers, which they shared and drank a 'health' to the newly married couple.

The service in the chapel ended, the Duke of Lennox and Charles Howard, Earl of Nottingham, escorted the Princess Elizabeth out of the chapel towards the Banqueting House. Thus, Lennox had the privilege of accompanying Frederick into the chapel and leading Elizabeth out. He joined the hundreds who cheered 'God give them joy, God give them joy' (548). At last a royal child had married, solidifying for the moment an order of succession. The joys of the day 'were declared in manie places, as well City and Court; for the bells of London rung generally in every Church, and in every street bonfires blazed abundantly' (552). Small wonder that several more days filled with celebrations, beginning with Thomas Campion's masque on Sunday evening and running at the tilt on Monday.

Poets reflected on this wedding, as some of the same ones, such as Heywood, Peacham, Donne, and Wither, had responded to Henry's death and funeral. Peacham, for example, attaches his 'Nuptial Hymns in Honour of this Happy Marriage' to his book *The Period of Mourning ... in Memorie of the Late Prince*. Nixon in *Great Brittaines Generall Joyes* includes 'Hymens Holiday', a set of verses about the wedding. He urges that this event be commemorated: 'Write, write you Chronicles of Time and Fame, / That keepe remembrances golden Registers.'[20] Nixon adds: 'This Wedding day (beginning of much blisse) / Set downe this day in Characters of Gold, / And marke it with Stone as white as milke' (B3). Similarly, John Taylor believes that 'Fames golden Trump will through the world proclame' this glorious wedding: 'Thus like a Scribe Fame waited to record / The Nuptials of this Lady and this Lord.'[21] These two, Taylor suggests, draw their royal blood from Emperors and Kings, 'Of Potent Conquerors, and famous Knights', enabling them to bring union to Christendom (D1). William Basse concludes his verses about Henry's death with a final stanza about Elizabeth's wedding: '*Isis* and *Rhene* are joyn'd in sacred vow; / And faire *Eliza's Fredericke's Valentine*. / The *Court* in joy attires hir splendant brow: / The *Country* shroves; And all in mirth combine.'[22] Heywood writes of Elizabeth: 'She enters with a sweet commanding grace, / Her very presence paradic'd the place'; and he adds: 'All eyes are fixt on her, the youthfull fry, / Amazed stand at her great Majesty.'[23] Waxing enthusiastic, Heywood claims that 'Had *Paris* seene her, he had nere crost the flood, / *Hellen* had beene unrapte, *Troy* still had stood'. In a word, the beautiful Elizabeth could have changed the course of history. Of Frederick, Heywood curiously focuses on his appearance, which the poet finds quite feminine: 'A mixed grace he in his visage wore, / And but his habit shewd what sex hee bore' (B3). But Heywood closes confidently and hopeful: 'The happy fortunes of these two prepare, / And let from them no comforts be debar'd / Blesse them with Issue, and a Royall Heyre' (C2) (see Figures 8 and 9).

George Wither in *Epithalamia: Or Nuptiall Poems* provides a perspective, a seeming eye-witness account, on all the celebration, beginning with a change in the weather itself and the mood of the

8 Engraving of Princess Elizabeth by Crispin van de Passe (1613)

court and city. Wither writes: 'The *Citie*, that I left in mourning clad, / Drouping, as if it would have still bin sad: / I found deckt up; in robes so neat, and trimme.'[24] The court's sorrow, responding to Henry's death, had cleared and transformed into a 'glorious fashion' (B2). Of the sea battle on the Thames, Wither writes that

9 Engraving of Prince Frederick, Elector Palatine, husband of Princess Elizabeth, by Crispin van de Passe (1613)

'*Mars* himselfe to, Clad in Armor bright, / Hath showne his fury, in a bloudles fight; / And both on land, and water, sternely drest' (B2). The poet also remarks on the fireworks: '*Cometts* and *Meteors* by the starrs exhald, / Were from the *Middle-region* lately cald.'

These entertainments Wither interprets later in the poem in terms of their purposes. For example, the fireworks 'May make you mind, *Jehovahs* greater wonders' (B4). Wither, unlike Heywood, sees in Frederick a potential warrior: 'I see him shine in steele' (B2v). The poet also calls him the 'truest *Valentine*'. Wither captures the scene in Whitehall: 'Now yon *Hall* their persons shroudeth, / Whither all this people crowdeth. / There they feasted are with plentie' (C2v). They share not only in the wedding but also in the masques that follow: '*Gods* and *Heroes* masked. / None yet saw, or heard in story, / Such immortall, mortall glorie' (C4). If Elizabeth indeed 'paradic'd the place', as Heywood claims, small wonder that the country 'shroves' (feasts, indulges in pleasure), as Basse suggests.

Having written an 'Elegie on the Untimely Death of the Incomparable Prince Henry' in which he worried about the loss of a centre, John Donne turned subsequently to 'An Epithalamion, Or marriage Song on the Lady Elizabeth' in which he seems more securely to have found his voice.[25] The poet begins by hailing 'Bishop Valentine', whose day the wedding commemorates; he then turns to work several changes on the idea of the *phoenix*, a concept and image linked to Lennox, King James, and in Webster's poem on the death of Henry to the prince himself. All the various birds are nothing compared to the phoenix; and 'thou [Valentine] this day couplest two Phoenixes' (p. 174); 'Two Phoenixes, whose joyned breasts / Are unto one another mutuall nests' (175). The speaker says that with rubies, pearls, and diamonds the princess can 'make / Thy selfe a constellation, of them All, / And by their blazing, signifie, / That a Great Princess falls, but doth not die' – the mystery of the phoenix. In the fourth stanza the poet implores: 'Come forth, come forth, and as one glorious flame / Meeting Another, growes the same, / So meet thy Fredericke, and so / To an unseparable union growe.' The flame nourishes them rather than consuming them. Donne works his way through the wedding ceremony and festivities and the impatience of the lovers to enjoy each other in bed, made explicit in section vi. The poet closes: 'And by this act of these two Phenixes / Nature againe restored is, / For since these two are two no more, / Ther's but one Phenix still, as was before' (177). The paradox resolves: two have become one, and nature rejoices. For the imaginative poet the marriage moves beyond politics and resolution of issues of succession and union of kingdoms; this marriage, additionally, renews all of nature.

In answer to the question, 'For, where is he?' in light of the reclining and awaiting bride, Donne the poet writes: 'He comes, and passes through Spheare after Spheare. / First her sheetes, then her Armes, then any where' (176). Those outside the chamber lay wagers about 'whose hand it is / That opens first a curtaine, hers or his' (177). This somewhat prurient interest in the wedding night finds its match in King James's own behaviour. Chamberlain reports: 'The next morning the King went to visit these young turtles that were coupled on St Valentines day, and did strictly examine him [Frederick] whether he were his true sonne in law, and was sufficiently assured.'[26] For all the beauty, spectacle, and enchantment of the wedding and its festivities, the king had not lost sight of the crucial matter of potential succession and an heir.

The court passed through sphere after sphere of masque entertainment, beginning on the wedding night with Thomas Campion's *The Lords' Masque*.[27] 'Masques were central to the ritual world in which early modern court life took place. They were staged at the very heart of Whitehall, at key moments in the court calendar.'[28] No moment could have been more 'key' in this court's calendar than this royal wedding; hence, the overflow of masques, with all of their excesses and extravagant expense. Such entertainments heightened the importance of the Stuart court in European eyes. John Taylor in *Heavens Blessing* attributes these entertainments to Mercury, who has opened the treasure of his subtle wit: 'And as a servant on this wedding waightes / With masques, with revels, and with triumphs fit, / His rare inventions, and his quaint conceites / … He in immaginary showes affords / In shape, forme, method, and applausfull words' (sig. D2). King James himself had arranged this masque in honour of Elizabeth and Frederick. A warrant, dated 4 May 1613, details some of the expenditures and materials required for this masque, for example: 755 and a half 'yards of tawny, white, crimson, colour de roy [purple] and black satin, employed upon the suits for Masquers'; '1 lb. 4 oz. of fine Venice gold and spangles … to be employed upon 8 plumes of feathers'.[29] In addition, several drawings by Inigo Jones, who worked with Campion, survive, showing the elaborate costumes of the masquers.[30] The text, not published until summer 1613, the accounts, reactions to the performance, and Jones's drawings enable readers to capture a partial version of what Lennox and others experienced on that charmed evening of 14 February, after the wedding ceremony and after the banquet. But who can tell the dancer from the dance?

In the Banqueting House at Whitehall the masque began by revealing a painted scene of a thicket and a cave from which emerged Orpheus, who confronts Mania, the goddess of madness, who '*appears wildly out of her cave. Her habit was confused and strange*' (105). Orpheus seeks to free Entheus, 'poetic fury', which he does after sending Mania and her twelve 'Frantics' away. The 'Lunatics *fell into a mad measure, fitted to a loud fantastic tune; but in the end thereof the music changed into a very solemn air*' (107). This action marked the first of several 'transformations', forming the major themes and activities of the masque. Released from the stigma of madness, Entheus will assist Orpheus to 'create / Inventions rare, this night to celebrate, / Such as become a nuptial'.[31]

After music '*appeared eight Stars of extraordinary bigness*', in front of whom stood Prometheus, *attired as one of the ancient heroes*' (108, 109). Entheus implores him to 'aid us to solemnize / These royal nuptials'. The Stars moved in '*exceeding strange and delightful manner*', only to vanish suddenly, replaced by eight Masquers, gorgeously attired, with crowns on their heads, '*embossed with flames of embroidery*' (110). On a bright and transparent cloud '*the Masquers led by Prometheus descended with the music of a full song*' (111). As this cloud vanished, the scene offered '*four noble women-statues of silver*' (111), who, upon Prometheus's words and a song, transformed into life, as Orpheus reports: 'statues have life and move' (112). As the Masquers woo these transformed ladies, four more statues appeared, '*transformed into women*' (113). The Chorus sang brightly: 'Live with thy bridegroom happy, sacred bride; / How blest is he that is for love envied' (114). With this and a dance Elizabeth and Frederick joined in the revels.

The masque also represented the royal couple as statues, standing on pedestals near an obelisk and bringing in Sibylla, who after a song uttered her prophecies in Latin. In one section she observes: 'One mind will join the two nations, one set of loyalties, / One worship of God, and one love' (116).[32] She calls for Jove to give force to her prayers and fidelity to her words, uttering special praise of Princess Elizabeth and underscoring the political and dynastic implications of this wedding: 'How full of divine grace she is! She has her father's features, / She, the future parent of male offspring … / British strength is added / To German strength: could anything be the equal of this?' Prometheus calls for an appropriate response: 'Then grace her trophy with a dance triumphant.' A final dance indeed concluded the masque.

In a letter to Ralph Winwood, John Chamberlain grumbles about the masque: 'The Lords maske likewise on the mariage night, though yt were very rich and sumptuous, yet yt was very long and tedious, and with many devises more like a play then a maske.'[33] But for Lennox and others, the masque seemed like a continuation of the wedding ceremony itself, especially in its reminder through various strategies, representations, and speeches of the idea of 'transformation'. Has not the court and England been transformed this day by this hopeful marriage? If statues can be transformed, why not lives, ideas, and countries? Fresh from seeing a new performance of *The Winter's Tale*, courtiers could see in these statues coming to life a recollection of Hermione at the end of that play, which also contains hopeful desires for the royal children, Perdita and Florizel. Different dramatic forms now intertwine with the actual events to underscore the renewing importance of transformation, as the future unfolds with bright prospects. A young prince may die, in life and in fiction, but another prince and princess overcome that grief and point to a resilient future. New day stars replace the night. Fiery dancers chase away darkness. Solace.

Following established tradition, the royal family, noblemen, and spectators gathered in the tiltyard at Whitehall Palace, just below Lennox's windows, on 15 February to see the King, Prince Charles, Frederick, the Duke of Lennox, and other nobles of the realm engage in running at the ring. The tiltyard, elaborately decorated, included many Heralds at Arms, the Yeoman of the Guard, and the King's Trumpeters, all in rich embroidered coats. Queen Anne with Elizabeth watched from gallery windows, accompanied by many noble ladies. First, King James, 'mounted upon a steed of much swiftness', began the activity; he took 'the ring upon his speare three severall times together, whereat the trumpets still sounded to the great joy of the beholders'.[34] Prince Frederick, 'upon a horse of … brave courage', took his turn, 'so lightly and so nimbly, that the whole assembly gave him high commendations' (550). Then Prince Charles followed on a Spanish jennet; he took the ring four times in five attempts. The Duke of Lennox and Earl of Arundel, with a few other lords, 'in honour of the magnificent Marriage, performed very worthy races, and many times tooke the ring'. Spectators of all kinds delighted in this chivalric activity, which added another layer of colour, spectacle, and celebration to the wedding, only slightly less idealistic than the masques.

Just a few hours after running at the ring, the tiltyard once again functioned as the assembling point for entertainment, this time for George Chapman's masque that evening, *The Memorable Masque of the two Honourable Houses or Inns of Court, The Middle Temple, and Lincolns Inn.*[35] This masque, sponsored by these two Inns of Court, took place in the Great Hall in Whitehall Palace. But it began in London's streets, not far from the Guildhall, moving from the Inns and the home of Sir Edward Phelips, Master of the Rolls, in Chancery Lane and making its way to Whitehall. This outdoor procession is unique in masques to this point in 1613. And what a display it offered, preserved in Chapman's text and in reports from John Chamberlain and the Venetian Ambassador, Antonio Foscarini.

The Temple of Honour functions as one of the essential features of the masque. The spectators might well have asked: how does one arrive at this Temple and what does Honour require? The first practical answer says that spectators arrive at this structure through London's streets. In a way, the masque will be another expression of chivalry, complementing what the court had seen that afternoon in the tiltyard. Chapman, with the help of Inigo Jones, suggests that one also arrives by means of the law, in keeping with the sponsorship of the Inns of Court.[36] Chapman's rich description of the street procession captures the dazzling spectacle, and it reinforces the intertwined relationship of London and the court.

'*Fifty gentlemen, richly attired and as gallantly mounted*' began the procession (75), followed by a mock-masque of '*baboons, attired like fantastical travelers*'. An array of 'Virginian priests', called '*Phoebades*', followed; '*then rode the chief masquers in Indian habits*', costumed in silver garments, '*richly embroidered with golden suns*'. The horses, clothed in spectacular garments, each '*had two Moors, attired like Indian slaves*', accompanying. The last chariot contained a strange character, named Capriccio, '*wearing on his head a pair of golden bellows*'; this chariot also carried Eunomia, the virgin priest of the goddess Honour, who appeared with Phemis, her herald, all elaborately costumed. Honour and Plutus filled out the chariot, Honour wearing a '*rich full robe of blue silk*' (77). This elegant procession finally made its way to Westminster. Chapman writes: '*the King, bride, and bridegroom, with all the lords of the most honoured Privy Council and our chief nobility, stood in the gallery, before the tilt-yard to behold their arrival*' (77). Lennox and the royal family then entered the palace and awaited the masque.

At the end of the hall appeared a great rock, next to which stood a silver temple, the Temple of Honour, reminding the courtly spectators of the concept of honour, so crucial to *1 Henry IV* and *Julius Caesar*, both performed at court recently. On the other side of the rock a grove emerged in which the baboons and other creatures of the antimasque began to appear. Chapman writes: '*Honour is so much respected and adored that she hath a temple erected to her like a goddess, a virgin priest consecrated to her (which is Eunomia, or Law)*' (80). Plutus, who has become a follower of Honour, engages in conversation with Capriccio, who has burst forth from the rock. Plutus asks him a pertinent question: 'But what makest thou, poor man of wit, at these pompous nuptials?' (84). Capriccio answers that he has come to do acceptable service; 'And my charge is a company of accomplished travellers that are excellent at antimasques'. After the baboons do their dance, 'being antic and delightful', they return to their tree; and Plutus bids farewell to Capriccio, sending him away with a wedge of gold. After this the full masque unfolds.

With Eunomia's help, Plutus gains access to Honour's Temple as she descends with her herald Phemis (Fame). Plutus suggests that the time has come to do their 'utmost rite' (86). Honour obliges, insisting that she has come across the 'Briton ocean' 'To do due homage to the sacred nuptials / Of Love and Beauty, celebrated here'. They will also perform the 'rites they owe / To setting Phoebus', that is, King James. Out of a mine of gold the 'Phoebades' emerge, singing and dancing as devotees of the sun. Honour argues that their allegiance should be directed to Phoebus; and all the participants in turn do obeisance to James, as the songs and dances hail him as the true sun. The Chorus even recognises his 'blest' mother, whose reburial in October 1612 the court recalled.

Eunomia addresses the Indian masquers, urging them to 'renounce / Your superstitious worship of these Suns', and instead turn their direction 'To this our Briton Phoebus' (89). The masque closes with a focus on Love and Beauty, namely, the bride and bridegroom. The Chorus sings: 'Love sparks made flame in Beauty's sky, / And Beauty blew up Love as high' (90). After a final song, Plutus invites all to 'holy feasts' (91). The great hall at the palace has become just such a fair temple, honouring the king and the royal wedded couple, and recalling England's interest in the Virginia colonies, for which a new charter had been issued in 1612. The law thus offers a way to true Honour, transforming even Plutus and opening the possibility of recognising the virtue of the royal couple. Foscarini, the Venetian Ambassador, sums up the evening appropriately: 'after great eulogies of the couple, pronounced by Riches and Honour, all the Masque began to dance a ballet, with such finish that it left nothing to be desired'.[37]

Lennox and the masquers for Francis Beaumont's *The Masque of the Inner Temple and Gray's Inn* could not initially use Foscarini's comment as a valid assessment: this performance left much to be desired. Originally planned for 16 February, it got delayed until that Saturday, 20 February – but not before it had moved from Winchester House in Southwark to Westminster by river on the 16th. Chamberlain describes the river voyage, paralleling the other Inns of Court who had moved through London's streets on Monday: 'they made choise to come by water from Winchester Place in Southwarke: which suted well enough with theyre devise, which was the mariage of the river of Thames to the Rhine: and theyre shew by water was very gallant by reason of infinite store of lights very curiously set and placed: and many boats and barges with devises of light and lampes'.[38] The elegant movement on the Thames provided a stunning spectacle; Beaumont writes: 'This voyage by water was performed in great triumph. The gentlemen masquers being placed by themselves in the King's royal barge with the rich furniture of state, and adorned with a great number of lights placed in such order as might make best show.'[39] In such array the entourage arrived at the privy stairs at Whitehall where the royal family and others waited. Entreated by the Inns of Court, Phineas Pett had been enlisted to help in this movement along the Thames; but he found the tide not to be friendly; and the 'company attending the maskers very unruly, the project could not be performed so exactly as was purposed and expected'.[40] Nevertheless, 'they were safely landed at the Privy Stairs at Whitehall'.

But the expected performance in the Great Hall did not occur. Beaumont says simply: the hall was full, 'whereby it was foreseen that the room would be so scanted as might have been inconvenient' (133). Therefore, lack of space sent the masquers away, despite the 'great expectation theyre was that they shold every way exceed theyre competitors that went before them'.[41] According to Chamberlain, space was not the only issue: 'but the worst of all was that the King was so wearied and sleepie with sitting up almost two whole nights before, that he had no edge to yt'. When Francis Bacon, the 'contriver' of the masque, complained that by this 'disgrace he wold not as yt were bury them quicke', the King responded: 'then they must burie him quicke for he could last no longer'. Chamberlain concludes: 'the grace of theyre maske is quite gon when theyre apparell hath ben alredy shewed and theyre devises vented so that how yt will fall out God knows, for they are much discouraged, and out of countenance'. The anticipated audience had thus already seen their stunning costumes, diminishing the impact of that spectacle. But by Saturday the performance space had been moved to the Banqueting House, and the masque went on then as planned, presumably with a now rested and alert king. A special feast served as partial compensation also. Foscarini reports: 'After the ballet was over their Majesties and their Highnesses passed into a great Hall especially built for the purpose, where were laid out long tables laden with comfits and thousands of mottoes. After the King had made the round of the tables everything was in a moment rapaciously swept away.'[42] Perhaps a pent-up hunger unleashed itself; elegance gave way to raging desire.

When King James entered the hall for the masque, he and the other spectators saw a mountain with four delicate fountains. Iris, Beaumont records, '*apparelled in a robe of discoloured taffeta figured in variable colours, like a rainbow*', appeared, pursued by Mercury, dressed in white, '*wings on his shoulders and feet*' (134). Iris insists that she has come 'To celebrate the long-wish'd nuptials, / Here in Olympia, which are now perform'd / Betwixt two goodly rivers' (135), echoing the masque in Act 4 of *The Tempest*. The contentious exchange between Mercury and Iris leads to the first antimasque, an array of four Naiads, who arise out of the fountains and dance; but Mercury, exerting his power, orders five Hyades to descend from the mountain and dance also. Cupids and then 'Statues' enter, the latter 'supposed to be before descended from Jove's altar' (137). Iris responds with the second antimasque, a curious group devoted to May games; these people, '*having such a spirit of country jollity as can hardly be imagined*', dance in a lively fashion, which greatly pleased the king, who called for it to be repeated, '*as he did likewise for the first anti-masque*' (139).

The masque proper called for Olympian Knights and Priests, located on the upper reaches of the mountain where they reside in '*pavilions*', which '*were to sight as a cloth of gold*' (140). At the uppermost reach of the mountain stood Jupiter's altar, '*gilt, with three great tapers upon golden candle-sticks burning upon it*'. Beaumont describes the Knights' costume: '*Arming doublets of carnation satin, embroidered with blazing stars of silver plate ... pumps of carnation satin*' and white feathers protruding from their helmets. The Priests wore '*Long robes of white taffeta, long white heads of hair*' (141). The Knights dance, and the Priests sing. Their second song suggests: 'at the wedding such a pair, / Each dance is taken for a prayer, / Each song a sacrifice' (141). The Knights call out the ladies of the court to dance, which they do in several different forms. The Priests then sing their final song: 'Peace and silence be the guide / To the man, and to the bride! / If there be a joy yet new / In marriage, let it fall on you, / That all the world may wonder!' (142). Each dance a prayer and each song a sacrifice: thereby the masquers bestow their blessing on the newlyweds and endow the evening with wonder – deferred but no less powerful.

The ten-day trajectory of spectacle and theatre produced an exhausting but thrilling experience – from fireworks to sea battles to the wedding itself to the three masques to the tiltyard. God, goddesses, Indian masquers, allegorical figures, country folk, Olympian Knights and Priests filled the masques, enriching the courtly experience and engendering spectacle, dance, and music. The splendour of the wedding itself rivalled the subsequent masques. Journeys of masquers through London's streets or at night along the Thames with lights blazing stirred wonder, as city and court converged. Themes of transformation, chivalry, honour, celebration, sanction for marriage, and praise of sovereign power permeated the entertainment. Looking back over this February experience and acknowledging its occasional imperfection, Lennox might well have agreed with the Venetian Ambassador's judgement: 'it left nothing to be desired'. A royal daughter had found a princely husband, and the country rejoiced beyond a common joy.

But not everyone rejoiced. Clearly missing from the wedding festivities was James's first cousin, Arbella Stuart, who in fact languished in the Tower. She had a sad existence, having been placed under a kind of house arrest during Queen Elizabeth's reign. Arbella's grandmother, Elizabeth Hardwick, Countess of Shrewsbury, kept a keen eye on her during her incarceration. Arbella's claim to the English throne worried both Elizabeth and then James, although she herself never made any moves to press her claim. But her position as a potentially serious claimant trapped her in a lifetime of political squabbles about her destiny and more specifically about marriage. Desperate for attention and freedom, Arbella even created a fictitious lover, about whom she wrote in her letters, to the alarm of Elizabeth. When James came to the English throne, she gained freedom and initial respect; indeed, she processed with other members of James's family in the magnificent royal entry pageant of 15 March 1604.

James's children loved her and stayed in close communication. Arbella also became a companion to Queen Anne; indeed, she served as godparent to their daughter Mary, born in 1605, as had Lennox. She danced in Jonson's early masque *The Masque of Beauty* (1605) and also in Daniel's *Tethys' Festival* (1610), the latter forming part of the celebration of Henry's inauguration as Prince of Wales. The Venetian Ambassador, Molin, who in 1607 had described and analysed the royal family, also included Arbella: 'She is twenty-eight; not very beautiful, but highly accomplished, for besides being of most refined manners she speaks fluently Latin, Italian, French, Spanish, reads Greek and Hebrew, and is always studying.'[43] Her intellectual and studious nature should have endeared her to James, but he seems to have paid little attention to her, never fulfilling his promise to restore her properties to her. Ambassador Molin noted that nothing had happened on that score: 'She remains without a mate, and without estate,'

James moved from benign neglect to direct confrontation when Arbella fell in love with William Seymour, future Earl of Hertford, and attempted to marry him. James summoned them both before the Privy Council and ordered them to give up all negotiations for marriage. Seymour's remote claim to the throne worried James. But the couple defied the king and married in 1611. When James found out, he had them imprisoned. If Anne intervened in Arbella's behalf, it all came to naught. They recklessly but courageously escaped prison, only to be captured. James sent Arbella to the Tower from which she did not emerge and died in 1615. She persisted in the belief that James would release her. In fact, sadly, she purchased four new and expensive gowns for Princess Elizabeth's wedding, but James did not let her attend. No rejoicing for Arbella; no February Valentine.

The wedding festivities did not end on 20 February; for on the 25th under the sponsorship of Prince Charles, Princess Elizabeth, and Prince Frederick, the Lady Elizabeth's Men performed John Marston's *The Dutch Courtesan* at Whitehall, possibly in the Cockpit. This play, dating from a few years earlier, had been published in 1605. (The play received another production at court on 12 December 1613.) Marston had by 1613 abandoned the theatre, had indeed entered the ranks of clergy, turning away also from his legal training at the Middle Temple. The younger members of the royal family had apparently decided that they wanted more entertainment and thus reverted to the pattern of the early weeks of 1613. Lennox and other court followers settled in to watch Marston's exploration of Malheureux's moral conflict as the enticements of the Dutch courtesan, Franceschina, challenge his otherwise upright and strict moral standards. Freevill and Beatrice meanwhile pursue their nuptial plans, the celebration of which includes an abbreviated masque in 4.1. The play struggles through various competing voices to define what constitutes love.

Freevill had himself first been enchanted by Franceschina, but by the play's opening scene he has decided to abandon her, pursuing what he calls 'lawful love' (1.2.91).[44] This action leaves an opening for Malheureux, who lamely announces: 'No love's without some lust, no life without some love' (143). He will become 'passion's slave'. The conversation between Freevill and Beatrice in 2.1 illustrates another dimension of love: fidelity, as Freevill claims that his vow to her is 'irrevocable' (29). Having received Beatrice's ring, Freevill informs Malheureux: 'Why, friend, philosophy and nature are all one; love is the center in which all lines close the common bond of being' (114–15). Malheureux assents, but the allures of Franceschina torment him. Her insistence that she cannot love him until Freevill dies shocks Malheureux, who nevertheless asserts: ''Tis as irrevocable as breath: he dies' (2.2.176). The courtly audience may be hearing an echo of an earlier performance of *Much Ado*, in which Beatrice in that play starkly commands Benedick: 'Kill Claudio.' Fortunately, Malheureux has not lost his moral sense, made evident in his soliloquy at the end of the scene where he acknowledges 'how easy 'tis to err'; therefore, he decides, 'My friend shall know it all' (224), echoing Camillo's decision to inform Polixenes of Leontes' evil intent in *The Winter's Tale*.

Thus in 3.1 Malheureux confesses to Freevill: 'I ha' been tempted to your death' (3.1.220). This leads Freevill to a strategy of using the nuptial masque as an occasion in which Malheureux may seem to challenge Freevill to a fight. Since this will be a ruse, they may 'laugh at folly' (257). The earlier moments of the scene have offered the bleak assessment of love and marriage by Crispinella, Beatrice's sister. The Servant announces in 4.1: 'The masquers are at hand' (3). Freevill and Malheureux challenge each other and exit, ready to carry out their plan. Although Freevill goes along with this plot and gives Beatrice's ring to Malheureux, he has something else in mind: to teach his friend a lesson. His decision to torment Malheureux finds its parodic parallel in the play's subplot, which displays Cocledemoy's several successful strategies of gulling Mulligrub, a vintner.

Franceschina first tricks Malheureux and has him arrested for 'killing' Freevill (5.1). Freevill meanwhile reveals himself to Beatrice, informing her of what has been going on (5.2). On trumped-up charges Cocledemoy succeeds in having Mulligrub placed in the stocks (4.5), an image that finds its counterpart in Malheureux's position, as he awaits execution for murder. But Freevill rescues him by revealing himself, insisting: 'to force you from the truer danger, / I wrought the feigned, suffering this fair devil / In shape of woman to make good her plot' (5.3.43–5). Instead, authorities haul Franceschina away to prison. A sobered Malheureux claims: 'I am myself. How long was't ere I could / Persuade my passion to grow calm to you!' (61–2). Even Cocledemoy relents and claims: 'honest Cocledemoy restores whatsoever he has got, to make you [Mullligrub] know that whatsoe'er he has done has been only … for wit's sake' (133–5). Relieved, Mulligrub says, 'I could even weep for joy!' (145); but Mistress Mulligrub adds: 'I could weep, too, but God knows for what!' (146). The play has found its moral compass and validated Freevill's claim that 'love is the center in which all lines close'.

Two days later, 27 February, the same group of royal young people sponsored a performance at court by the Children of the Queen's Revels of George Chapman's *The Widow's Tears*, a play earlier acted by the same group at Blackfriars Theatre in 1609. Having had his masque performed at court on 15 February,

Chapman now offers a play. He loosely based this play, published in 1612, on the story of the Widow of Ephesus found in Petronius's *Satyricon*. Chapman adopts the familiar theme of women's inconstancy, made also apparent in the exchange between the Player Queen and Player King in *Hamlet*, Act 3, scene 2. Tharsalio woos and wins the Countess Widow, named Eudora, whose husband has recently died and who vows to remain faithful to his memory. Lysander, Tharsalio's brother, believes firmly in the faithfulness of his wife Cynthia, but nevertheless puts her devotion to the test when he pretends to have died. The question of the relationship of Lysander and Cynthia comes to dominate the second half of the play. The play asks: what are the obligations of married love?

Tharsalio announces his intentions from the beginning, as he embraces Confidence as his guide. Despite Eudora's vows, underscored by Cynthia who insists that Eudora will 'in memory of him … preserve till death the unstain'd honor of a widow's bed' (1.1.85–6), Tharsalio believes that such widow's tears are at best 'short-liv'd' (135).[45] Therefore, he approaches Eudora brazenly; but she initially rebuffs him. He also plants seeds of doubt in Lysander's mind, based on 'human frailty' (204). He asks Lysander: 'Do you enjoy the sole privilege of your wife's bed?' (226–7). Lysander's faith in Cynthia rests on 'ignorance and credulity', Tharsalio claims. Thus, the play sets in motion two narrative strands that examine fidelity; but Tharsalio's is the easier path, as he quickly wins Eudora, whose resistance withers. He therefore announces: 'the great Countess is mine, the palace is at your service, to which I invite you all to solemnize my honor'd nuptials' (3.1.80–2). Surprised, Cynthia asks: 'Is there probability in this, that a lady so great, so virtuous, standing on so high terms of honor, should so soon stoop?' (98–9).

Act 3, scene 2 presents a masque in honour of the marriage. A whole chorus of Sylvans approaches, and the 'device is rare', Argus says (3.2.13). Hylus, Lysander's son, plays the part of the god Hymen, who descends to be among the Sylvans. Eudora joins in the festivities: 'let's dispose ourselves / To entertain these Sylvan revelers, / That come to grace our loved nuptials' (35–7). After everyone dances, Hymen praises the great bride and bridegroom and their nuptial joys, to the acclaim of all. The Jacobean court surely heard echoes of the experiences that they had enjoyed in the recent wedding festivities.

But underneath this joy, Chapman's play explores the increasing tension in Lysander's mind about his wife; finally, he and Tharsalio agree to test Cynthia by arranging Lysander's fake death, a situation that slightly echoes Marston's play. Having learned of her husband's 'death' and attended his funeral, Cynthia takes up residence in his tomb, where the remainder of the play's action takes place. When Act 4 opens, she has already been there four days. But unexpectedly, Lysander, disguised as a soldier, also comes to the tomb. Little by little he wins the confidence of the 'widow', and she falls in love with him. He suggests that she should 'enjoy the fruits of life' (4.2.89). But he pays a price for all of this, namely, his loss of faith in her. He exclaims: 'This mirror of nuptial chastity, this votress of widow-constancy, to change her faith, exchange kisses, embraces, with a stranger' (5.1.118–19).

Finally, Tharsalio explains to Cynthia what has been going on: 'The soldier was your disguis'd husband. … This was a project of his own contriving to put your loyalty and constant vows to the test' (316, 319–20). Alarmed, she nevertheless decides that she has an advantage, leading to a double irony: she knows about Lysander, but he does not know that she knows. The final moments sort out the relationships; and Tharsalio closes: 'So, brother, let your lips compound the strife, / And think you have the only constant wife' (705–6). Because Cynthia does not speak for the last two hundred lines of the play, she offers little assurance about her future with Lysander. Perhaps she recoils from a likely answer to the question she had incredulously asked about Eudora's sudden acceptance of Tharsalio's advances: can a 'lady so great, so virtuous, standing on so high terms of honor, … so soon stoop'. In other words, have the widow's tears (her own) been efficacious?

On 1 March, Charles, Elizabeth, and Frederick sponsored another play, the anonymous *Raymond Duke of Lyons*, at Whitehall, performed by Lady Elizabeth's Men. Then King James sponsored two more plays at court: on 2 March, *1 The Knave*, and on 5 March, *2 The Knave*, performed by the Prince's Men. (The texts of these three plays do not survive.) Thus, for two weeks after the final wedding masque, the court continued to enjoy dramatic performances. At this point Prince Charles and Prince Frederick left Whitehall and journeyed to Oxford and Cambridge. Frederick received sumptuous entertainment at Oxford and in his own hand matriculated himself as a member of the university.

At Cambridge he and Charles saw two different plays performed, one of them lasting between seven and eight hours, according to John Chamberlain. They also heard theological and philosophical disputes. John Hacket captures the scene at Trinity College: 'His [Dr Nevile's] Table was Graced with the Company of Prince *Charles*, Prince Elector *Frederick* the Bridegroom, Count *Henry* of *Nassaw*, *Lodwick* Duke of *Lenox*, with a most comely Concourse of Nobles and Gentlemen. ... In two distinct Nights a Comick and a Pastoral Fable, both in *Latin*, were Acted before their Highnesses, and the Spectators, by the Students of the same College.'[46] Chamberlain adds, however: 'The King is very angrie and out of love with our Cambridge men for theyre questions at the Palsgraves beeing there specially whether *electio* or *successio* were to be preferred in king-doms, and is out of patience that yt shold be so much as argued in schooles.'[47] James clearly preferred that he alone be allowed to ruminate on kingship and succession.

On 24 March, the annual Accession Day Tilt took place at Whitehall with Lennox as one of the principal participants. In Chamberlain's view, 'Yesterday was the great tilting at court, where there was more gallantrie both for number and braverie then hath ben since the King came in' (440). Lennox, and the earls of Arundel, Rutland, Pembroke, Dorset, and Montgomery, and six lords were among the tilters. Chamberlain says that 'they all performed theyre parts very well specially Sir Harry Rich with Sir Sigismond Alexander'. But rain hindered the spectacle 'to the disgrace of many fine plumes'.[48] Sir Henry Rich and his brother Sir Robert Rich offered a speech to the king, one written by Ben Jonson. The poem offers the brothers' 'lives, their loves, their hearts' to the king.[49] Jonson's verse also interprets the emblems that the brothers pre-sented; for example, Robert 'Presents a royal altar of fair peace; / As an everlasting sacrifice'. Henry offered a 'prospective' glass, which when looked at correctly enables the knight to appear as a new creation to the king's eyes. The other tilters presented their *imprese*, 'whereof some were so dark, that their meaning is not yet understood, unless perchance that were their meaning, not to be understood', Wotton suggests (2: 17). (*Imprese* were allegorical or symbolic visual designs, typically accompanied with mottoes of some kind, such as can be found in the tournament in Shakespeare's *Pericles*.) Wotton further says that the 'two best, to my fancy, were those of the two Earls brothers [Pembroke and Montgomery]: the first a small exceeding white pearl, and the words, *Solo candore valco*. The other a sun casting a glance on the side of a pillar, and the beams reflecting, with this motto, *Splendente refulget*'. This Accession Day tournament joined the earlier one on 15 February as part of the nearly three-month-long courtly entertainments, all prompted by Princess Elizabeth's wedding.

Shakespeare intersects this tournament explicitly. He designed the *impresa* for Francis Manners, the socially ambitious Earl of Rutland, obviously at the earl's request. For this artistic endeavour Shakespeare received a payment of 44 shillings. The earl's steward's records also include a payment of 44 shillings to the actor Richard Burbage, who painted the *impresa*.[50] Thus, two of the King's Men earned income from the Accession Day tilt and, thereby, participated in it, as Burbage clearly had performed in the many dramatic performances at court over the past several weeks. London 1613 included the most renowned playwright and the most prominent actor, here in the immediate aftermath of the wedding.

Given all of the dramatic performances and Shakespeare's acquaintance with the royal family, it is hard to imagine that he chose to remain away in Stratford while all of this took place in Whitehall. In all likelihood, this King's Man tapped into much of the court entertainment, at least as a spectator, and of course as playwright for many of the plays, which his acting company performed. Clearly, Shakespeare was in London in early March 1613, for on the 10th he purchased the Blackfriars gatehouse, a highly desirable piece of property and the only residential and substantial property that Shakespeare ever owned in London. This gatehouse rose above the strong eastern gate of the former Dominican priory; it lay about 200 yards away from the Blackfriars Theatre, where the King's Men performed, and it offered easy access to the Thames and a short journey to the Globe. Shakespeare put down £80 in cash, leaving a remainder of £60, to be paid by September. He thus joined his friend Richard Burbage and competitor Ben Jonson as a property owner in Blackfriars. The gatehouse, like the Holbein Gate where Lennox resided, had residential rooms. One can imagine Shakespeare occupying his new property, perhaps at least through March, if not beyond.[51] Such a place in Blackfriars would have been nearly irresistible, placing him among his actor friends, near his business interests, and in proximity to all the Whitehall festivities in early 1613.

A few weeks after the Accession Day tournament, the royal family began its journey with Elizabeth and Frederick to send them on their way to Germany; the long festivity had ended, and now the reality of departure loomed. Lennox travelled with the royal party because James had appointed him to accompany the princess to her new home; the king included also the Earl of Arundel, Viscount Lisle, and Lord Harrington (Elizabeth's former guardian) to travel with her. The week after Easter, on Saturday 10 April, the entourage began its movement from Whitehall to Greenwich, but not before the Venetian Ambassador, Antonio Foscarini, had a chance to bid the newlyweds farewell. At Whitehall, he first met Frederick, who then escorted him to the Princess's room. 'The Princess then in familiar fashion and smiling talked of her going to a fair country as she understood, but she did not know if it was as fair as this.'[52] Foscarini went on to meet with King James, who asked the ambassador if he had seen the children. 'He seemed to feel their departure keenly, and said he hoped to see them soon again and with offspring; they were both born in the same year and in the month of August and had not yet finished their seventeenth year. All this he said with great tenderness' (526).

On Tuesday 13 April, the royal party journeyed on to Rochester; here the King and Queen said their farewells to Elizabeth and her husband. The Venetian Ambassador, Foscarini, reports that the crowd that met them along the route was 'incredible'. Throughout Kent 'they will be met and accompanied by the infantry of eight thousand and horse to the number of two thousand. The King has given orders that all the horse are to be in uniform and he has chosen the cloth, the lace and the plumes. The cost will exceed one hundred and twenty thousand crowns.'[53] James had never before travelled in this part of England. The royal parents left, but Charles went on with his sister to Canterbury where he bade farewell.

Elizabeth now rested in Canterbury, separated for the last time from her parents and brother. From there she wrote a profoundly personal letter to King James on 16 April. It put into perspective the effects of those glittering masques, fireworks displays, and play performances that surrounded her opulent wedding. Elizabeth wrote:

> Sire, I now feel the sad effects of separation and distance from your majesty. My heart, which was pressed and astounded at my departure, now permits my eyes to weep their privation of the sight of the

most precious object, which they could have beheld in this world. I shall perhaps, never see again the flower of princes, the king of fathers, the best and most amiable father, that the sun will ever see. But the very humble respect and devotion, with which I ceaselessly honour him, your majesty can never efface from the memory of her, who awaits in this place a favourable wind, and who would return again to kiss the hands of your majesty, if the state of affairs, or her condition would allow it, to show to your majesty with what ardent affection she is and will be, even to death.[54]

This remarkable letter, as effusive and affectionate as any that James received from his children, underscores a separation that Elizabeth had begun to feel. She would never write quite so warm a letter to her father again. She would never see her father or any other member of her immediate family again. Happy with her new husband but saddened at leaving England, the youthful Elizabeth went to face the unknown in a strange land: more than an ocean would separate her from her parents and brother Charles.

At Margate, Elizabeth and Frederick readied to make their departure on 23 April, a day on which Lennox and other members of the Order of the Garter were to engage in activities associated with the feast of St George, but bad weather prevented this and thwarted the princes' journey. Finally, on Sunday 25 April, they set sail, reaching Flushing on 29 April. Foscarini anticipated their trip: 'They will embark on board a galleon of one thousand four hundred tons, which the late Prince caused to be built and which preserves his name. It is thought to be the most beautiful ship England ever had.'[55] Two pinnaces will carry ammunition, and 'there will be an escort of six royal galleons and others to the number of sixteen. At sea half way across they will be met by the Dutch fleet' (524). Appropriately enough, one of the ships that attended the fleet had the name of *Phoenix*.[56] Elizabeth and Frederick sailed on the *Prince Royal*, built under the leadership of Phineas Pett, who also made the journey, as he reports. Pett accompanied the Lord Admiral, and they travelled with the royal party as far as Flushing. On 2 May, he and the Lord Admiral took leave of Elizabeth and began the return journey to England. Frederick had left Elizabeth on 30 April in order to go to the Palatinate. Elizabeth began a journey of several weeks, receiving marvellous entertainment and hospitality everywhere, accompanied by Lennox and the entire entourage.

The leisurely, circuitous journey to Germany included a tour through part of the Low Counties with entertainment in Amsterdam, Haarlem, and Utrecht. An anonymous account reports the reception in Amsterdam on 13 May: the 'first welcome was a volley of 600 Great-shot, sent from the ships; and then being landed, the Burgers of the Towne stood ready in Armes, to receive her on the shore' where they led Elizabeth to her lodging, pausing to view 'two rich and sumptuous Pageants, erected in the streets'.[57] A few days later, the party reached Germany where, for example, at Oppenham four elaborate triumphal arches lined the streets, presenting such allegorical figures as Fortitude, Virtue, Fortune, Hope, Concord, and Faith, indicated by their emblematic properties. Lennox recognised these figures from various pageants and entertainments that he had seen in Scotland and England.

On 6 June, Elizabeth entered Franckendal, which 'the *Palsgrave* hath given to her for her Joynter' (B4). The Burgers met the Prince and Princess 'in a war-like manner, attiring themselves like *Turks, Poles,* & *Switzers*, and so with a solemne and orderly march conducted them to their Lodgings' (B4–B4v). The city offered two pageant arches, one presenting several German kings and the virtues that each represented, and the second depicting Fame at the top of the arch with the qualities Constancy, Justice, Wisdom, and Magnanimity located across the scaffold. On the first evening, the royal party saw a 'Regall Throne', illuminated by a hundred lamps, representing a 'figure of that *Throne of Salomon*, when he entertained the *Queene* of *Sheba*' (B4v). And the next night they witnessed a spectacular re-enactment of the Siege of Troy, including a castle representing Troy and the army of Greeks outside the walls. After being initially repulsed, the Greeks 'subtilly sounded a *Retreat*, and seeming to retire, lay hidden in Ambush, leaving a Horse of extreame proportion and greatnesse before the wals' (B4v–C1). Unwittingly, the Trojans drew the horse into their walls, and then the Greeks attacked, remaining 'Conquerors, and in that Triumph marched away'. The city itself had triumphed with these extraordinary entertainments.

On 8 June, the entourage reached Heidelberg, the final destination of this part of Elizabeth's experience. Many shots of ordnance greeted the royal couple, a sign of the citizens' 'love, joy, and dutie' (C1). The throngs had come 'especially to behold *Her*, upon whom all their eyes were fixed with love and admiration' (C1v). The city had erected several arches, each containing its mute argument of visual meaning. Near the university, for example, the faculties of medicine, philosophy, theology, and law, each had prepared a scaffold saluting its particular art and the royal couple. After this procession, Elizabeth arrived at the castle, where she met for the first time Frederick's mother and received gracious entertainment there.

During the next three days the tiltyard became the focus of activity, although on the first day poor weather rendered the tournament impossible. But the sun emerged the following day; and so did Frederick, dressed to represent Jason, who entered the tiltyard first, along with Lennox and others. A stunning visual spectacle unfolded, including a procession of allegorical and mythological figures. For example, Jupiter appeared in a chariot, 'drawne by two *Griffons*, and those *Griffons* guided by *Mercury*, who sate as Coach-man' (C2). Next came Juno in a chariot, drawn by peacocks and guided by Iris. Attended by appropriate companions, the God of Husbandry and Neptune, god of the sea, entered; and on a rock three mermaids sat singing and playing their instruments. Arion, playing his lute and sitting on a sea-horse, soon followed; and behind him came the Seven Deadly Sins, chained and driven forward by a dragon, spitting fire all the way. Frederick then appeared as Jason in a ship, which contained the Golden Fleece, 'which *Jason* fetcht from *Greece*; and at the sterne *Envy* was dragg'd, eating her owne heart' (C2v). Mars, Hercules, Venus, and Cupid all preceded the imperial chariot bearing Victory; and 'Next unto *Victory* entered *Diana*, in a Chariot made like a Forrest, set out and adorned with living Birds and Beasts', with satyrs and nymphs following (C3). Astounded by the spectacle, the spectators readied themselves for another day in the tiltyard.

On the next bright day, Frederick once again appeared as Jason, this time on horseback, surrounded by many supporters: six squires, eight trumpets, seven footmen and their horses. Mythological figures followed, such as Apollo and Bacchus. Midas with his ass's ears entered, as did Marsyas 'and a *Satyre* fleaing off his skinne, because hee durst contend with *Apollo*, in Musicke' (C3v). Then the Nine Muses, seated on Mount Parnassus, followed, and after them the Three Graces, accompanied by Hercules and Mercury. Just to make the entertainment complete, 'three being attyred in the habits of *Turkes*' appeared, watched over by six squires with lances. Elizabeth, Lennox, and other members of the English party might

well have thought of these tiltyard experiences as a glorious extension of the prolonged wedding festivities. They certainly would have
been familiar with what they saw, including those Turks. Heidelberg
had outdone itself with entertainment. As a kind of respite, on 12
June, Frederick, German princes, Lennox, and others 'hunted the
Deere with Lances' (C4). Whatever visual overload they had experienced, they could now discharge in vigorous hunting.

But on 14 June, this all came to an end. On this day the Duke
of Lennox and other English members of the entourage took their
leave of Princess Elizabeth and Frederick. For Lennox it had to be
especially poignant: not only had the exceptional festivities concluded but also he was separating himself from this person whom
he had known since her birth. As her father had left her at Rochester,
so now Lennox, her father's representative, left her at Heidelberg.
Alone now, but obviously with her husband, this teenaged royal
princess would have to make her life on a new Continent, one still
very strange to her, and she would have to make it without her faithful supporter Lennox. As she wrote to her father from Canterbury,
she could now say of the departing Lennox: she felt 'the sad effects
of separation and distance'. All the events, festivities, and pageants
in Holland and Germany pointed to a new future for Elizabeth and
Frederick, but they also looked to a past that would be no more.

George Goring, a minor diplomat in the English delegation,
underscored the looming isolation of Princess Elizabeth when he
wrote to Sir Thomas Edmondes, Ambassador in Paris, on 13 June
1613, that he would be surprised 'if all her Highnes trayne, there
will at six moneths ende remayne six persons. For some shee likes
not, others not the countrye.'[58] Goring adds: 'shee hath not one with
her whoe is able vppon any occasion to advise her for the best, or to
persuade or disuade'. Some possess will but 'want wit, others wit but
noe will, and a third kinde voyed of both' (91b). Goring wonders
'what this may grow to'. History validates Goring's concern.

Thomas Howard, Earl of Arundel, his wife, and thirty-six attendants, including Inigo Jones, also bade farewell to Elizabeth. They
travelled part of the way with Lennox, but then directed their
journey to Italy, their ultimate destination. Arundel had participated in Elizabeth's wedding, bearing the king's sword; he also took
part in the tilt that took place the day following the wedding. He
had danced in Jonson's masque *Hymenaei* (1606) for the wedding
of his relative Frances Howard and the Earl of Essex. Along with

Lennox, Arundel had performed in *Prince Henry's Barriers*, part of the celebration of Henry's investiture as Prince of Wales in 1610. In May 1611, he became a member of the Order of the Garter, along with Prince Charles and Robert Carr, eventually Earl of Somerset. An important constituent of the powerful Howard clan, Arundel exercised considerable influence at court. From Gilbert Talbot, the Earl of Shrewsbury, his wife's father, Arundel learned much about art collecting and began to establish himself as one of the most important art collectors in Jacobean England.

The passion for art took him to Italy in 1613 and explains the presence of Inigo Jones, already well known for his designs for court masques, including two for Elizabeth's wedding. He had begun his collaboration with Jonson in 1605 with the *Masque of Blackness*. He had also travelled extensively in Italy and spoke Italian fluently; thus he could be of great value to Arundel. In the words of one scholar: Arundel 'began in that year [1613] an extended tour of Italy which was to alter the whole cast of English culture'.[59] Simply, the discoveries, purchases, and knowledge gained in Italy changed the course of art collecting in England, first by making it fashionable. Arundel and Jones moved throughout Italy: Vicenza, Bologna, Florence, Siena, and including a long stay in Rome, where they engaged in excavations in the Forum, unearthing some ancient statues – which may have been 'planted' there by Roman authorities. The Arundel party spent the summer of 1614 in Genoa but returned to England in September, following the death of Henry Howard, Earl of Northampton, Arundel's great-uncle. In addition to many treasures, Jones brought back extensive knowledge of Italian architecture and notebooks full of drawings that he had made. The value of this Italian sojourn in 1613–14 can hardly be overstated in terms of Jones's artistic development and Arundel's legacy.

Paralleling Elizabeth's festive experiences, Queen Anne began a progress in late spring 1613, making her way towards Bath to take the waters there and perhaps to escape thinking too intently about the departed daughter. King James accompanied Anne only as far as Hampton Court, as she pressed on, stopping on 27 April at Caversham near Reading at Cawsome House, the residence of Sir William Knollys, who entertained her there in shows devised by Thomas Campion, who had, of course, written the masque presented on 14 February. This show began with a conversation between a Traveller and a Cynick, the latter arguing for the private, ascetic life. But the *'fantastick Traveller in a silken sute'* laid out a different case, finally persuading the Cynick to embrace social life.[60] The two then went by horseback to the park gate, where two Keepers greeted them: *'with them stood two* Robin-Hood men *in sutes of greene striped with blacke'* (237). A Keeper and songs welcomed the Queen. In the lower garden Anne encountered a Gardener, who spoke to her: 'Most magnificent and peerelesse Diety, loe, I the surveyer of Lady *Floras* workes, welcome your grace' (240). A song ushered the queen into the house.

After supper, the Traveller, Cynick, and Gardener reappeared, this time to be joined by Silvanus in the opening of a masque. Silvanus entered the hall, dressed with his lower part *'like a Goate, and his upper parts in an anticke habit of rich Taffatie, cut into Leaves'* (245). He bowed to the Queen and acknowledged her, offering her 'the fresh-air'd groves, / Those pleasures which greene hill and valley moves' (245). As his speech ended, suddenly a great noise brought in eight Pages with green torches, and then eight Maskers appeared. The whole entertainment dissolved into dance and music with Queen Anne joining in. On the next afternoon, 28 April, the Gardener again confronted the queen in the lower garden, as she readied to leave. The Gardener pleaded: 'Stay, Goddesse, stay a little space, / Our poore Countrie love to grace' (247). Since they cannot detain her, they send their love with her: 'While we the sad time prolong / With a mournefull parting song.' This song of three voices dispatched the 'Author of our joy'.

While Elizabeth was arriving in Heidelberg, Queen Anne arrived in Bristol and stayed there 4–8 June. The mayor and others welcomed her into the city. The main entertainment, however, focused on a battle on the Severn river. Records of the city contain a number of entries concerning the festivities, especially the building of a bower from which the queen could witness the sport. Financial records reveal extensive expenditures. John Chamberlain, writing to Dudley Carleton, observes: 'there was a Shew made on the river at high-water against the mouth of the river at the Gibb; and there was built a scaffold in Canons' Marsh finely decorated with ivy-leaves and flowers for her Majestie to sit in and see the fight'.[61] Chamberlain estimates the crowd at thirty thousand persons, stretched along the riverside. Before that, hundreds of citizens welcomed Anne into the city's streets, where an Orator first greeted her with much praise, extending the city's 'true Love' that proceeds from the subjects' hearts.[62] Robert Naile reports at the end of the first day's entertainment: 'Thus did her graces Court excel, with great renowne and fame, / Where thousands for to see her face, to *Bristoll* flocking came' (sig. B4v).

Reminiscent of the mock battle presented as part of the wedding festivities in February, this one at Bristol also contained a skirmish between Turkish and Christian forces.[63] Naile provides in the poem a somewhat virulent account of the Turks, recalling other analyses of the Turks; he seems at points especially to have in mind Richard Knolles's work and to remember some details from the Battle of Lepanto.[64] Naile not only provides a version of the sea battle but also an interpretation that situates the ongoing struggle between Turks and Christians. He comments specifically on the plight of English merchants caught in the struggle with aggressive Turkish ships on the open waters: 'many a Christian Marchant man, hath knowen' the loss of 'all their goods (O barberous cruelty!)' (sig. C2v). Naile contrasts the humane treatment by Christians towards others to that of the Turks, those 'tiranizing Lords / Barbarian-like'. He chastises Christians who have let the 'proud *Ottoman*', the 'cursed race', the 'accursed Infidels' gain control over lands (C2v). Naile also regretfully acknowledges that sometimes Christians can rival Turks in their unkindness; he nevertheless urges: 'Unite your Forces Christian like from *Europe* to expell / Proud *Ottoman*, too dangerous a neighbour neare to dwell' (C3). He laments that he does not have Virgil's talent to capture this event in its epic quality, blurring the line between the fiction of this sea battle in Bristol and the larger real-world conflict between Turks and Christians.

Naile begins his account of the battle: 'Formost of all an English Ship came stemming with the tyde, / And right before her *Graces* Tent at Anchor did she ride' (C3v). While at anchor, the English 'gan discry from farre / Two Turkish Gallies well prepar'd, most mighty men of warre'. The 'Turks' cry out: 'What will yee yeeld, or else sinke and be drown'd?' (C4). But the English Christian sailors respond: 'We had much rather lose our lives then lose our liberty.' Naile writes of the Turks jumping into the water, and he claims that the "silver waves were stain'd with crimson blood' (C4), a detail that may recall Knolles's account of the Battle at Lepanto. Victory, meanwhile, 'Now on the Christians, then on Turkes, did looke impartially'. Some of the Turks took down the flag of the English ship, enraging the Christians: 'Their valiant hearts were more inflam'd by Turkes disgracefull soyle [spoiling]' (D1). The battle finally abated as the Christian forces prevailed. The Turks even left some of their troops behind, 'Which captives brought before her *Grace*, on bended knees did crave / For mercy, which her *Majestie* with pardon freely gave' (D1). Another source records: 'some of the Turks remained prisoners and were presented to her Majesty, who laughing said, that they were not only like Turks by apparel, but by their countenances'.[65]

Anne thus became part of the drama, much as Queen Elizabeth had in a similar pageant in Bristol in 1574, in which she had decided the issue between war and peace. Anne enjoyed the battle: 'This Fight was so excellently formed for the time, that delighted her Majesty much; and she said, she never saw any thing so neatly and so artificially [artfully] performed.'[66] Naile interprets the scene as representing England's ability to stamp out conspiracies and 'privie plots' against the state: 'Loe here behold by this triumph, as in a mirror plaine, / How mighty *Jove* against all foes our quarrell doth maintaine' (D1). This analysis recalls that of John Taylor and others of the battle between Christians and Turks on the Thames witnessed by the royal family on 13 February, a victory that apparently underscored England's military might. Naile draws an additional truth from this mock encounter: 'Their vaine attempts and boundles thoughts, he turnes to their decay / Entrapped in the selfe-same snare, they did for others lay.'

The next day the queen took her leave, but not before sending the mayor a diamond ring. As she rode from the city, 'joyfull hearts expressed were, when they beheld her face, / And with loud voyces did cry out, *The Lord preserve your Grace*' (D1v). Dismounting from his horse, the Mayor on bended knee bade Anne farewell. The citizens of Bristol have demonstrated their love and loyal hearts, according to Naile, which 'Envy cannot staine' (D2). And they have challenged and defeated the menacing Turks, represented in the fictional and dramatic sea battle.

By 19 July, the cathedral city of Wells had received word of Queen Anne's planned visit; thus the city authorities began making plans, which mainly involved enlisting the co-operation of the various guilds. City records, the only source of information about this pageant, indicate, for example, what the mayor and other dignitaries should wear. The city formed a committee 'to give allowance for the matters of the Shewes whether they bee fit or not And every companie to be Contributorie as they have binne in tymes past to the shewes aforesaid'.[67] The queen arrived on 20 August and moved through the city streets, encountering various pageant devices, reminiscent of medieval drama, especially the cycle plays in which the appropriate guild would be matched to a corresponding scene.

Thus, the first company group, comprising Hammermen, Carpenters, Joiners, Coopers, Masons, Tilers, and Blacksmiths, presented a streamer with their arms and 'Noath buildinge the arke. Vulcan workinge at the Forge. Venus carried in a Charriott and Cupid sitting in her lapp with his bowe bent. A morrice Daunce. The Dragon which devoured the virgins' (fol. 376). The Shearmen and Tuckers offered a streamer with their arms. The third group of Tanners, Chandlers, and Butchers showed a cart of 'old virgins', the chariot drawn by men and boys; and 'St Clement their saint rode allsoe with his booke And his Frier rode allsoe who dealt his almes out of his masters Bagge'. The Cordwainers presented St Crispian; and the Taylors showed 'Herod and Herodias and the daughter of Herodias who daunced for St John Baptiste hedd. St John Baptiste beheaded.' The final company, the Weavers, offered a morris dance, a giant and a giantess, and 'St George with his knightes who slew the dragon and rescued the virgin'. No evidence exists of speeches, but presumably some people addressed the queen, who certainly experienced an array of religious subjects, held together by the guilds' lineage. The Venetian Ambassador, Foscarini, in Wells for the festivity recorded his impressions: 'I thus saw games, hunting and, finally, public representations, all carried out at the expense of the city.'[68] He adds: 'In passing from place to place, all the streets were full of people and blessings and good wishes were showered upon the queen, who thanked everyone and gave her hand to many to kiss' (37). Anne told Foscarini that she would remain in the area for a month.

After leaving Elizabeth in Heidelberg in mid-June, Lennox made his way to France where by early July he had audiences with the queen on the subject of a possible marriage partner for Prince Charles. The Venetian Ambassador, Zorzi Giustinian, reports: 'He has taken this route on his return, by order of his king, in order to assure Her Majesty of his master's cordial friendship. These words he expressed in his first audience.'[69] Many apparently thought that Lennox had come to France mainly to visit his mother and friends; therefore, the visit was kept rather unofficial. But Lennox, according to a letter from John Beaulieu in Paris to William Trumbull in Brussels in mid-June, did provide an account of his recent journey with Elizabeth: 'Their Report of their glorious Journey with the Princesse, and of her Reception and Entertainments made her in all the Places where she hath passed, but especially in the Prince her Husband's Country and Palace, is … Honourably and Magnificent in all respects.'[70] King James had urged Lennox to proceed carefully in France. The ambassador further comments in mid-July: 'Lennox has been obliged to speak very cautiously, simply sounding the disposition of the queen and others. Finding this good he sent immediately to England, and he expects to receive instructions to set the matter on foot' (14). The negotiations did not get very far at this point; after all, Charles was only thirteen years old. Finally, in mid-August, Lennox left France for England after another interview with the French Queen.

Only one small cloud interfered with Lennox's joy through the experience on the Continent: he had hoped to be made Duke of Richmond before his departure. Chamberlain writes: 'The Duke of Lennox is gon over with the Lady Elizabeth somwhat malcontent that he could not prevayle in a purpose he had to be made Duke of Richmond, and so an English peere of parlement.'[71] Finding this process difficult, Lennox, according to Chamberlain, 'hath geven yt over for the time' (449). Lennox would have to wait ten more years before receiving this much-desired English title; he then became the only Duke with a Scottish and an English title. James did bestow on him the title Earl of Richmond in October 1613.

When he returned to London in August 1613, Lennox had much occasion to think back over the past eight months, so rich with festivity and joy. At the beginning of the year in early January, Sir Thomas Lake had written to Dudley Carleton: 'The black is wearing out, and the marriage pomps preparing. The winter has been stormy and rainy.'[72] The glorious wedding, masques, festivities, tilts, and journeys had erased whatever lingered of melancholy. Not even the burning of the Globe Theatre on 29 June could dampen Lennox's spirits, now secure in the effects of Princess Elizabeth's wedding, which had indeed been a Valentine to the whole nation. Lennox could echo John Donne's image of a new 'phoenix' arising in the kingdom, or embrace the words of Antonio Foscarini, speaking of the festivities: 'it left nothing to be desired'. Political succession in the kingdom now seemed secure.

Notes

1 Anthony Nixon, *Great Brittaines Generall Joyes* (London, 1613), sig. C3.

2 *The Letters of John Chamberlain*, ed. Norman E. McClure, 2 vols (Philadelphia: American Philosophical Society, 1939), 1: 416.

3 *Letters of John Chamberlain*, 1: 399.

4 For an account of the wedding festivities, see Jerzy Limon, *The Masque of Stuart Culture* (Newark: University of Delaware Press, 1990), pp. 125–69.

5 John Taylor, *Heavens Blessing and Earths Joy* (London, 1613), sig. C4v.

6 *Letters of John Chamberlain*, 1: 421.

7 *The Magnificent Marriage of the Two Great Princes* (London, 1613), sig. A2v.

8 *Magnificent Marriage of Two Great Princes*, sig. A2v.

9 Taylor, *Heavens Blessing*, sig. B1v.

10 For an account of the appearance of 'Turks' in civic pageants, see my '"Are we turned Turks?": English Pageants and the Stuart Court', *Comparative Drama* 44 (2010): 255–75.

11 *Autobiography of Phineas Pett*, ed. W. G. Perrin (London: Navy Records Society, 1918), p. 102.

12 Taylor, *Heavens Blessing*, sig. A4.

13 *Letters of John Chamberlain*, 1: 423.

14 *Calendar of State Papers Venetian, 1610–1613* (London: HMSO, 1905), 12: 498.

15 Nixon, *Great Brittaines Generall Joyes*, sig. B3v.

16 I follow the account as found in John Nichols, *The Progresses, Processions, and Magnificent Festivities of King James the First* (London 1828), 2: 542. Nichols reproduces *The Magnificent Marriage of the Two Great Princes*, cited above, along with other interpolated contemporary material.

17 *Letters of John Chamberlain*, 1: 423. For a twentieth-century complaint about the wedding, see David Harris Willson, *King James VI and I* (New York: Oxford University Press, 1956). Willson writes: 'There followed a week of festivities which were elaborate, tedious, poorly managed and grossly extravagant. Why King James … permitted such lavish, vulgar and senseless waste is difficult to understand' (p. 286). Ask the Duke of Lennox or members of the royal family about this 'senseless waste' and one would get an incredulous response.

18 Continued quotations from John Nichols, *The Progresses of King James*, 2: 546.

19 Bishop Montagu served as Dean of the Chapel Royal for many years. He also brought together the materials to form *The Workes of King*

James, published in 1616, for which he wrote a most interesting prefatory essay.

20 Nixon, *Great Brittaines Generall Joyes*, sig. B2v.

21 Taylor, *Heavens Blessing*, sig. D2v.

22 William Basse, *Great Brittaines Sunne-set* (London, 1613), stanza 22.

23 Thomas Heywood, *A Marriage Triumph* (London, 1613), sig. B2v.

24 George Wither, *Epithalamia: Or Nuptiall Poems* (London, 1613), sig. B1v.

25 Quotations from this poem come as found in *The Complete Poetry of John Donne*, ed. John T. Shawcross (New York: Doubleday, 1967).

26 *Letters of John Chamberlain*, 1: 424.

27 Quotations from Campion's masque come from *A Book of Masques in Honour of Allardyce Nicoll*, eds. T. J. B. Spencer and Stanley Wells (Cambridge: Cambridge University Press, 1967). *The Lords' Masque* is edited by I. A. Shapiro, pp. 95–123.

28 Martin Butler, *The Stuart Court Masque and Political Culture* (Cambridge: Cambridge University Press, 2008), p. 9. Butler's excellent study focuses on the political implications of the masques.

29 Cited in the edition by Shapiro, noted above, p. 101.

30 These can be found in *Inigo Jones: The Theatre of the Stuart Court*, eds Roy Strong and Stephen Orgel (Berkeley: University of California Press, 1973), 1: 240–52.

31 For a critical discussion of this masque see Stuart Curran, 'James I and Fictional Authority at the Palatine Wedding Celebrations', *Renaissance Studies* 20 (2006): 51–67, David Norbrook analyses a proposed masque, '*The Masque of Truth*: Court Entertainment and International Protestant Politics in the Early Stuart Period', *Seventeenth-Century* 1 (1986): 81–110. Norbrook believes that Prince Henry was involved in planning this masque that was not performed. His analysis derives from the French text by D. Jocquet, published in 1613. See also Martin Butler's discussion in *The Stuart Court Masque*, pp. 197–9.

32 Translation provided in Curran, 'James I and Fictional Authority'.

33 *Letters of John Chamberlain*, 1:428.

34 Nichols, *Progresses of King James*, 2:549.

35 For Chapman's masque, I follow the text found in *Court Masques: Jacobean and Caroline Entertainments 1605–1640*, ed. David Lindley (Oxford: Oxford University Press, 1995). For an analysis, see Martin Butler, *The Stuart Court Masque*, pp. 200–3. He does not pay attention to the procession to Whitehall. I discuss the processional parts of these masques in 'Court Masques about Stuart London', *Studies in Philology* 113.4 (2016): 822–49.

36 For some of Jones's drawings see Orgel and Strong, *Inigo Jones*, 1:

253–63. This edition provides a list of expenditures for the masque, which totalled £1,182.

37 *Calendar of State Papers Venetian*, 12: 532.

38 *Letters of John Chamberlain*, 1: 426.

39 The text of Beaumont's masque I take from *A Book of Masques*, cited in note 27. This quotation comes from p. 132 in this edition prepared by Philip Edwards. See Martin Butler's brief discussion, pp. 199–200. Butler does observe: 'Of the performed masques, only this one envisaged the alliance as having military consequences' (200).

40 *Autobiography of Phineas Pett*, p. 103.

41 *Letters of John Chamberlain*, 1: 426.

42 *Calendar of State Papers Venetian*, 12: 533.

43 *Calendar of State Papers Venetian*, 10: 514.

44 Marston, *The Dutch Courtesan*, ed. M. L. Wine (Lincoln: University of Nebraska Press, 1965). All quotations will come from this edition.

45 Chapman, *The Widow's Tears*, ed. Ethel M. Smeak (Lincoln: University of Nebraska Press, 1966). All quotations will be from this edition.

46 John Hacket, *Scrinia Reserata* (London, 1692), p. 24. Hacket also reports the theological disputations that took place.

47 *Letters of John Chamberlain*, 1: 440.

48 Henry Wotton's letter to Sir Edmund Bacon, found in *The Life and Letters of Sir Henry Wotton*, ed. Logan Pearsall Smith (Oxford: Clarendon Press, 1966), 2:17.

49 *Ben Jonson*, ed. Ian Donaldson (New York: Oxford University Press, 1985), p. 448.

50 Reported in *The Life and Letters of Sir Henry Wotton*, 2: 17.

51 S. Schoenbaum, along with other biographers, insists that Shakespeare used this property only as an investment; see his *William Shakespeare: A Compact Documentary Life* (New York: Oxford University Press, 1977): 'It was, apparently, an investment pure and simple' (p. 273). Katherine Duncan-Jones more recently has argued to the contrary: *Ungentle Shakespeare: Scenes from His Life* (London: Arden, 2001), p. 246. I agree with her position that Shakespeare probably spent some time in the gatehouse. I have a fantasy of Lennox and Shakespeare having a discussion about their respective gatehouses.

52 *Calendar of State Papers Venetian*, 12: 525.

53 *Calendar of State Papers Venetian*, 12: 523.

54 *The Letters of Elizabeth Queen of Bohemia*, ed. L. M. Baker (London: Bodley Head, 1953), pp. 32–3.

55 *Calendar of State Papers Venetian*, 12: 523.

56 According to Phineas Pett in his *Autobiography*, p. 104.

57 *The Magnificent, Princely, and most Royal Entertainments given to the High and Mightie Prince, and Princesse* (London, 1613), sig. B1v–B2.

All quotations will come from this text. Another version of this account received publication in Edinburgh in 1613. Additional material about the wedding, the activities associated with it, the trip to Germany, and reactions in Scotland and Denmark can be found in *The Palatine Wedding of 1613: Protestant Alliance and Court Festival*, eds Sara Smart and Mara R. Wade (Wiesbaden: Harrassowitz, 2013).

58 British Library, Stowe MS 174, f. 91. I have modernised Goring's comments somewhat.

59 G. P. V. Akrigg, *Jacobean Pageant, or, The Court of King James I* (New York: Atheneum, 1974; originally published, 1962), p. 274.

60 *The Works of Thomas Campion*, ed. Walter R. Davis (Garden City, NY: Doubleday, 1967), p. 236. All quotations for this entertainment will come from this edition.

61 Cited by John Nichols, *The Progresses of King James the First* (London, 1828), 2: 646.

62 Robert Naile, *A Relation of the Royall Magnificent, and Sumptuous Entertainment, given to the High, and Mighty Princesse, Queene Anne* (London, 1613), sig. B2. All quotations come from Naile's longish, rhyming couplet poem that captures the event.

63 See Bergeron, '"Are we turned Turks?"'.

64 Richard Knolles, *The Generall Historie of the Turkes* (London, 1603). Other editions appeared in 1610, 1621, 1631, and 1638.

65 Nichols, *Progresses of James*, 2: 647.

66 Nichols, *Progresses of James*, 2:647.

67 Wells, Town Clerk's Office, *Wells Acts of the Corporation 1553–1623*, fol. 376. All quotations will come from this manuscript source.

68 *Calendar of State Papers Venetian, 1613–1615*, 13: 36.

69 *Calendar of State Papers Venetian*, 13: 4–5.

70 In Ralph Winwood, *Memorials of Affairs of State in the Reigns of Q. Elizabeth and K. James I* (London, 1715), 3: 465.

71 *Letters of John Chamberlain*, 1:444.

72 *Calendar of State Papers Domestic* (London, 1858), 9: 166.

6

Two great stars

No court is an island unto itself, nor is a city, even if walled. Rather, each interpenetrates the other. For example, London's public theatre companies, principally the King's Men, performed regularly at the Jacobean court, indeed, an impressive number of times in early 1613. In that case, 'Shakespeare' remained at court this year. The king's governing Privy Council engaged in ongoing contact with London's mayor and aldermen, each making requests of and responding to the other. After all, London had for centuries been known as the *camera regia*, the king's chamber. As such, London sponsored and financed the exceptional royal entry pageant for James, performed in city streets on 15 March 1604. Along those streets, among the thousands of spectators, stood the King's Men in livery provided by the Jacobean court. Boundaries between court and city thus blur at such moments.

The mid-seventeenth century provided a dubious spate of books that lambasted the early Stuarts, among them Arthur Wilson's *The History of Great Britain*. In a rare dispassionate moment Wilson rightly observes: 'The City of *London*, and the Court at *White-hall*, like two great Stars in Conjunction, had one and the same influence and operation.'[1] These two great stars each had its own sphere of cultural, political, and economic influence; but they reflected the light of the other. A simple example: the King's Men performed Shakespeare's *1 Henry IV* during the extraordinary outpouring of drama at court in early 1613. Later that year, Matthew Law and the printer William White produced a quarto text of *1 Henry IV*, to be sold at Law's shop in Paul's Churchyard. The wedding of Princess Elizabeth may have prompted a new edition of Edmund Spenser's *The Faerie Queene*, which honours her namesake Queen Elizabeth. William Welwood dedicated his *An Abridgement of all Sea-Lawes* first to King James and then a second dedication to the Duke of Lennox, the quintessential courtier.[2] Such dedications are not especially unusual. But in 1613, London's mayor Thomas Middleton, Grocer, also became the object of a epistle dedicatory by Richard Johnson in his *Looke on me London*. Here Johnson writes approvingly of Middleton: 'in the first yeare of the Kings Majesties Reigne … you made your Visitations in the Suburbs … to enquire after evil livers, and by Justice strove to root out iniquity'.[3] Middleton's actions receive the approbation of this Puritan writer. Writers and printers thus look to both great stars.

In 1613, Stephen Harrison's *Arches of Triumph* appeared in a new edition, having been first published in 1604. The new edition, however, contains only the engravings, not the original text, as if, nearly ten years after the event, the public needed only a visual reminder. Harrison's book may stand as a kind of marker of the interrelationship of the court and public spheres in Jacobean England. The book's magnificent engravings capture the appearance of the seven triumphal arches that stood in London's streets on the occasion of the plague-delayed pageant for King James, almost a year after his accession to the English throne. Through the city streets the king, Queen Anne, Prince Henry, Arbella Stuart, the Duke of Lennox, and other court figures moved, pausing at each arch for dramatic entertainment, written by Ben Jonson and Thomas Dekker, with one speech prepared by Thomas Middleton. Harrison's reissued text, perhaps also spurred by the celebrations for Elizabeth's wedding, calls attention to the pivotal year 1613 and the end of James's first decade as King of England, or, as he would doubtless have preferred, King of Great Britain.

The discussion here focuses on print and performance, which underscore London's vibrancy and help round out the cultural picture of 1613. Many of the publications by London's printers had connections to the court, and so did numerous performances. The king had his printer, Robert Barker, but the City had dozens. This abundance confirms the idea that books 'are not … merely commodities: as carriers of ideas, of languages, of cultural memory, they pulse with the very life force of a society—its beliefs, values, and anxieties'.[4] The scores of books published in 1613 reinforce print's power, a power that the court also clearly understood. Publications and performances in London's theatres burnish the brightness of the City's star. Anyone could wander among the many book stalls and shops near St Paul's and find an astounding array of published texts in 1613. As writers wrote and printers churned out texts, old social and economic boundaries began to blur, books functioning as agents of change. Along with the theatres, books expanded the cultural landscape, offering a complementary sphere of power that brought the City in conjunction with the court.

One area of a kind of performance clearly reflects a court interest: namely, sermons. King James loved hearing the great preachers of his day, such as Lancelot Andrewes; he often heard at least two sermons on Sunday. Of published sermons in 1613 there seemed no end; and they ranged from those of George Abbot, one of the Bible translators and created Archbishop of Canterbury to succeed Richard Bancroft, who had guided the translation, to the lowliest cleric. Publishing sermons became a means of expanding audience and enhancing a reputation. They included sermons lamenting Prince Henry's death, celebrating Elizabeth's wedding, and discoursing on various subjects, ethical and religious.

Many had first been delivered at St Paul's Cross, that special place in the north-east corner of the churchyard. 'The open-air pulpit in the precincts of St Paul's Cathedral known as "Paul's Cross" can be reckoned among the most influential of all public venues in early-modern England. In a world where sermons generally counted among the conventional means of adult education … Paul's Cross stands out as London's pulpit of pulpits; indeed it lays claim to being the "public pulpit" of the entire realm, and was arguably more of a stage than a preaching station.'[5] Large crowds gathered, sometimes thousands of persons, to listen to the sermon and participate in this public spectacle that offered, like drama, 'recreation' – and possibly 'solace'.

Just a few weeks after Elizabeth and Frederick's wedding, the Cambridge-educated Thomas Adams on 7 March mounted the pulpit at Paul's Cross to exhort the crowd to righteous living by avoiding hypocrisy, which he described as a kind of thievery. Adams had assumed the post of vicar at Willington, Bedfordshire, in 1612, by grace of its patron Thomas Egerton, Baron Ellesmere. He became renowned among his contemporaries as an excellent preacher. The chance to preach at Paul's Cross could not be ignored, an opportunity that John Donne did not bypass in 1616. Having reached countless listeners, Adams then decided to publish his sermon, which appeared in two editions in 1613, entitled *The White Devil,*

Or the Hypocrite Uncased. Possibly Adams responded to the title of John Webster's play, first performed and published in 1612; perhaps Adams had seen or read the play.

Whether the sermon as published resembles the one preached in March cannot be known, but the text itself runs to sixty pages, which would create a lengthy experience in the churchyard. Adams makes a point of addressing readers in a prefatory statement in which he attempts to answer whatever critics he has, acknowledging that some 'have the Title sticking in their stomacks; as if Christ himselfe had not called Judas a Devill; and likened an Hypocrite to a Whited Sepulcher' – a white Devil, in other words.[6] He further defines this in the sermon proper, saying of Judas: 'A Devill hee was, blacke within and full of rancour, but white without' (1), precisely the meaning that Webster had in mind. This sermon, full of erudition, including Latin and Greek quotations, and extensive marginal notes, clearly designed for print, has an elaborate organisation with multiple points and subpoints. It focuses on the vices that Adams finds objectionable and sinful, noting that no society exists free of Judas figures. Among the many writers cited, he manages to quote from Ovid in his commentary on Achilles. In this venue Adams makes the case against the 'white devil' much as Webster had done in a different form and place. Adams's sermon illustrates something of the pull of magnetic preachers exercising their skill in the public sphere several miles from Whitehall. The printed text adds another dimension to the circulation of cultural influence and power, enabling the churchyard sermon to resonate among readers.

A measure of the ability of print to extend an idea can be found in King James's important address to Parliament on 21 March 1610, wherein he ruminated on the nature of kingship and government. At the close of the speech the king broached the subject of reforestation and urged the passage of a new statute for preservation of woods. James argued: 'The maintenance of woods is a thing so necessary for this Kingdom, as it cannot stand, nor be a Kingdom without it.'[7] Every part of the kingdom depends on a reliable and abundant supply of wood; therefore, deforestation represents a definite social and economic threat. Not incidentally, it might also interfere with royal recreation. The king observed the connection between an adequate supply of wood and shipping, without which trade deteriorates; and trade, James insists, 'is a maine pillar of this Kingdome'. Without flourishing and abundant forests wildlife becomes threatened. Thus, James challenged Parliament: 'Ye have reason therefore to provide a good Law upon this subject' (324). In order to further the ecological cause, James also issued a Proclamation, 'Articles to be performed by vertue of our Commission of Sale annexed, touching Forrests, Parkes, and Chases'. James's worry and prescient environmental concern had nevertheless by 1613 received little support from Parliament.

But the king did find a stalwart champion of reforestation in Arthur Standish, who beginning in 1611 regularly published treatises on the subject, such as his *The Commons Complaints*, the 1612 edition of which carried James's support. Standish followed this in 1613 with *New Directions of Experience to the Commons Complaint*. The busy title page basically outlines Standish's purpose in the volume as he intends to sketch a programme for reforestation. This edition also contains a formal announcement from the King, who acknowledges the author's good intentions: 'We have therefore beene pleased to give allowance to this Booke, and to the Printing thereof.'[8] James advises Gentlemen to receive this book willingly 'and others of ability, who have grounds fitting for his projects, it shall much content Us'. The king's endorsement has encouraged Standish to persevere 'in so needefull and more then [than] necessary businesse' (sig. A3).

Standish has himself canvassed the country personally in an effort to determine the current status of the forests; he even knows how many acres England contains and how much firewood the country needs. Careful protection of the forests 'so farre from the losse or hurt to land … may rather greatly better and improve it' (A3v). Standish acknowledges the king's interest and involvement in this ecological problem, and he refers specifically to the 1610 address to Parliament. This guide book thus offers practical means for improving the status of the forests, and Standish sounds the alarm about doing nothing. In a word, in order to sustain wealth and civilisation such as England enjoys, the country must act to preserve the diminishing woods. This printed book in effect allows the king to speak on this crucial subject and keep alive his Parliamentary request.

Maintaining forests could at moments, however, be at odds with the necessity for sufficient arable land – the other side of environmental concern. Into this issue stepped the prolific Gervase Markham, known to the Duke of Lennox for the dedication of the book *Cavelarice* to him. Poet, prose writer, translator, and dramatist,

Markham embraced many subjects, which included horsemanship, veterinary medicine, domestic economy, military training, and letter writing. Thus, in 1613 he published *The English Husbandman*, his guide to farming. Markham saw the subject of husbandry as underserved by English writers, and he took his inspiration from the likes of Virgil. He claims on the title page that this is 'A worke never written before by any Author'. Markham explores the quality of soils, the kinds of ploughs that should be used for each soil, the art of planting, grafting, and gardening. *English Husbandman* serves as a guide book, complete with copious illustrations, especially of farming implements. Like Standish, he has explored the countryside extensively and thus writes from experience. Markham also lays out the argument for the economic necessity of the farmer, this 'Master of the earth', as Markham calls him.[9] According to Markham, husbandry helps hold together the country and the monarchy itself.

Had the urban-dwelling Londoner's interest not included husbandry, this person could have found among the city's book stalls another work by Markham, also published in 1613: *Hobsons Horse-load of Letters: Or A President for Epistles*. This, too, functions as a guide, a how-to book. Markham claims on the title page: 'A worke different from all former publications'.[10] This disingenuous statement ignores the enormously popular book by Angel Day, *The English Secretary*, first published in 1586 with several subsequent editions, which contained many examples of letters that a reader might then copy, modify, or at least be guided by. Markham ranges from business letters, to those issuing a challenge, to love letters. One could find a model for a 'merry mad Letter to a merry mad wench, chaste, and ingenious'; or letters of friendship; or, pertinent to Jacobean London, 'An Epistle for procuring the Order of Knighthood'. The systematic mind that could discourse on multiple kinds of ploughs could just as readily, apparently, devise a range of model letters.

A Londoner might also encounter many actual letters, especially those that emanated from voyages of discovery and colonisation, in particular the New World settlement in Virginia at Jamestown, established in 1607. Since the Elizabethan period, the country had begun to embrace voyages of exploration, like the journeys of Sir Francis Drake and Sir Walter Ralegh. In the early years of James's reign, aristocrats and merchants came together to form the joint-stock Virginia Company of London, under the auspices of the king, who granted the first royal charter in 1606 and subsequent ones in 1609 and 1612. James established a Commission to oversee the function and activities of the Virginia Company. Many obvious members of the aristocracy, such as the earls of Pembroke, Montgomery, and Southampton, subscribed to the company; and so did more ordinary citizens and merchants, and even many of London's guilds. Although Lennox did not join the company, he as a member of the Privy Council, as the Charter of 1612 makes clear, engaged in jurisdiction over the company. Indeed, with the king's blessing the Privy Council granted power and authority to the newly established Commission. In 1613, James issued an order, granting the Virginia Commission the right to establish a lottery for the purpose of raising revenue. Print in 1613 served to bolster efforts to support the Virginia Company.

The voyage of 1609, comprising five hundred colonists led by Sir Thomas Gates and Sir George Summers, provoked many letters and publications in England, mainly because this effort, sent to reinforce the Jamestown colony, ran into horrendous storms that drove the boats to Bermuda. Only in May 1610, one year later, did the ships reach their ultimate destination. Then began the outpouring of reports; the whole experience seemed miraculous because the group, trapped on Bermuda, had been presumed to be dead. Sylvester Jourdain's *Discovery of the Bermudas* (1610), and the Council of Virginia's *True Declaration of the state of the Colonie in Virginia* (1610), generated great excitement and probably influenced Shakespeare in writing *The Tempest*, performed recently at court in early 1613. William Strachey's letter, known as the *True Report of the Wrack*, dated 15 July 1610, enjoyed wide circulation, although not published until 1625.

Jourdain's text of 1610, now entitled *A Plaine Description of the Barmudas*, received new publication in 1613, although this time anonymously and greatly expanded. A certain 'W. C'. (probably William Crashawe) wrote the lengthy epistle dedicatory to Sir Thomas Smith, Treasurer of the Virginia Company. The dedication briefly summarises the journey, its problems, and its adventures. The author insists that Bermuda 'is one of the sweetest Paradises that be upon the earth'.[11] This report desires to give hope and heart to the Virginia Company and the colonies, by encouraging a positive view. The addition to Jourdain's original text has the title 'An Addition sent home by the last Ships from our Colonie in the Bermudas'.

Although written in the first person, the text does not reveal the author's identity. It reports on another journey, which began in April 1612; by July, the travellers had reached Bermuda. The writer documents the bounty of the island and seeks to debunk the earlier reports of the place as 'enchanted and kept with evill and wicked spirits' (E3v). This book serves as a kind of sales pitch, designed to encourage support for the Virginia Company and to make travelling and settling in the New World a desirable idea.

Alexander Whitaker's *Good Newes from Virginia* (1613) fulfils a similar purpose. Whitaker had gone to Virginia in 1611 to offer religious guidance and support. Thus, the 'good news' that he reports takes the form of an elongated sermon, the 'gospel' of providential operation in the Virginia colonies. Whitaker had the honour of leading Pocahontas to conversion and baptism in 1614. The text actually begins with a long dedication, written by William Crashawe, a friend of Whitaker's, a fellow preacher and a member of the Virginia Company. Crashawe explains Whitaker's purpose of going to Virginia: 'to assist that Christian plantation in the function of a Preacher of the Gospell'.[12] Crashawe writes of the 'miraculous' deliverance from Bermuda for those who had been driven to the island's shores. Whitaker certainly sees God's providence at work, and he remains optimistic about the native people's religious understanding. He therefore urges his readers to be generous, 'to cast your almes on the waters of *Virginia*' (H2v); after all, the colony belongs to God. Whitaker's purpose echoes Jourdain's, and print expands the appeal.

Some explorations, with royal support, of course, went elsewhere, especially South America, where Ralegh had earlier explored Guyana. In February 1609, Robert Harcourt, with the encouragement of Prince Henry, received the king's commission to journey to Guyana. He left England in April of that year, reaching Wiapoco on 17 May 1609. Harcourt took with him his brother Michael, two Guyana natives, one of whom had lived in England for fourteen years, and about sixty other adventurers. He records this experience in *A Relation of a Voyage to Guiana*, published in September 1613. His narrative resembles many of the other travel accounts; but he begins the text by dedicating it to Prince Charles: 'Having had tryall (most worthy Prince) of your most renowned Brother Prince Henrie, his many favours towardes mee, and princely furtherance of my humble sute unto his Majestie your royall Father'.[13] Harcourt seeks continued support from Charles: 'I therfore (in all humble reverence) present the prosecution of this high Action unto your gracious Patronage' (A2v–A3). The return of Michael Harcourt from Guyana in 1612 with marvellous stories about goldmines and precious stones prompted Robert to ask Prince Henry to urge his case with James in order to be given an exclusive monopoly for control of Guyana, and the king agreed. This new stir about Guyana doubtless caused Robert to publish his account.

Harcourt writes with extensive detail about his adventures in Guyana, which for him lasted only from May until August. He found the natives to be friendly, many remembering Ralegh's earlier experience with them, but they did complain about Ralegh's failure to return. Harcourt explained to them about Queen Elizabeth's death and King James's arrival as new king of England. The natives readily agreed to provide housing and food, although they worried that they might not have enough. Harcourt reassured them and further promised that with the king's authority he and settlers would protect them from their enemies. He writes favourably of their assistance in exploring the region and describes what they found. To his consternation Harcourt learned that the drink casks aboard his ship were deteriorating, apparently being of poor quality; therefore, he needed to leave soon in order to make it safely back to England. He set sail in August, leaving behind his brother, and arrived in England on 17 December 1609. Harcourt closes his account with the familiar justification of such adventures; that is, countries should undertake them only 'for the glory of God ... for the honour of their Soveraigne ... [and] for the benefit and profit of their Countrey' (sig. K2). The natives might have been tempted to respond to this idealised concept by suggesting that these 'were but words'.

Can one write about Guyana and other parts of the world without actually travelling to them? Samuel Purchas, an ordained priest and appointed chaplain to Archbishop George Abbot in 1613, would answer with a resounding 'yes'. The proof can be found in his copious *Purchas His Pilgrimage*, published in 1613 but dedicated by Purchas to the archbishop on 5 November 1612, the day before Prince Henry's death. In the Ninth Book, Chapter 3, he offers a brief history of Guyana; in the edition of 1614, he directly refers to Robert Harcourt's exploration of Guyana. Purchas on the title page calls his book a 'theologicall and geographicall historie',[14] which seems a reasonably good description. He creates, he writes to Abbot, a 'Perambulation over the World', making it his personal pilgrimage (sig. ¶2v) by linking the ancient and modern worlds. This is 'my first Voyage of Discoverie', Purchas claims, bringing together the work of hundreds of treatises, documents, and histories. Clearly in 1613, England, at least the publishing world, seemed ready for such a synthesis that builds on current fascination with exploration and travel and goes beyond on-the-ground accounts. Purchas begins to move in the direction of imaginative fiction.

Purchas admits in the 'To the Reader' section that his interest in religion governs the approach to this geographical history. He writes that he does not 'intend an exact Geographie, in mentioning every Citie with the degrees of longitude and latitude'; rather, he focuses on every country and its characteristics. Purchas acknowledges limitations. He constructs three sections, Asia, Africa, and America, with multiple books and chapters in each, which survey the cultures of nations. He starts with no less than Creation and the Flood, moving in Chapter 9 to a 'Geographicall Narration of the whole Earth in generall, and more particularly of Asia' (sig. A1).[15] He writes of the Hebrew nation, of Arabs, Saracens, and Turks – the latter a perennially favourite topic. The two books on America cover 'New France, Virginia, Florida, New Spain, with other Regions of America' (A4), including Guyana. Daunting in scope, fearless in detail, and generous in analysis, Purchas's *Pilgrimage* stands at a pivotal moment in England's understanding of the known world, reinforcing the achievement of 1613.[16]

While enchantment with travel remained vibrant, one could also travel through imaginative poetry, some already discussed in the form of elegies written for Prince Henry. Topics for poetry coincidentally track the plays presented at the Jacobean court in 1613. A major new volume of poetry appeared this year, namely., William Browne's *Britannia's Pastorals*. As noted earlier, Browne had contributed an elegy to accompany the one by Christopher Brooke in *Two Elegies* (1613), devoted to Prince Henry to whom Browne had originally intended to dedicate his pastoral. Instead, he dedicates the book to Edward, Lord Zouch, a member of the Privy Council. Browne, a follower of Edmund Spenser, could, of course, have found in the book stalls this year a new edition of *The Faerie Queene*. In his poetry Browne seems also to be indebted to Michael Drayton's *Poly-Olbion*, published the previous year and reprinted in 1613. Drayton in fact contributes a commendatory poem to Browne's long poem.

Written in rhyming couplets, *Britannia's Pastorals* contains five 'Songs', each mixing pastoral romance, tragicomedy, allegory, and myth. No coherent narrative thread holds together the discrete parts. Browne announces his task: 'My *Muse* for loftie pitches shall not rome, / But onely pipen of her native home.'[17] No far-flung travels here; rather, Browne's poem rests firmly on his native Devonshire soil. It has a requisite number of shepherds and shepherdesses, love intrigue, betrayal, unrequited love, danger, attempted rape, attempted suicide, and intervention of gods. The poem begins with Marina and her unrequited love of Celandine, who soon drops out of the narrative. Distressed, Marina abandons the idea of love and tries to commit suicide, but fails, being rescued by a god. In Song 2, a 'cruel swain' wounds Doridon and abducts Marina, who must travel with him. At the end of Song 3, a series of 'swains' offer twelve different 'gifts' to and about love, including increasingly elaborate poetic diagrams, which demonstrate the interlocking nature of love. Song 4 contains the most elaborate allegory, beginning with Riot, who resembles Furor from Book 2 of Spenser's *Faerie Queene*. In this allegorical moment, Truth emerges in the person of Aletheia, whom Browne describes fully. This Song ends in the Vale of Woe. The final Song includes the elegy for Prince Henry, the poem's most explicitly topical moment. Idya (England) mourns the prince's death and cries out: 'Is Henry dead, and doe the Muses sleepe?' (90). The poem ends with Remorse placing Riot in fetters and bringing all to the House of Repentance, which resembles the House of Holiness in Spenser's Book 1. This House transforms Riot into the courtly lover Amintas. One could call the poem Browne's or England's 'Pilgrimage', cloaked in an intricate romance narrative and containing an idealised setting that leads to reconciliation, resembling in some ways *The Winter's Tale*.

By radical contrast, Thomas Sampson's *Fortunes Fashion* explores the practical world of fifteenth-century English politics in its roughly 160 stanzas of six lines each, containing four lines of alternating rhyme followed by a rhyming couplet. Perhaps the publication of an edition of *Richard III* in 1612 or *1 Henry IV* in 1613 prompted Sampson to turn to the subject of history. Through the persona of Lady Elizabeth Gray, eventually Queen Elizabeth, wife of Edward IV, Sampson presents a first-person narrative of her experience, which tracks closely Shakespeare's version in *Richard III*, except the focus remains on Elizabeth, whose voice begins simply enough: 'I was king Edwards wife, a wofull Queene, / As in this history may plaine be seene'.[18] She captures the vulnerability she felt as a widow and how she came to accept Edward's love. Elizabeth traces the courtship with Edward, the trouble about his apparently being betrothed to Lady Bona of France, and the conflict with Warwick about this issue.

The remainder of the poem traces a pattern of transitory and fleeting pleasure to be followed by events of great pain, including the capture of Edward, his escape, and his eventual death, which left Elizabeth and her children extremely susceptible to the ambitious villainy of Richard, Duke of Gloucester (soon to become King Richard III). Everything that follows bears out her worry as she documents the rise of Richard and his evil deeds, especially the killing of her two sons. Even in sanctuary, Elizabeth could not escape Richard's machinations. The poem continues to Elizabeth's death, which interestingly she documents: 'My corps being dead, to Windsor was convaid' (F3). Then the poet intervenes: 'Then did this Queene returne unto her rest, / And vanisht, leaving to my memorie / Here to relate what she to me rehearst' (F3). For the first time in the poem we hear this other voice, who now claims to report what the queen had told him; and this speaker makes clear his attempt to restore Elizabeth's status. Poetry's power recuperates Elizabeth's lost reputation, forcefully and poignantly presented through her voice, which struggles to comprehend the tragedy that surrounds her.[19]

Pastoral romance, historical tragedy, and now satire, captured in the poetry of John Taylor and George Wither. The year 1613 had been a busy one for Taylor, henceforth to be known as the 'Water Poet': he had published an elegy for Prince Henry and then his account of Elizabeth's wedding, and King James had named him one of the King's Watermen. Unlike the serious poetry that he had already written or that of Browne and Sampson, Taylor also turned to a playful, ironic, and satiric tone and context when he published *Odcombs Complaint: Coritats Funeral Epicedium* and subsequently *The Eighth Wonder of the World*. Both poems poke fun at Thomas Coryate, the renowned traveller who had published *Coryat's Crudities* in 1611 about his extensive travels throughout Europe. Taylor decided to create the mischievous myth that Coryate had died. He turns on its head the serious and meaningful elegy that he had written about Henry.

In the address to gentlemen readers, Taylor begins: 'No sooner newes of Coriats death was com, / But with the same, my Muse was strooke dom: / For whilst he lived, he was my Muses subject.'[20] Thus, out of a gander's quill, Taylor has fashioned a pen with which he has written 'this following worke of woe' (A1v). And so the 'tragick story' unfolds. The low matter of Coryate's supposed death by drowning receives a high style. The poet's description of him (A3) further deflates Coryate's image. In the watery tomb, Coryate encounters various sea gods and goddesses, except that the fish and sharks 'feed on Coriat' (B1v). Taylor concludes: 'affection makes me cry, / Sorrow provokes me sleep, griefe dries mine eye' (B2). The poet wittily offers Coryate's epitaph in the 'Barmooda tongue' and in the 'Utopian tongue' (B2v, B3). Should readers be unable to translate the Bermuda tongue, they can track down the author, who 'dwelleth at the olde Swanne neere London Bridge, who will teach them (that are wiling) to learne' (B4v).

Taylor continues in this vein in *The Eighth Wonder*, which accounts for Coryate's miraculous escape from drowning. Coryate had been bound for Constantinople and eventually arrived there where he encountered a warm welcome. Indeed, the king dubbed him a knight and performed the ceremony with the very sword of Priam, albeit a bit rusty. Coryate thus has an explicit link to an ancient and glorious history. Taylor closes with a farewell to Coryate: 'Now Coriat, I with thee have ever done, / My Muse unto her journies end hath wonne' (C3v).[21] Shoppers in London's book stalls must have been highly amused with this spat between the acknowledged traveller and the waterman, who had become a poet. Satire has a potential to undo any serious enterprise, including travel.

George Wither could rival Taylor's industry in 1613. He had arrived in London in 1606, a young man determined to be a poet. In 1613, he wrote an elegy in response to Henry's death, and he wrote *Epithalamia*, which celebrates Elizabeth's wedding in February. The latter encompasses almost the entirety of the festivities, as if Wither had participated in them. He interspersed these poetical exercises with his *Abuses Stript, and Whipt, or Satirical Essaies*, a volume which enjoyed five editions in 1613 alone, attesting to its popularity and possible notoriety, sufficient to lead to his imprisonment for several months, during which time he nevertheless continued to write. The two books of *Abuses Stript* consist of satirical essays – rhyming couplet poems – that explore many vices or shortcomings to which people succumb. Wither focuses on behaviour, as opposed to cause, unlike other more psychological approaches. By exposing these problems, he intends to bring about change in behaviour; thus, the satirical essays offer correction and instruction

If Wither's morality appears traditional, his approach to the text is not. For example, he includes the increasingly common paratextual epistle dedicatory and address to readers. But Wither decides to dedicate *Abuses Stript* to himself. Wither outlines seven reasons why he has chosen to proceed in this manner. In the midst of his youthful fervour, he makes salient points, such as admitting that he probably could not have found a patron; he has therefore committed this book to his own protection. Wither turns to address the reader and begins by warning: 'Do not looke for *Spencers*, or *Daniels* wel composed numbers, or the deep conceits of now flourishing *Johnson*, no'.[22] Instead, readers will find a plain, simple style that contains no 'feigned Allegories', or 'darke riddles', or 'Parables' (B1v), such as exist in Spenser's well-composed numbers.

After thirteen pages of prefatory material, Wither finally turns to the task of examining vices and shortcomings. The sixteen satires in Book 1 and the four in Book 2 range across the usual problems, such as inordinate love, lust, hate, envy, revenge, choler, jealousy, covetousness, ambitions, inconstancy, and presumption. All of these in varying measures Wither claims to have experienced. He begins with problems associated with love because that passion 'is most *Naturall*' (D1). The poet observes that the male wooer may even tell his beloved 'tales of Castles in the ayre' (D3v), perhaps recalling Sir Petronel Flash in *Eastward Ho!* and his approach to Gertrude, who journeys eastward to a non-existent castle. The lover may indeed have picked up approaches from plays 'he heard at *Curtaine* or at *Bull*' (D3v). In Satire 5, 'Of Revenge', Wither again makes reference to drama. Jealousy, the focus of Satire 7, may grow out of misdirected or an over-abundance of love, as it may also derive from choler, the subject of Satire 6. Jealousy Wither defines in the opening lines as proceeding 'out of a too-much *love* with *feare*' (F4v), a concept that Shakespeare's Othello understands.[23] Wither expands a definition of jealousy's operation: 'But adde a *feare* of loosing of our joy, / And that we love so dearely, 'twill destroy /

All our delights' (F4v). The poet offers a trajectory that traces the path of jealousy from a solid, trusting relationship to a change that produces fear, doubt, suspicion, and finally a complete, annihilating disruption of love, now abused, stripped, and whipped. As a satirist, Wither perceives the morally destructive nature of the vices that he examines and compellingly warns of their peril. Thus, Wither approaches satire in a direction that differs considerably from Taylor. Readers would thus have been impressed with the scope of poetry available in this public sphere, ranging from elegies, epithalamiums, and historical narrative (Sampson) to romance (Browne) and satire (Taylor and Wither) and everything in-between.

The theatre, offering topics that parallel the year's poetry, served as the principal public performance venue. The year 1613 flourished as an exceptional year in terms of performances, publication, and composition of drama. Obviously, many dramatic performances took place at court in 1613; but thousands of citizen spectators also saw drama produced in theatre buildings, open-air structures and indoor ones – a public marketplace differing from but related to the book shops. The playwrights of these public plays had themselves some kind of connection to the court, if only to have had plays performed there. Most of the plays performed at court in 1613 had already had public performance, many by the King's Men. The public theatres offered opportunities for new plays, such as Shakespeare and Fletcher's *Henry VIII* and *Two Noble Kinsmen*, discussed earlier, which likely responded to court events, primarily Elizabeth's wedding.

King James, of course, had put all of the London adult acting companies under royal patronage shortly after arriving in London, assuring a link between the court and the city.[24] This system of theatre patronage extended, not surprisingly, to the Duke of Lennox, who moved in and out of the public sphere. Certainly his duties as nominal head of the Privy Council compelled him to dwell in the stir of political discussion, such as involvement with decisions by and for the Virginia Company and its exploration and settlement in the New World. Lennox served as patron of the Duke of Lennox's Men, an acting company, which mainly performed as a touring group. He expanded his connection to the theatre by intervening in behalf of George Chapman whose play *The Conspiracy of Charles, Duke of Byron* (1608) had provoked the ire of the French Ambassador, necessitating Chapman's apparently living in Lennox's house for a while; at the least, Lennox provided protection for Chapman, much as Lennox's brother Esmé Stuart offered Jonson a place of residence and patronage. In response, Chapman penned an elegant dedicatory sonnet in praise of Lennox in his translation of Homer's *The Iliad*. The poem begins:

> Amongst th' Heroes of the Worlds prime years,
> Stand here, great Duke, and see them shine about you:
> Informe your princely minde and spirit by theirs;
> And then, like them, live ever; looke without you,
> For subjects fit to use your place, and grace.[25]

Chapman reflects his indebtedness as a recipient of the duke's largesse, whose deeds do not derive from or reside in self-love. Chapman closes: 'To this soule, then, your gracious countenance give; / That gave, to such as you, such meanes to live.' As patron and supporter of various writers, Lennox learned much about publication and the texts that emerged in 1613.

The interconnection of print and theatre can be captured in the image of the indefatigable John Taylor who delightfully attacked Coryate in verse but also managed to find time to write a commendatory poem to accompany Thomas Heywood's *An Apology for Actors* (1612), the only significant document that provides a critical understanding and analysis of the extraordinary place of drama in Jacobean London. Heywood, already an established dramatist from the Elizabethan period onward with a well-known remarkable play, *A Women Killed with Kindness*, pushes back against Puritan and other forces arrayed against the theatre. Thus, in *Apology*, he offers a rousing defence of the theatre, beginning with the argument that 'playing is an ornament to the citty, which strangers of nations repairing hither report of in their countries'.[26] Heywood firmly embraces a didactic function for drama: 'there is neither tragedy, history, comedy, morrall, or pastorall, from which an infinite use cannot be gathered' (228). Eventually, Heywood seems to have attempted these different genres, perhaps testing his theory. As noted earlier, Heywood had in 1613 published an elegy for Prince Henry and *A Marriage Triumphe*, an epithalamium for Elizabeth and Frederick's wedding.

Heywood's *The Silver Age* and *The Brazen Age* and the other 'Ages plays' can be seen as dramatisations of *Troia Britannia*, his masterful poem of 1609. In the course of five plays, Heywood works his way from *The Golden Age* (1611) to the two parts of *The Iron Age* (not published until 1632 but written during the time of the earlier plays, possibly even in 1613). *The Silver Age* had been performed at court on 12 January 1612 by the King's Men and Queen's Men. All the Ages plays had public performance, about which Heywood boasts in the address 'To the Reader' in *1 The Iron Age*: 'Lastly, I desire thee to take notice, that these were the Playes often (and not with the least applause,) Publickely Acted by two Companies, uppon one Stage at once, and have at sundry times thronged three severall Theaters.'[27] The acting companies were probably the Queen's Men and King's Men; and the theatres were likely the Red Bull, the Curtain, and perhaps the Globe or Blackfriars. Crowds thronging to the public theatres to see these plays surely came in large measure for the sheer spectacle or the delight of seeing gods and goddesses mixing and mingling with mortals, reminiscent of some masques. Spectators could not have flocked to the theatre to experience narrative coherence; about that Heywood seems at best indifferent. Indeed, Heywood gives new meaning to 'episodic'.

In *The Silver Age*, published in 1613, Heywood creates Homer as a would-be choric figure, who attempts to provide a link among the disconnected parts. Act 1 focuses on King Pretus, who begins by imprisoning his brother Acrisus. After his queen Aurea seductively tempts Bellerophon, Pretus banishes him. Other than the opening dumb show of Act 2 in which Perseus mistakenly kills Acrisus, Heywood abandons this story, and instead turns to the gods, beginning with Jupiter, who descends in a cloud and engages in conversation with Ganymede. Much confusion ensues as Jupiter pretends to be Amphitrio and thus gains access to Alcmena, while Ganymede pretends to be Socia. Heywood seems to be recalling a comedy by Plautus. Juno and Iris '*descend from the heavens*' (121 SD), leading Juno to confront Jupiter, who, after much thunder and lightning, appears '*in his glory under a Raine-bow*' (122 SD).

The final Act 3 begins with the birth of Hercules, who immediately kills the snakes that Juno has sent and then goes to kill a lion. This Act explores Hercules's adventures and those of Ceres, who soon enters the play with her daughter Proserpine. The final moments refocus on Hercules, who defeats Cerberus and enchains him. Another spectacle follows: 'Hercules *sinkes himselfe: Flashes of fire; the Divels appeare at every corner of the stage with severall fire-workes*' (159 SD). Hercules attempts to rescue Prosperine but fails; a final council of the gods allows Pluto to keep her, thereby denying Ceres' claim and desire. Heywood seems especially interested in creating a rich spectacle, recalling the kind of spectacle that the court had encountered in technically demanding masques. Surely spectators at *The Silver Age* struggled to make sense of this play that whips from subject to subject without much care for transitions.

Although the title page of *The Brazen Age* indicates a five-act structure, the actual text makes no such divisions. Like the previous play, this one also ranges across a wide and diverse array of topics from the mythic past and includes many exotic stagecraft moments, all attempting to underscore a diminution of the world from silver to brazen. With a quasi-focus on Hercules, the play starts with the miraculous birth of Meleager, recalled by the mother Queen Althea. Heywood then wrenches the story to Venus and Adonis. Because of neglect, Diana has sent a treacherous boar, who becomes the object of the hunt, joined by Adonis and many others. Theseus and Nestor bring in the wounded Adonis, whom Venus poignantly laments. Althea kills herself with Meleager's sword after she has killed him with a fiery brand. Witnessing this disaster, Jason decides to depart and to begin his quest for the Golden Fleece.

The scene shifts to Troy with the entrance of Hercules, Jason, and the Argonauts. Heywood devotes attention to Jason and Medea, whose father Oestes plans to kill Jason. Heywood offers this startling stage direction: '*Two fiery Buls are discovered, the Fleece hanging over them, and the Dragon sleeping beneath them: Medea with strange firey-workes, hangs above in the Aire in the strange habite of a Conjureresse*' (217). Jason successfully obtains the Golden Fleece, and Medea aids his escape by scattering the limbs of her brother to thwart her father. The play's final section returns to Hercules, who is now enamoured of Omphale, the Lydia Queen. A poisoned shirt kills Hercules, but not before he tears down trees and kills Omphale. Hercules even amazingly manages to place himself on a pyre, and Jupiter strikes him with a thunderbolt, burning him. Spectators surely marvelled at the play's riveting episodic stories and wondrous spectacle. They had made their way through London's scruffy, dirty streets, arriving at the theatre for an afternoon of escape into the mythic world of gods and goddesses and amazing theatrical feats. What they 'learned' about personal behaviour, the utility of drama, can only be imagined.

George Chapman moves clearly into the realm of tragedy with his *Revenge of Bussy D'Ambois*, performed at the Whitefriars Theatre, according to the 1613 title page. This play forms a conscious sequel to his earlier *Bussy D'Ambois*, dating from the early Jacobean years. Chapman's *Widow's Tears* had been performed at court earlier in 1613, and his *Masque of the Inner Temple* had, of course, formed part of the wedding festivities. Chapman had additional court connections through his association with the Duke of Lennox, as noted earlier. Chapman's play, unlike the setting and narrative of Heywood's plays, focuses on France's political world and the conflict over the rights of the king. It includes the supernatural, particularly the ghost of Bussy, but otherwise stays firmly tied to practical action and the battle between warring court factions. Chapman wrestles with how one can function successfully in a thoroughly corrupt world. From this conundrum emerges the idea of revenge, as Chapman taps into a well-established English tradition, derived mainly from Seneca. Clermont D'Ambois becomes the major protagonist, accepting the role of avenging his brother's death.

Renel, a Marquesse in the French court, laments a former orderly glory: 'things most lawfull / Were once most royall; Kings sought common good' (1.1.19–20).[28] This assessment creates a kind of marker for judging the spirit and morality of the play world. The voices of Renel, Clermont, and Tamyra sound the play's recurrent themes: moral decay, reality masked by misleading theatrical action, and revenge. Clermont joins Baligny, who has brought Clermont's challenge to Montsurry, in a discussion about the court, concluding: 'They are the breathing sepulchres of noblesse' (2.1.154). This moral decay makes the situation ripe for revenge and restitution; and thus Clermont determines to kill Montsurry, while King Henry wants to get rid of Clermont, who speaks about the orderly structure of God's universe and the necessity of observing order (3.4.45f). Divine providence that should assure a righteous king stands in stark contrast to the play's action and the workings of fortune.

Act 5 begins with the ominous appearance of the Ghost of Bussy D'Ambois. In short order, the king, who has worried about Guise, has him murdered (5.4) and justifies the action. Clermont makes his move against Montsurry in 5.5 and succeeds in killing him, thus satisfying the Ghost's desire. But the appearance of the Ghost so disturbs Clermont that he cannot justify continuing to live. Clermont closes with a metaphor of being on a ship and sailing toward death's shore as he kills himself. Encountering this sad scene, Charlotte D'Ambois urges all to retreat from the world, this morally suspect world that has affected all adversely.

At least, Clermont exhibits moral purpose and heroic character. Those qualities John Marston ignores in *The Insatiate Countess*, published in 1613, but doubtless written earlier and performed, like Chapman's play, at the Whitefriars by one of the children's companies. Marston's *The Dutch Courtesan* had been performed twice at court in 1613. If courtiers who had seen that play chanced upon *The Insatiate Countess*, they would recognise some similarities, except that Marston and his collaborators move the play in a decidedly tragic direction. To claim that Isabella, the protagonist in Marston's play, lacks moral conviction risks understatement; she moves through the play focused on apparently insatiable desire and lust, in what amounts to a domestic tragedy. The play also has a fully developed subplot that seems to turn the main plot on its head. Both plots challenge an understanding of love and marriage.

The Insatiate Countess begins with a sober stage direction: '*The Countess ... discovered sitting at a table covered with black, on which stands two black tapers lighted, she in mourning.*'[29] Isabella's husband has recently died, and she receives solace from Roberto, Count of Cyprus, who offers several moral bromides for dealing with grief. The Countess interrupts him with the startling observation: 'I mourn thus fervent, 'cause he died no sooner: / He buried me alive' (1.1.46–7). Thus, by line 75 she kisses Roberto and begins her seduction. He responds affirmatively and enthusiastically. Spectators seem to encounter 'the widow's tears'. As Isabella extinguishes the tapers, she claims: 'this taper, due unto the dead, / I here extinguish, so my late dead lord / I put out ever from my memory' (98–100) – end of grieving. Henceforth, the Countess becomes a serial lover, liberated from any sense of commitment.

Act 2 opens with a wedding masque during which Isabella falls in love with Guido, whom she views in the most heroic and idealised terms (2.1.210–24). Thus, she says that when she goes to the nuptial bed with Roberto, 'I'll think't my love, and die in that delight' (258). Isabella sends a love letter to Guido even as she admits that her husband 'is a noble gentleman, / Young, wise, and rich' (2.3.54–5). When Guido enters, she confesses her love, which

'Hath power to draw me through a wilderness' (76). Guido eagerly accepts Isabella's advances, creating a moral wilderness, a hallmark of this play.

Having secured Guido's love, Isabella nevertheless lets her wandering eye fall on his dear friend Gniaca, whom she describes as a 'rare shaped man' (3.2.31). Thus, she begins all over again, abandoning one love in pursuit of another – an insatiate countess indeed. Perplexed and troubled by the betrayal of his friend, Gniaca nevertheless cannot resist: 'You have prevailed, I'm yours from all the world' (108). Guido's closing soliloquy renders a trenchant analysis of Isabella, 'poor in soul and fame, / I leave thee rich in nothing but shame' (187–8). Not satisfied with Gniaca's love, Isabella wants revenge and asks Gniaca to kill Guido, who, she claims, has defamed her. From her servant Anna, Isabella learns that Gniaca has not honoured her request; undaunted, she seizes on the next man to appear, Don Sago, who immediately acknowledges her beauty and takes on the task of revenge, only to be imprisoned.

The final act begins with Sago being escorted into the court of Don Medina, who will render judgement, and Guido's body being brought in. Medina decides to pardon Sago but not Isabella, who enters with her hair down, wearing a crown of flowers and carrying a nosegay. She remains unrepentant and defiant. Unexpectedly, her husband Roberto, now a friar who has escaped the world's corruption, enters and wrings from her an acknowledgement of what she has done. Indeed, she asks his pardon in one of her few heartfelt speeches. Roberto responds: 'Let thy death / Ransom thy soul' (193–4). Isabella mounts the scaffold and quickly meets her execution. Perhaps she hears in her mind Guido's words: 'I leave thee rich in nothing but shame' (3.4.188). Shame and amorality remain much in evidence. Attempts to love and stay faithful in marriage take a serious beating in Marston's play. In the opening scene, Isabella extinguishes the tapers of mourning; she then proceeds to snuff out all chances of a moral life. Marston travels a long way from his more playful *Dutch Courtesan*.

In one of the finest Jacobean tragedies, John Webster presents quite a contrast to *Insatiate Countess* in *The Duchess of Malfi*, which, although not published until 1623, likely had a performance in 1613 by the King's Men at Blackfriars. It seems probable that Webster was writing the play in late 1612 and interrupted his writing in order to prepare the elegy for Prince Henry, *A Monumental*

Column. The play has a number of connections to Webster's *The White Devil*, published and written in 1612. Although *Duchess* certainly has its sordid moments, the tragic focus on the Duchess shines a bright light on moral, defiant, and heroic behaviour. She does not have to ransom her soul by death; rather, death magnifies the beauty of her life. When the Duchess says, 'I am going into a wilderness' (1.1.360), she may seem to echo Isabella in Marston's play.[30] But the Duchess enters only a risky social wilderness; she does not lose her moral compass. Both women are widows at the beginning of their respective plays, and both soon acquire husbands. There the similarity ends. The Duchess understands commitment in love and marriage; Isabella obviously does not. Therefore, the Duchess can exhibit heroic stature in death; Isabella has no reservoir of strength or character. Webster's Duchess faces the evil forces of her brothers, Ferdinand and the Cardinal, and Bosola; whereas Isabella faces primarily herself as antagonist.

The play's opening scene sketches the personalities of the principal characters. Ferdinand finds himself imprisoned in irrational fantasies and psychosexual desire for his sister. The Cardinal fares no better, being totally corrupt; and Antonio says of him: 'The spring in his face is nothing but the engend'ring of toads' (159–60). By contrast, the Duchess, according to Antonio, spends her days 'practiced in such noble virtue' (201). Bosola enters the employ of Ferdinand and the Cardinal, who want him to spy on their sister because they would not have her remarry. The 'reasons' remain hidden, but they surely range from incestuous desire to wanting to obtain her property. The remainder of the scene presents the encounter between the Duchess and Antonio in which she gives him a wedding ring. Puzzled, Antonio cannot imagine that she intends the ring for him. But the Duchess says succinctly: 'We now are man and wife' (493). They embrace the risk of this relationship, and they remain unwaveringly committed to each other through all the tribulations that follow in the wilderness that they experience.

The crucial 3.2 moves along a trajectory from playfulness to threatening confrontation to self-conscious performance to revelation, all with the Duchess at the centre. The first fifty-five lines begin innocently enough with playful banter and kisses exchanged between Antonio and the Duchess in the bedchamber in the presence of her servant Cariola. Antonio and Cariola withdraw while the Duchess continues to comb her hair. Unknown to her, Ferdinand enters the room and immediately gives her a poniard, saying: 'Die then quickly! / Virtue, where art thou hid?' (3.2.72–3). His menacing remarks continue; and he refuses to answer the Duchess's question: 'Why might not I marry?' (111). Ferdinand provides no answer, but says, 'I will never see thee more' (144); and he departs. The Duchess recovers quickly and tells the arriving Antonio that he must prepare for their departure. When Bosola enters, she tells him that Antonio has betrayed her trust with the household accounts; and she outlines the accusations when other household officers arrive. This self-conscious performance creates a palpable fiction as the Duchess announces, 'I would have this man be an example to you all' (192). This theatrical moment has successfully convinced the group, except not Bosola, who moves into a long speech that praises Antonio, an assessment that delights the Duchess, who suddenly reveals: 'The good one that you speak of is my husband' (274). She admits that she has had three children by Antonio. Bosola takes all of this in stride, urging the Duchess to 'feign a pilgrimage / To our Lady of Loreto' (307–8); and she gratefully says: 'Sir, your direction / Shall lead me by the hand' (311–12). Being led by Bosola only assures the arrival into a wilderness of deceit and danger.

By the end of Act 3, Ferdinand's forces banish and imprison the Duchess, and separate her from Antonio. She understands the challenges she will face and steels herself for this adventure: 'There's no deep valley but near some great hill' (145). Certainly a deep valley opens for her in Act 4, beginning with her encounter in the darkness with Ferdinand, who claims that he has come to make peace with her, but gives her a *'dead man's hand'* (4.1.43 SD), which has a wedding ring on it. No sooner has she discovered the horror of this 'gift' but she encounters *'the artificial figures of Antonio and his children, appearing as they were dead'* (55 SD). Bosola insists that they are dead; and she responds: 'I account this world a tedious theater, / For I do play a part in't 'gainst my will' (84–5).

A parade of madmen accost her in 4.2; and then Bosola arrives, looking like an old man, who informs the Duchess: 'I am come to make thy tomb' (4.2.114). But through these torments and the arrival of the Executioners, the Duchess resolutely insists: 'I am Duchess of Malfi still' (138). They may kill her, but they cannot defeat her. They strangle her, Cariola, and the children. Offended, Bosola starts his moral ascent, and Ferdinand descends into complete madness. Along the way the Cardinal manages to poison his mistress Julia, all confirming the early assessment of them as living in a moral cesspool. But in the natural darkness, Bosola mistakenly kills Antonio (5.4), leading Bosola to a desperate conclusion: 'We are merely the star's tennis balls, struck and bandied / Which way please them' (56–7). In the final scene, mayhem takes over as Bosola fatally wounds the Cardinal; Ferdinand attacks the Cardinal and fatally wounds Bosola, who then kills him. This play takes characters and spectators on a tragic voyage. But the purposely evil action finds its counterpart in the resolutely moral action of the Duchess, Antonio, and eventually Bosola.

The heroic, moral action of a female protagonist also dominates Elizabeth Cary's *The Tragedy of Mariam*, published 1613, although written a few years earlier. Lennox knew her husband, Henry Cary, whom she had married in 1602, and who became a courtier and member of the Bedchamber, along with Lennox. Eventually he became Viscount Falkland. Cary's play has the distinction of being the only play, not a translation, written by a woman in the Shakespearean era. Cary's neoclassical play, based on a Senecan model, became a 'closet play', never intended for performance. Cary, a distinguished scholar and speaker of multiple languages, did some translating and read widely and deeply, including the work of the ancient Josephus, on whom she based her play.

Mariam tells the story of this Jewish woman, who has married Herod, ruler of Jerusalem in the first century BCE. Herod had got rid of his first wife Doris, who nevertheless haunts the play, as does his sister Salome, who becomes a kind of 'vice' figure, one given over to malicious and evil designs. When the play opens, Herod has returned from his second journey to Rome, there to defend himself before Augustus Caesar. Salome convinces her brother that Mariam has been unfaithful to him and plots his overthrow and death. For Mariam's part, she has learned that Herod has left an order for her death, should he be killed. All of these understandings and misunderstandings cloud Herod and Mariam's relationship, despite its initial love. Mariam spends much of the play in contemplating her marriage, the place of women in this society, and her own destiny. She also opposes male tyranny, exemplified in Herod's actions. The play moves a long and tragic way from Mariam's opening soliloquy, the entirety of the play's first scene, in which she says: 'And more I owe him [Herod] for his love to me, / The deepest love that ever yet was seen.'[31] Clearly she has misjudged the malevolence of those arrayed against her. As Act 4 closes, she moves to her execution. The Nuntio in Act 5 provides Herod a vivid account of Mariam's death. Herod speaks unceasingly of his remorse for her death, and he curses himself as a 'vile monster' as the play ends. Like the Duchess of Malfi, Mariam has been resolute and moral but a powerless martyr against malicious forces.

The performance of Ben Jonson's *The Alchemist* at court in early 1613 opened the royal spectators to an amusing and critical perspective on the City of London. The year further offered several performances in public theatres and publications of plays that focus on London with a benign but satiric perspective, wrenching the theatre world away from dark tragedies or plays of exotic gods and goddesses. (George Wither and John Taylor illustrate well the function of satire in poetry.) Nothing displays the ambiance of the Guildhall better than these Jacobean comedies about London, ones often referred to as 'city comedies'. Many of them centre on members of the city's guilds. About these guilds the court would know much; after all, King James became a member of the Clothworkers guild in the summer of 1607, and Prince Henry and the Duke of Lennox became Merchant Taylors that same summer. In 1606, King Christian IV, King of Denmark, came to London to visit his sister, Queen Anne. Henry Roberts reports on part of the king's experience: he 'tooke his Coach with his companie, and passed on to the Exchange, viewing the beawtie of Cheapside, and the riches of the inhabitants, the Goldsmiths, Mercers, and other wealthy trades, all the way setting their commodities to sale'.[32] In order for the Danish king to appreciate the splendour of London, he needed to visit the Guildhall area as well as Whitehall.

Membership in one of twelve principal guilds (or 'livery companies') conferred citizenship, and from these guilds came the Aldermen and the Mayor of London. In the Mercers' company, for example, the guild of highest prestige among the twelve, members included the first Earl of Pembroke, Sir Thomas Gresham, Sir Lionel Cranfield, and the Earl of Bedford: Whitehall mingling with Guildhall. Connections between the guilds and the theatre world abound also. David Kathman lists over fifty theatre people who held membership in a guild, including Ben Jonson (Bricklayer), Anthony Munday (Drapers), John Heminge (Grocers), John Lowin (Goldsmiths), Richard Tarlton (Haberdashers), and John Webster (Merchant Taylors).[33] Like the noblemen, these actors and playwrights did not necessarily practise the trade of their guild, but they enjoyed the privileges accorded them. Thus, playwrights well understood the life of the guilds, and they exploited the foibles and ambitions of London's guildsmen and citizens.

Performed in summer 1613, *Eastward Ho!* had first been performed by the Children of Her Majesty's Revels at Blackfriars in 1605, the year of the play's publication. This play, written by Chapman, Marston, and Jonson, encountered difficulties from the authorities; and all three playwrights spent some time in prison. Allegedly the play had given offence to King James because of some slight to the Scots. Jonson seems to have been released rather quickly, perhaps the result of his seven letters written to noblemen, including Lennox's brother, Esmé Stuart, one of Jonson's patrons, to whom Jonson wrote: 'be pleased to take this protestation, that, next his Majesty's favour, I shall not covet that thing more in the world than to express the lasting gratitude I have conceived in soul towards your Lordship'.[34] Chapman in one of his letters mentions Stuart's help in gaining Jonson's release. Chapman himself in the letters that survive wrote to the king and two letters to the lord chamberlain; in all likelihood, he also wrote to his protector, the Duke of Lennox, who would assist him later in bringing about his release from prison in another scrape with authorities over a play. London's theatre world and Whitehall's court clearly intersect. In 1613, all three dramatists enjoyed recognition from the court through performances of their plays. Why another production of *Eastward Ho!* in 1613 remains a mystery; perhaps actors wanted to tap into the fully developed genre of 'city comedy' that had taken root, this play being one of the earliest.

Eastward Ho! focuses on the family of William Touchstone, a member of the Goldsmiths, an important guild. Touchstone has a wife, two daughters, and two apprentices. Their lives intersect with Sir Petronel Flash, 'a new-made knight'. (His status clearly refers to the many knights created under James by which men purchased knighthood.) Gertrude, Touchstone's socially ambitious daughter, wants to hitch her wagon to Sir Petronel's presumably rising star: she wants more than anything else to be a 'lady' with all the imagined advantages this status would give her. Ambition meets ambition. They marry in the play's early moments. Her father rightly believes that this arrangement will come to naught; and her sensible sister Mildred chides her for putting off her 'city tire' (1.2.11).

Meanwhile, Touchstone grants freedom to the apprentice Golding and intends for him to marry Mildred, thereby maintaining appropriate ties to the city and to the guild.

The other apprentice, Quicksilver, discharged from Touchstone's service, takes up with Security and others who have a different kind of agenda: to become 'knight adventurers'. They might even stow away on a ship bound for Virginia. Thus, in the midst of the workaday world of London, some characters begin to embrace romantic fantasies – the dramatists' means of spoofing pretentious social behaviour. A blow to such fantasy comes quickly in Sir Petronel's admission that all his castles are 'built with air' (2.3.9). As Gertrude sets out eastward, dressed in new finery and in an elegant coach with a footman named Hamlet (!), she will ride toward an illusion. For Gertrude, who makes her departure eastward in 3.2, this castle offers great hope and a validation of her desire to be a lady.

Sir Petronel has his own fantasy: to find gold in Virginia. Such a plan forms the basis of 3.3, which takes place at the Blue Anchor Tavern and includes much discussion of Virginia. In such an atmosphere, Petronel turns away the warning from the watermen that a journey tonight would be dangerous, insisting, 'We'll have our provided supper brought aboard Sir Francis Drake's ship' (144–5). Romance meets romance, wrapped in satire. As 4.1 makes clear, the men have shipwrecked in the Thames at the Isle of Dogs. But Petronel assumes that they have arrived in France, and he begins immediately speaking French.

In his opening speech in 4.2, Touchstone heaps scorn on these adventurers and the illusory castle, which his daughter has pursued. Meanwhile, Golding has achieved new status in the city: he will be named deputy to his alderman. Touchstone contemplates, in his own romantic fantasy, that Golding's name shall be 'written upon conduits, and thy deeds played i' thy lifetime by the best companies of actors' (4.2.72–4). He taunts the newly arrived Gertrude: 'Your Ladyship is welcome from your enchanted castle' (109). But Gertrude remains defiant: 'Though my knight be run away, and has sold my land, I am a lady still' (114–15), sounding like the Duchess of Malfi. Empowered, Golding sends Petronel and Quicksilver to prison; from there Touchstone hears Sir Petronel's desperate plea: 'Forgive me, father' (5.5.124). Touchstone offers forgiveness, as he does to his humbled daughter Gertrude. Touchstone sees these developments as a victory not only for sensibility but also for

London's values. He makes the play's moral judgement in a closing speech: 'The usurer punished, and from fall so steep, / The prodigal child reclaimed, and the lost sheep' (196–7). Touchstone's moral smugness forms the play's final irony as excessively romantic fantasies have run aground, like a boat in the Thames.

Francis Beaumont, who had written one of the masques for Elizabeth's wedding and with Fletcher several plays performed in 1613, takes a radically different approach to satiric comedy in *The Knight of the Burning Pestle*, dating from 1607–8 but first published in 1613. Not only does the playwright situate the play in London but also he further restricts the action to a theatre building where the audience and the characters watch a play attempt to unfold. Beaumont creates a sophisticated, self-reflexive drama that satirises London life but overlays this critique with numerous self-conscious conventions of romance. No other comedy of the period comes close to Beaumont's trenchant and artful analysis of drama itself within the confines of a play. Apparently, audiences, however, did not respond favourably to productions by the Children of the Revels at Blackfriars. This information comes from Walter Burre's epistle to Robert Keysar, a wealthy Goldsmith who financed the child actors. Burre, the publisher, writes in the 1613 quarto edition that the audience 'who for want of judgement, or not understanding the privy mark of irony about it … utterly rejected it'.[35] Burre has thus rescued the play from oblivion – the power of print. Without grasping the play's 'privy mark of irony' no audience would have a chance of understanding *Burning Pestle*.

Ostensibly, the actors have arrived to present *The London Merchant*; thus, a Prologue begins in the Induction but only speaks three lines before being interrupted by a Citizen in the audience. This Citizen, a Grocer, first objects to the play's title, then recalls the titles of several plays that have been performed in this theatre, all having some connection with London life. The Citizen states his desire simply: 'I will have a grocer, and he shall do admirable things' (33–4). The Grocer's wife and the Citizen climb on to the stage, soon joined by Rafe, their apprentice, also an amateur actor. In his first speech, he quotes Hotspur's speech on honour from Shakespeare's *1 Henry IV* (1.3.201ff). The Prologue, who has begun to lose control, asks what this new play should be called. The Citizen suggests *The Grocers' Honour*; but the Prologue has a better suggestion: *The Knight of the Burning Pestle*. So the play becomes without completely surrendering the original play. The only quasi-consistent narrative of the play centres on the Merchant Venturewell, his daughter Luce, Jasper the apprentice and Luce's lover, Master Humphrey a would-be suitor, and the Merrythought family. The linear development of this love plot keeps being interrupted by the episodic intersecting activities of the Citizen, his Wife, and Rafe, who becomes a 'knight' and 'grocer-errant'.

Act 1 opens with a discussion between Venturewell and Jasper about Luce, whom Jasper wants to marry, much against her father's wishes. Venturewell thinks Jasper unworthy and no match; besides, he has found a rich husband for her, namely, Humphrey. Incredulous, Jasper complains that Humphrey 'hath little left of nature in him' (1.1.34). Venturewell sends Jasper away; and thus begins the traditional love story of an intransigent father, who must be overcome if Jasper and Luce can satisfy their love. In all of Humphrey's speeches, he unfailingly speaks in rhyming couplets, perhaps documenting Jasper's comment that he has 'little left of nature in him': he's all art. And Rafe is all chivalric romance: he enters reading the prose romance *Palmerin of England*, from which he quotes. In order to have the accoutrements of a knight, Rafe designates his fellow apprentices Tim as his 'squire' and George as his 'dwarf'. Thus equipped, Rafe can venture forth for heroic adventure.

This he does in the next act, in which he becomes embroiled in the triangular struggle among Jasper, Humphrey, and Luce, presumably in Waltham Forest. Meanwhile, Jasper confronts Humphrey in the forest, accusing him of being 'an arrant noddy' (228); and he beats Humphrey. The Citizen's Wife does not approve; indeed, she addresses Humphrey: 'Come hither, Master Humphrey; has he hurt you?' (254). A 'Boy' from the original play enters and objects to the Citizen's idea that Rafe will fight with Humphrey. But the Citizen replies abruptly: 'Plot me no plots' (266). Jasper even snatches away Rafe's pestle and knocks him down, to which the Wife cries: 'Run, Rafe; run, Rafe; run for thy life' (311). The seeming imitation of life keeps being overcome by theatrical artifice.

Rafe, turning his thoughts to valiant adventure, decides to challenge the 'giant', about whom he has heard; and he invokes Susan, the cobbler's maid in Milk Street, for help. Inspired by Susan, Rafe sallies forth and defeats the giant, forcing him to recant his ill (460). In Act 4, the Citizen asks: 'What shall we have Rafe do now, boy?'

(4.1.27); and they concoct the idea that Rafe shall court the Lady Pomponia, a king's daughter with golden hair. But when she offers her 'favour' for him to wear in his shield, Rafe resists because she represents the Antichrist and false traditions. Besides, he must remain faithful to Susan of Milk Street. In the Interlude that closes Act 4, Rafe appears as a 'May lord' in order to address London and praise Grocers. What remains? Beaumont decides to conclude the love story of Jasper and Luce by first having Jasper appear as a 'ghost' to Venturewell. The ghost instructs the merchant to let the lovers marry and to beat Humphrey, which he promptly does. At the wife's insistence Rafe appears with a troop of soldiers and gives them a rousing speech. The Citizen complains: 'I do not like this. … Everybody's part is come to an end but Rafe's, and he's left out' (267–8). But the Wife has a final idea: let Rafe come out and die, which he does, over the objection of the Boy, who finds this inconsistent with a comedy. Rafe appears with a forked arrow through his head and reviews all that he has done. He closes poignantly: 'I die; fly, fly, my soul, to Grocers' Hall' (328). Rafe has done his episodic best. The Citizen offers a kind of apt summary for *Burning Pestle*: ''Tis a pretty fiction i'faith' (314) – pretty *fictions* might be a more accurate description of this at times convoluted play that keeps asking: how does one construct a play?

No longer concerned with a fictional Grocer, as in Beaumont's comedy, the year 1613 produces an actual Grocer, named Thomas Middleton, who became Mayor. The playwright Thomas Middleton had an exceptional year, which intersected the life and mayoralty of Thomas Middleton, Grocer. For the dramatist, one could call it 'the year of Middleton'. His first play, *The Phoenix*, had been performed at court in 1604. Subsequently, Middleton wrote several 'city comedies': *Michaelmas Term* with Quomodo the Draper; *A Trick to Catch the Old One*; *A Mad World, My Masters*; and *Your Five Gallants*. In 1613, Middleton wrote his best comedy, *A Chaste Maid in Cheapside*, the culmination of his city comedies, performed some time in mid-1613 at the Swan Theatre. He also wrote a superb Lord Mayor's Show, *The Triumphs of Truth*, and a brief pageant for the opening of the New River. The rich connection of playwright and Mayor changed the dramatist's professional life, leading him ever deeper on the complementary road of civic involvement and the production of seven Lord Mayor's Shows, and the appointment in 1620 as City Chronologer.[36] Middleton thus moved away from fictional representations of London towards actual engagement with city and guild authorities. He began to participate in the creation of London's history, to write *for* London, not just *about* London.

Thomas Middleton, Grocer, born in 1549 in Wales, had by 1575 become apprenticed to a Grocer. In 1582, he gained admission to the Grocers' company, which in 1592 elevated him to its livery ranks. He was a founding member of the East India Company and a supporter of the Virginia Company. In May 1603, London's authorities elected him to the post of Alderman; but, when he sought an 'exemption' to taking this position, the Lord Mayor and Aldermen imprisoned him in Newgate prison. The City's records reveal a letter, dated 11 June, from King James to the city officers, 'complaining of their conduct in committing Thomas Middleton to Newgate, for refusing to serve the office of Alderman ... and directing them to release him immediately'.[37] The authorities relented, and Thomas Middleton gained release. Shortly thereafter, King James knighted Middleton. Whitehall and Guildhall once again come into conjunction. And playwright meets Grocer.

The narrative and chronological arc of *A Chaste Maid* moves from Lent toward Easter. In 1613, as discussed earlier, Princess Elizabeth's wedding on 14 February took place three days before Ash Wednesday. Her departure from England to her new home and life on the European continent began in April shortly after Easter. Middleton in the play seems to have this frame in mind, as he does the Lenten strictures. Three questions encapsulate the play's essential issues. First, Yellowhammer, a Goldsmith, in his shop asks: 'What is 't you lack, gentlemen?' (1.1.99). In the same scene he also asks: 'What's your price, sir?' (116). And the Second Promoter asks the Country Wench: 'What time of year is 't, sister?' (2.2.142).[38] The city, in its material abundance and tolerant if not corrupt morality, provides the place to satisfy whatever one lacks. This runs counter to Lent, which, of course, requires one deliberately and wilfully to 'lack' something. In commercial London everything seems to be for sale, including Lent itself; the only question is the price.

The play's action takes place in Cheapside, that area of London east of St Paul's Cathedral. Like other city comedies, Middleton's has a clear merchant-class environment. But this play will not include journeys to an illusory castle or would-be journey to Virginia or a grocer-errant engaged in chivalric, romantic quests. Middleton's comedy assumes a satiric perspective, taking to task merchant ambition, learning, Puritans, family life, and pompous knights. Yellowhammer, a Goldsmith, has a wife Maudline, and a daughter Moll, who loves Touchwood Junior, and an inept son Tim, a Cambridge University student. As in *Burning Pestle*, the father here does not want his daughter to marry Touchwood; instead, he prefers that she marry Sir Walter Whorehound – the very name raises serious questions about the wisdom of this choice. Middleton complicates this situation with the Allwit family, already indebted to Whorehound in profound ways, and the barren Kixes, who desire children but produce none. Touchwood Senior, meanwhile, produces multiple children, sometimes two in one year – fecund beyond reason.

Chaste Maid explores *error*, both in the sense of 'mistake' and of 'wandering'. The play's opening three scenes establish the three principal families. The play begins in Yellowhammer's Goldsmith's shop with conversation between Maudline and Moll about marriage, soon joined by Yellowhammer who notes the arrival of Sir Walter Whorehound, who brings with him his 'landed niece brought out of Wales, / Which Tim our son, the Cambridge boy, must marry' (1.1.43–4). Sir Walter enters with 'niece' in tow, planning to turn her 'into gold'. He further instructs this niece that in London she 'must pass for a pure virgin' (112) – a would-be chaste maid in Cheapside. When Yellowhammer asks, 'What's your price sir?' (117), he seems to ask the play's essential question.

If the Yellowhammer household makes errors in judgament, the Allwit household makes errors knowingly. Mistress Allwit has become pregnant again, and Allwit (a willing cuckold, a 'wittol') rejoices in his good fortune in a curious and in ways chilling speech (1.2.10ff), which parodies Psalm 23. Allwit says: 'I thank him [Whorehound], he's maintained my house this ten years, / Not only keeps my wife, but a keeps me' (16–17). That is, Sir Walter has provided all the necessities of the household – good fire in winter and plentiful food – and has fathered all the children. These conditions the husband and wife fully understand and accept. Indeed, Allwit says: 'I am as clear / From jealousy of a wife as from the charge' (49–50). On the contrary, Sir Walter becomes jealous of Allwit, fearful that he has slept with his own wife. Middleton thus turns conventional family life upside down. But Sir Walter holds over them the threat of marrying and thus wrecking their cosy arrangement.

Middleton provides a different angle in the relationship of Touchwood Senior and his wife. They produce so many children that Touchwood Senior decides to separate so as to lessen the chance of more. The scene shifts to Sir Oliver and Lady Kix who have the opposite problem, as Lady Kix makes clear: 'To be seven years a wife and not a child, / O, not a child!' (2.1.136–7). Feeling desperate, Sir Oliver would 'give a thousand pound to purchase fruitfulness' (144), underscoring how everything seems to be for sale in the play.

In 2.2 Allwit prepares for the christening of his new child and announces that he will serve as one of the godparents ('gossips'), to which Sir Walter concurs: 'The better policy, it prevents suspicion' (2.2.35). Unintentionally, Sir Walter then in an aside articulates a moral centre for this rather amoral play: 'When man turns base, out goes his soul's pure flame, / The fat of ease o'er-throws the eyes of shame' (39–40). Just how inverted values have become gets reinforced in the remainder of the scene with the appearance of the two Promoters, ones designated to keep watch to be sure that no one violates Lent. In fact, of course, they have readily accepted bribes to look the other way, including Master Beggarland, who, as the First Promoter says, 'You know he purchased the whole Lent together' (134). The Puritans who come for the Allwit christening in 2.3, in which Allwit wears one of Sir Walter's suits, underscore their own selfish interests, reinforced in 3.2 in which they satiate their gluttonous desire for food and drink. Allwit consoles himself: 'Had this been all my cost now, I had been beggared' (3.2.61). News comes at the end of the scene that Sir Walter intends marriage. Allwit rightly understands that this marriage will destroy the life that he and his wife have created: 'all the work will break' (212).

A kind of 'work' occupies Touchwood Senior, who returns to the Kixes with his special potion, guaranteed to produce a child. Sir Oliver and Lady Kix fight over who bears responsibility for their barrenness. Lady Kix urges Touchwood: 'bring us into love again' (74). He has brought the 'drink' with him, 'a little vial of almond-milk', he admits in an aside (89). He instructs Sir Oliver to drink it and then ride for at least five hours. Instead of riding away, Lady Kix must take the potion lying down. 'A-bed sir?' she asks, and Touchwood responds affirmatively (151–2).

Act 4 focuses on love, first Tim's for Sir Walter's niece. Obtuse characterises Tim, documented several times in the play, here in two conversations: the first with his Cambridge Tutor and second with the Welsh gentlewoman, whom he greets in Latin, which she does not understand. She responds in Welsh, totally confusing Tim, who decides that she must be a scholar and that they will make a 'learned couple' (4.1.132). Tim rushes away to pursue marriage with this woman. The end of the scene includes Allwit, who has come disguised to Yellowhammer to prevent a possible marriage between Sir Walter and Moll. He, ironically, makes the case on moral grounds, observing that Sir Walter is 'an arrant whoremaster' who has fathered numerous children (226). Not surprisingly, this information does not deter Yellowhammer, who admits to having had a whore himself and a bastard. But some characters occasionally claim moral conviction. Sir Walter, for example, enters 5.1, slightly wounded from a recent scuffle with Touchwood Junior, which has produced moral conversion in Walter. Thus, he begins to rail against Allwit and his wife. But in a breath-taking turn, Allwit accuses Sir Walter: 'You have been somewhat bolder in my house / Than I could well like of … / I thought you had been familiar with my wife once' (144–7). The scales have fallen from Sir Walter's eyes, and he departs. Good riddance, the Allwits decide; they will move on to the Strand somewhere with all their rich household stuff and start over – no lasting moral and material consequences for them.

Birth and death occupy the play's final scenes. The Kixes announce in 5.3 that a 'child is coming' (14). On the other hand, Touchwood Junior, rather like Jasper in *Burning Pestle*, has sent a letter to the Yellowhammer household announcing his death; and Moll has also apparently died. The play closes with their 'funerals'. When Moll and Touchwood Junior spring from their coffins, all rejoice in amazement. The parents relent, as Yellowhammer insists, 'I stand happy' (5.4.61). Alas, Tim has married the Welsh gentlewoman. Even her nineteen mountains have turned out to be illusory. That marriage, that error in judgement, cannot be resolved favourably. Instead, all must simply celebrate, and so Yellowhammer invites everyone to dinner to be 'kept in Goldsmiths' Hall' (121), near the Guildhall.

Had they, Lennox, or anyone else entered Goldsmiths' Hall on Foster Lane in 1613, they would have seen the heraldic shield of the guild with its female figure, described as a 'demi-virgin' (a chaste maid in Cheapside), on top, holding a balance and a touchstone, the means by which to verify gold's quality. The motto across the bottom reads: *Justitia virtutum regina* (Justice is queen of virtues). The touchstone of moral justice in *Chaste Maid* remains more absent than present in this play in which one can purchase Lent, abandon morality, and invert family values. Only Yellowhammer's benign gesture at the end throws any light on the Goldsmiths' beautiful shield.

In the Goldsmiths' Hall in 1613, one might also have found a portrait or some acknowledgement of the contribution of Sir Hugh Myddleton, Goldsmith, who helped bring a new fresh water supply to London in a project that joined Whitehall with the Guildhall. The opening of the 'New River' Thomas Middleton celebrated in a brief pageant at the location of the river's entry into Islington, then north of London, on Michaelmas Day, 29 September 1613, the same day in which the guilds elected Sir Hugh's brother Thomas, Grocer, as Lord Mayor of London – Goldsmith and Grocer, echoing *Chaste Maid* and *Burning Pestle*. On this day, aldermen, other authorities of the city, and the labourers who built the canal gathered at the cistern in Islington for Middleton's entertainment, *The Manner of His Lordship's Entertainment*.[39] Long before 1613, many had recognised the pressing need for a new, reliable, clean water supply to complement the springs, cisterns, and the River Thames, which formed the basic sources of water. The need became increasingly urgent in the burgeoning and rapid growth of London. As early as the 1598 edition, John Stow in his *Survey of London* had acknowledged the absolutely essential need for water in such a city. The City of London might be secure within its wall, but without sufficient water it would perish. The Thames, for example, had become increasingly problematic because the water had to be pumped into the city, and pollution vitiated the water's quality.

The idea of bringing water into London from the northern outreaches dates back to the Elizabethan period. After many futile starts, Hugh Myddleton finally stepped forward to rescue the languishing and seemingly doomed project. He signed the first agreement with the City of London on 21 April 1609 and a new one on 28 March 1611. Work had begun in earnest in 1609, but it experienced a twenty-two-month work stoppage and other problems. Dozens of people became actively involved in the project, and a number made financial investments. But eventually it took the intervention of King James to save the plan from its financial problems. On 2 May 1612, representatives of the king and Myddleton drew up a formal indenture: Whitehall and Guildhall in co-operation. The basic agreement called for James to contribute half the expenditure, past as well as future. Many people, therefore, including the king, helped make the New River possible. This understanding renders suspect the title page's claim that the canal resulted as the 'sole invention, cost, and industry of that worthy Master Hugh Myddleton of London' (961). Thus, in late September, this 40-mile canal that brought water from Chadwell and the Amwell spring north of London began to flow into Islington – hence the celebration.

The city authorities engaged Middleton to write an appropriate, brief entertainment. This consisted mainly of lots of noise from 'warlike music of drums and trumpets' and a single speech. As all gathered in Islington, a troop of 'labourers, to the number of threescore or upwards, all in green caps' marched several times around the cistern, representing those who had worked on the project. These labourers complement Sir Hugh's efforts. Together they formed an economic and social community, epitomised now in the gathering, which comprised city leaders and ordinary workers.

Middleton writes of 'perfection', which means both successful completion of the project and the project's 'flawless, faultless' character. In a sense, this entertainment completes, 'perfects' the New River. An anonymous speaker, representing the whole group, spoke in rhyming couplets, praising the skill of the workers, and the 'cost, art, and strength' that sustained them. He refers to the difficulties that beset this undertaking, including 'Travail, and pains, besides the infinite ways / Of malice, envy, false suggestions' (961). Here the speaker clearly alludes to the obstacles that Sir Hugh had to overcome, which included opposition from landowners and some members of Parliament; and yet, by 'one man's industry, cost, and care' the project came to a successful conclusion. 'Perfection draws / Favour from princes, and from all applause' (962), the speaker observes. He also reaches for the 'clerk's book', which records each group of labourers. The speech closes: 'Now for the fruits then: flow forth precious spring, / So long and dearly sought for.' With these final words the 'flood-gate opens, the stream let in into the cistern, drums and trumpets giving it triumphant welcomes' (962). The playwright honours the city's understandable self-congratulation and elevates Sir Hugh Myddleton as a stalwart entrepreneur, undaunted by forces arrayed against him. In all likelihood, Middleton enjoyed the irony of his artistic position as both endorser and critic of the city's habits and attitudes. He no longer resides on the fictional periphery of civic life; he has now become intensely involved. The perfect invention is not Myddleton's alone but also Middleton's and the king's.[40] Two great stars join.

On 29 October 1613, the Grocers presented the Lord Mayor's Show in honour of the inauguration of Thomas Middleton; they hired the dramatist Middleton to write the pageant, which he called *The Triumphs of Truth*. It took place on the day after the Feast of St Simon and St Jude, as such pageants had since the mid-sixteenth century. The guild to which the new mayor belonged bore the responsibility for honouring him with an elaborate entertainment. Rivalry had developed among the guilds to present an exceptional pageant, outdoing previous ones. Since the establishment of the office of Lord Mayor in the twelfth century, the new mayor had to travel to Westminster to take the official oath of office: Guildhall and Whitehall intermingle in City business. The processional route typically began in the morning at the Guildhall, moved down the Thames to Westminster, returned, and made a formal entry through the City's streets with closing ceremonies at the Guildhall and religious services at St Paul's. In the Lord Mayor's Show of 1612, at which Prince Henry was expected and which Prince Frederick and Lennox in fact attended, Dekker constructed an elaborate, allegorical pageant. Middleton followed suit in 1613 with one even more extensive and colourful. Indeed, at a cost of roughly £1,300, Middleton's was the most expensive in the Jacobean period.[41]

Records of the Grocers' Court Books reveal unusually early deliberations on 5 February 1613 about preparations for a mayoral pageant, surveying the need for banners, streamers, and other ornaments 'set in readiness in convenient time in honour of the next worthy Magistrate that shall be chosen out of this Company'.[42] Also in February, the Master, Wardens, and others gave consideration to a 'Device or project in writing set down' by Anthony Munday. Various playwrights and others submitted proposals to the guild for consideration. If chosen, the dramatist would then negotiate the specific services that he would perform, echoing similar arrangements for the court masques. Entries in 1613 indicate that Munday received the gross sum of £149 for his 'device', providing apparel, securing players, and arranging transportation. Middleton got £40 'for the ordering overseeing and writing of the whole

Device'. Records show a payment of £4 to the printer Nicholas Okes for printing the text, probably the usual run of five hundred copies. The artificer John Grinkin received £310 for the construction of all the pageant devices – the ship, chariots, five islands, and all the carpentry work, painting, and fireworks (965).

Of 'public' events in 1613, nothing could surpass Middleton's Lord Mayor's Show in terms of audience numbers: thousands of citizens lined London's streets and along the Thames toward Westminster. For its physical demands, its spectacle, required technical skill, and imagination, Middleton's pageant surely rivals the masques that actors had performed at court for Elizabeth's wedding. Even the newly arrived Russian Ambassador, Aleksei Ziuzin, attended the mayoral pageant, as ambassadors regularly attended court masques or fought over the right to attend. Ziuzin's account pays particular attention to the river journey, a part of the pageant to which Middleton gives scant notice in his text. Ziuzin notes the mayoral barge and adds: 'And before the ship and behind and on the sides, over the whole river, sailed on many boats, the King's gentlemen, and knights, and aldermen, and merchants, traders, and the bodyguard of the King's court, and all sorts of people of the land in bright costume.'[43] According to the Ambassador, a 'great salute' greeted the mayor at the royal palace, accompanied by Lennox and the King's gentlemen and knights. In London's streets 'went people in masks with palms, and they carried palms with fireworks, and they threw from them sparkling fire on both sides because of the great press of people, that they might give way' (978). Throngs of people, brightly collared banners, drums and trumpets, and planned dramatic entertainment in the streets make for an extraordinary late October day. The pageant in Cheapside differs radically from *Chaste Maid*; indeed, it seems the obverse of the comedy, its allegorical seriousness contrasting markedly with the satiric perspective of the Cheapside comedy.[44]

Middleton begins the text with an epistle dedicatory, directed to the new mayor. He refers to the mayor's 'many great and incident dangers, especially in foreign countries in the time of your youth and travels' (30–1). Today's inauguration establishes Thomas Middleton, the mayor, 'in this year's honour, crowning the perfection of your days, and the gravity of your life, with power, respect, and reverence' (33–5). Then the playwright makes a connection to himself: 'in that myself, though unworthy, being of one name with

your lordship, notwithstanding all oppositions of malice, ignorance, and envy, should thus happily live, protected by part of ...
mercy' (35–8). Having overcome unspecified difficulties as a writer,
Middleton offers this pageant. No matter how magnificent, these
triumphs can only be but 'shadows to those eternal glories that
stand ready for deservers' (42–3). From the first moments in the text
Middleton embraces a religious perspective for the event, one that
might indeed 'perfect' the mayor's life.

Not only does Middleton praise and honour the mayor but also
he commends the Grocers. He begins: 'But to speak truth' (69),
the care that the guild exhibited 'hath been seldom equalled and
not easily imitated' (70–1). Indeed, such attention pervaded 'the
whole course of this business, both by the wardens and committees'
(72–3). Middleton praises the Grocers' 'maintenance to scholars,
soldiers, widows, orphans, and the like' (555–6). The guild did not
spare expense 'so the cost might purchase perfection, so fervent
hath been their desire to excel' (74–6). (The idea of 'purchasing'
perfection may ironically echo *Chaste Maid*.) The words 'truth,
perfection, and error' recur in the pageant, where indeed Middleton
establishes a dramatic battle between Truth and Error.

Early in the morning at the Guildhall, the mayor confronted
London, 'a grave feminine shape', who appeared from behind a
silk curtain, holding in her left hand a key of gold while wearing a
crimson robe. She greeted the mayor: 'I am thy mother' (131), who
has 'Set wholesome and religious laws' before him (142). These
virtues derive from and embody truth, but error also exists among
the 'sons' who have been disobedient. London offered the mayor the
key of gold; and she gave him a final moral charge: 'all pollution, /
Sin, and uncleanness must be locked out here' (188–9). This caring
mother points the way for the mayor's approach to office, and she
offers support.

After the return from Westminster, Truth's Angel and Zeal
greeted the mayor at Baynard's Castle; both allegorical figures were
on horseback and spectacularly costumed. But close behind the
mayor 'Stood Error's minister that still sought to blind thee' (225).
By the time the mayoral party arrived at Paul's Chain, a lane on
the south side of the cathedral, Error had come in a chariot, which
contained many of his 'infernal ministers'. Error, dressed in grey,
carried 'symbols of blind ignorance and darkness, mists hanging at
his eyes' (248–9). A gruesome Envy accompanied Error, 'eating of a

human heart … attired in red silk, suitable to the bloodiness of her manners' (250–2).

For sheer seductive power nothing surpasses Error's first speech (255–318). If Error cannot look attractive, he can certainly sound enticing. Error turns upside down the world articulated by London earlier in the pageant, at first by a kind of poetic imitation of London's speech. If spectators heard only the opening lines of Error's speech, they would hear a seemingly benign voice. This disingenuous quality gives way to Error's true intent as he adumbrates a programme for exercising power and gaining wealth, the seductive charms of high office. By line 270, 'And let thy will and appetite sway the sword', no doubt remains about Error's purpose. The final movement of this impressive speech concentrates on the 'evils' and limitations of Truth, such as her narrow, austere life. Error, by contrast, offers pleasure and delight. Middleton has drawn stark moral boundaries from which the mayor must make a choice in this psychomachian drama.

Indignant at Error's speech, Zeal drove the chariot away in order to make room for Truth, who wears a white satin garment and a robe of white silk 'filled with the eyes of eagles, showing her deep insight and height of wisdom' (327–8). She wears on her breast a pure round crystal, carries a sun in her right hand, and in her left a 'fan, filled all with stars' (336). With such brightness she can drive away Error's darkness and ignorance. Zeal interprets her remarkable emblematic costume, as Middleton taps into rich iconographical traditions, such as found in Henry Peacham's *Minerva Britanna*, published in 1612 and dedicated to Prince Henry. Truth addresses the mayor, claiming to be his guide, and she offers clear moral instruction. The representation of truth and error takes another twist in the appearance of a King of Moors, his queen, and attendants in Paul's Churchyard. The Grocers' guild had joined with the East India Company, of which the mayor was a member, to expand their trade – a probable reason for including a Moor. Like Othello, this Moor has become a Christian, thanks to the English merchants and traders. Beneath his dark exterior resides a transformed soul. Having once pursued error in false religion, the Moor has been brought to the Christian faith. Middleton clearly means this as a compliment to the Grocers, noted for their foreign trade and benign influence on other cultures.

Moving into Cheapside, the mayor found London's Triumphant Mount near the Little Conduit, but its beauty Error had obscured with a mist and a group of 'monsters'. Fortunately, Truth challenged this situation, commanding: 'Vanish, give way' (524). With this powerful order, 'the cloud suddenly rises and changes into a bright-spreading canopy, stuck thick with stars and beams of gold' (525–7). The spectators then saw London, surrounded by Religion, Liberality, and Perfect Love. Part of the mount displays the 'charitable and religious works' (553) of London, especially those of the Grocers. At the back of the mount reside Chastity, Fame, Simplicity, and Meekness, all with appropriate symbolic costume. But when the Triumphant Mount reached the Cross in Cheapside, Error again successfully cast a pall over it. So the battle raged.

Finally that evening near the mayor's house, the mount appeared completely beautified; and London spoke a final time to the mayor, reminding him of how she had greeted him early in the morning. Truth speaks last, providing additional moral instruction and underscoring how the mayor must carry out his office in full brightness: 'There is no hiding of thy actions now' (747). She praises the guild for 'Counting all cost too little for true art' (758). Truth urges the mayor to embrace all virtues: 'Faith in thy heart and plenty in thy hall, / Love in thy walks, but justice in thy state, / Zeal in thy chamber, bounty at thy gate' (763–5). Middleton closes the pageant with a technically spectacular event. Zeal, who burns 'in divine wrath' (775), seeks and receives permission from Truth to set fire to Error's chariot. 'At which a flame shoots from the head of Zeal, which, fastening upon that chariot of Error, sets it on fire, and all the beasts that are joined to it' (779–81). With such spectacle Middleton challenges the technical displays in Heywood's 'Ages' plays and the court masques. The glowing ashes of Error's chariot testify to the complete victory of Truth and to the imaginative zeal by which the playwright has approached his task in London's streets. In this Cheapside the dramatist, actors, artisans, and the guild have indeed been able to 'purchase perfection'. Thomas Middleton, the mayor, retains vibrant glowing embers of memory of this spectacle. Doubtless, he found it to be perfect. So apparently did his son, also named, of course, Thomas Middleton, who gave Middleton the playwright 10 shillings in November 1613, a likely gift of gratitude.[45]

The public sphere fills the space between Westminster and the City of London with incomparable works of art: poetry, theatre, pageants, and publications of infinite variety. Taken together, these performances and publications forge a powerful cultural force that enlivened and enriched life in Shakespeare's London, whether in Cheapside, the book shops near St Paul's, or across the river on the south bank where rowdy theatres created a new world, extending inevitably into Whitehall. At first glance, the court and city might seem in opposition, as indeed they sometimes were; but the performances and publications in London complement the various cultural activities at Whitehall, thereby creating an important bond between the two worlds. Neither Whitehall nor Guildhall can survive as a self-contained entity. Economic, political, and cultural pursuits in each keep bumping against the other, enhancing, perhaps 'perfecting' the other, to use Middleton's term. The wondrous image of the boats on the Thames on the evening of 16 February participating in a royal wedding, underscores this cultural link, as Beaumont created this flotilla to move from Southwark, not far from Guildhall, to the privy stairs at Whitehall shimmering images of light along the river destined for the palace but originating in the city precincts – a court masque for a royal wedding that nevertheless must arrive from the city. The publications and performances that follow in subsequent months reinforce the metaphor of two great stars in conjunction, light reflecting light.

Notes

1 Arthur Wilson, *The History of Great Britain* (London, 1653), p. 72.

2 William Weldwood, *An Abridgement of all Sea-Lawes* (London, 1613), sig. A2 and A3.

3 Richard Johnson, *Looke on me London* (London, 1613), sig. A3.

4 Marta Straznicky, 'Introduction', in *Shakespeare's Stationers: Studies in Cultural Bibliography*, ed. Marta Straznicky (Philadelphia: University of Pennsylvania Press, 2003), p. 6. See also Graham Rees and Maria Wakely, *Publishing, Politics, and Culture: The King's Printers in the Reign of James I and VI* (Oxford: Oxford University Press, 2009); Zachary Lesser, *Renaissance Drama and the Politics of Publication: Readings in the English Book Trade* (Cambridge: Cambridge University Press, 2004); Douglas A. Brooks, *From Playhouse to Printing House* (Cambridge: Cambridge University Press, 2000); Lukas Erne, *Shakespeare and the Book Trade* (Cambridge: Cambridge University Press 2013).

5 W. J. Torrance Kirby, 'The Public Sermon: Paul's Cross and the Culture

of Persuasion in England, 1534–1570', *Renaissance and Reformation* 31 (2008): 6; the article appears, pp. 3–29. For a more extensive study, see Arnold Hunt, *The Art of Hearing: English Preachers and Their Audiences, 1590–1640* (Cambridge: Cambridge University Press, 2010).

6 Thomas Adams, *The White Devil* (London, 1613), sig. A4. Quotations come from this edition.

7 *The Political Works of James I*, ed. Charles Howard McIlwain (Cambridge, MA: Harvard University Press, 1913), p. 323.

8 Arthur Standish, *New Directions of Experience* (London, 1613), sig. A2v. All quotations come from this edition. Another one, also published in 1613, does not contain the announcement from James, and it has a slightly different title.

9 Gervase Markham, *The English Husbandman* (London, 1613), sig. A3. Amusingly, in 1617, Markham signed an agreement with the Stationers' Company to publish no more books on diseases and cures of various animals.

10 Markham, *Hobsons Horse-load of Letters* (London, 1613).

11 *A Plaine Description of the Barmudas* (London, 1613), sig. A3. Quotations come from this text.

12 Alexander Whitaker, *Good Newes from Virginia. Sent to the Counsell and Company of Virginia* (London, 1613), sig. A3.

13 Robert Harcourt, *A Relation of a Voyage to Guiana* (London, 1613), sig. A2. Quotations come from this edition.

14 Samuel Purchas, *Purchas His Pilgrimage, Or, Relations of the World* (London, 1613). Quotations come from this 1613 edition. Subsequent editions appeared in 1614, 1617, and 1626. Purchas is equally well known for his massive compendium *Purchas His Pilgrim*, first published in 1619, and other editions followed.

15 Purchas seems to anticipate Sir Walter Ralegh's *History of the World*, published in the next year 1614, which also begins with the Creation and Flood.

16 Of marginal interest is Anthony Sherley's *Sir Antony Sherley His Relation of His Travels into Persia* (London, 1613). This was published several years after Sherley's journey through Italy, much of the Middle East, and settling in Persia, where the king made him a *Mirza* and made him his ambassador to the princes and states of Christendom. The Earl of Essex had urged Sherley to make the journey first to Italy to support Don Cesare d'Este of Ferrara and then on to Persia. Much of the account only promotes Sherley's presumed virtues, providing little information about the places that Sherley visited, since he focuses mainly on himself, although he has much to say about the Persian king. By 1613, he had long since left Persia, had served the Spanish government, had gone to Russia, and eventually returned to England.

17 William Browne, *Britannia's Pastorals* (London, 1613), p. 2. Quotations come from this edition. For an excellent discussion of this poem see Michelle O'Callaghan's analysis in her book *The 'shepheards nation': Jacobean Spenserians and Early Stuart Political Culture, 1612–1625* (Oxford: Clarendon Press, 2000), pp. 86–101. O'Callaghan observes: 'The political climate of 1613 enabled Browne to look to the court as a national cultural institution that could inspire his "country" epic. Book I has a coherency that arises out of the use of a tragicomic structure to accommodate differences within a reformed Arcadia' (p. 101).

18 Thomas Sampson, *Fortunes Fashion, Portrayed in the troubles of the Ladie Elizabeth Gray* (London, 1613), sig. A4. Quotations are from this edition.

19 William Leighton also contributed a volume of poems, *The Teares or Lamentations of a sorrowfull Soule* (London, 1613), which he dedicated to Prince Charles. Leighton was one of the King's Pensioners. These poems about the soul's struggles were meant to be sung. This volume concludes with 'Adams fall', which articulates the doctrine of free will. The later 1614 edition indeed includes musical settings by the likes of John Dowland, William Byrd, Orlando Gibbons, and Leighton. See additional discussion of music in 1613 in Chapter 2 and the commentary on music for Prince Henry.

20 John Taylor, *Odcombs Complaint: Or Coriats Funerall Epicedium: or Death-song* (London, 1613), sig. A1. Quotations come from the 1613 edition.

21 John Taylor, *The Eighth Wonder of the World, Or, Coriats Escape* (London, 1613).

22 George Wither, *Abuses Stript, and Whipt, Or Satirical Essaies* (London, 1613), sig. B1. All quotations come from this original quarto..

23 For a discussion of Wither and the play, see my 'George Wither's Response to *Othello*', in *The Text, the Play, and the Globe*, ed. Joseph Candido (Madison, NJ: Farleigh Dickinson University Press, 2016), pp. 265–83.

24 For an excellent discussion of the patronage of drama, see the essays in *Shakespeare and Theatrical Patronage in Early Modern England*, eds Paul Whitfield White and Suzanne R. Westfall (Cambridge: Cambridge University Press, 2002).

25 George Chapman, *Homer Prince of Poets* (London, 1609), sig. Dd1.

26 Heywood, *An Apology*, in *English Renaissance Criticism: The Renaissance*, ed. O. B. Hardison, Jr (New York: Appleton-Century-Crofts, 1963), p. 226.

27 *The Dramatic Works of Thomas Heywood*, ed. R. H. Shepherd (1874; rpt New York: Russell & Russell, 1964), 5: 264. All quotations from the plays will come from this edition and be cited by page number.

28 *Bussy D'Ambois and The Revenge of Bussy D'Ambois*, ed. Frederick Boas (Boston: D. C. Heath, 1905). All quotations come from this edition of Chapman.

29 John Marston, *The Insatiate Countess*, ed. Giorgio Melchiori (Manchester: Manchester University Press, 1984), 1.1.1 SD. All quotations will come from this Revels edition.

30 *The Duchess of Malfi* in *English Renaissance Drama*, ed. David Bevington (New York: W. W. Norton, 2002). All quotations will come from this edition.

31 *The Tragedy of Mariam*, eds Barry Weller and Margaret W. Ferguson (Berkeley: University of California Press, 1994), p. 71. All quotations will come from this edition.

32 Henry Roberts, *Englands Farewell to Christian the Fourth* (London, 1606), sig. B2.

33 David Kathman, 'Grocers, Goldsmiths, and Drapers: Freemen and Apprentices in the Elizabethan Theater', *Shakespeare Quarterly* 55.1 (2004): 1–49.

34 Jonson's and Chapman's letters can be found in Appendix 3 of *Eastward Ho!*, ed. C. G. Petter (London: Ernest Benn, 1973), p. 131. All quotations from the play come from this New Mermaids edition.

35 Francis Beaumont, *The Knight of the Burning Pestle*, ed. Michael Hattaway (New York: W. W. Norton, 1986), p. 3. All quotations come from this New Mermaids edition. For additional discussion of the prefatory material in the early quartos, see my 'Paratexts in Francis Beaumont's *The Knight of the Burning Pestle*', *Studies in Philology* 106 (2009): 456–67.

36 The exceptional interconnections between Middleton the dramatist and Middleton the Grocer-Mayor form the subject of my 'Thomas Middleton, Thomas Middleton in London 1613', *Medieval and Renaissance Drama in England* 27 (2014): 17–39.

37 *Analytical Index to the … Remembrancia, Preserved among the Archives of the City of London*, ed. W. H. Overall and H. C. Overall (London, 1878), p. 3.

38 Thomas Middleton, *A Chaste Maid in Cheapside*, ed. Linda Woodbridge in *The Collected Works of Thomas Middleton*, gen. eds Gary Taylor and John Lavagnino (Oxford: Clarendon Press, 2007). All quotations will be from this edition.

39 *The Manner of His Lordship's Entertainment*, ed. David M. Bergeron in *The Collected Works of Thomas Middleton*, gen. eds Gary Taylor and John Lavagnino (Oxford: Clarendon Press, 2007), pp. 959–62. All quotations will come from this edition. This entertainment has sometimes been referred to as 'The New River Entertainment'.

40 The text of Middleton's pageant lives on in Anthony Munday's 1618

revision of Stow's *Survey of London*. For a discussion of this curious development, see my 'Afterlives: Thomas Middleton and Anthony Munday', *Studies in Philology* 111 (2014): 65–82.

41 For a history of the Lord Mayors' Shows, see Tracey Hill, *Pageantry and Power* (Manchester: Manchester University Press, 2010).

42 Cited in *The Triumphs of Truth*, ed. David M. Bergeron, in *The Collected Works of Thomas Middleton*, p. 965. All quotations from the guild and from this pageant come from this edition. Quotations from the pageant will be cited by line numbers; the text of the pageant occurs on pp. 968–76.

43 The Russian Ambassador's account appears with the text of the pageant, cited above, p. 978, in *The Collected Works of Thomas Middleton*. The text was edited by Maija Jansson and Nikolai Rogozhin, and translated by Paul Bushkovitch.

44 For a comparative discussion of these two dramatic events, see my 'Middleton's Moral Landscape: *A Chaste Maid in Cheapside* and *The Triumphs of Truth*', in *'Accompaninge the players': Essays Celebrating Thomas Middleton, 1580–1980*, ed. Kenneth Friedenreich (New York: AMS Press, 1983), pp. 133–46. For additional discussion that brings together all of Middleton's 1613 dramatic output in light of economic concerns, see Ceri Sullivan, 'Thomas Middleton's View of Public Utility', *Review of English Studies* 58 (2007): 162–74.

45 This information comes from Gary Taylor's 'Thomas Middleton: Lives and Afterlives', *The Collected Works of Thomas Middleton*, p. 42.

Divorce, wedding, and murder

Thomas Middleton, the playwright, honoured Thomas Middleton, Grocer and Lord Mayor, with the magnificent *The Triumphs of Truth*, a mayoral pageant staged in London's streets on 29 October 1613. These two could not have anticipated that in a few months they would again be joined in a planned dramatic entertainment, but this time in honour of a court wedding. This collaboration underscores yet again the permeable boundary between Whitehall and the City of London. The city's streets would shine with a courtly procession, led by the Duke of Lennox; and an indoors masque at the Merchant Taylors' Hall would cap the wedding celebration. Obviously no one knew at the beginning of 1613 or during the heady days of Princess Elizabeth's February wedding that the year would end with another major aristocratic wedding, sponsored and funded by King James. But to get to that moment on 26 December, the participants had to pass through a messy divorce and an even messier murder in the Tower. Participating in the festivities for this wedding of Robert Carr and Frances Howard, Lennox had much reason to think about and recall the events that constituted the narrative trajectory of 1613, as the year that began with drama and a royal wedding ended with a court-sponsored wedding. That arc was, however, anything but smooth and unfailingly pleasant.

The production of Shakespeare and Fletcher's *Henry VIII* in late June 1613 intersects the narrative in unanticipated ways. This play's performance stands almost precisely between the February and December weddings, offering both retrospective and prospective views. It clearly resonates with the royal wedding of Elizabeth and Frederick, perhaps having been written in response to it or at least informed by it. The play's ending celebrates the birth of Henry's daughter Elizabeth and looks forward to the eventual arrival of the

Scottish king. But Henry, of course, had first to divorce Katherine, his wife of some twenty years and mother of his surviving child, Mary, and then marry Anne Boleyn, who gave birth to Elizabeth. The debate about divorce – legal, political, and religious – delineates the king's struggle with his moral conscience; indeed, the word 'conscience' becomes a prominent term in the play. For example, the Lord Chamberlain says: 'It seems the marriage with his brother's wife / Has crept too near his [Henry's] conscience' (2.2.15–16). But Suffolk responds in an aside: 'No, his conscience / Has crept too near another lady' (16–17). The king himself closes this scene: 'But conscience, conscience! / O 'tis a tender place, and I must leave her' (141–2). After Katherine's remarkable appearance in 2.4, which stirs Henry's admiration, the king attempts to articulate the vexing issue of the legitimacy of his daughter Mary.

The moral and legal issue about Mary can seem at moments a convenient matter to assuage Henry's conscience and open the possibility of divorce. In any event, twenty years of a successful marriage get set aside in favour of a new wife. Anne's coronation, the focus of 4.1, and the christening of Elizabeth at play's end ratify the new marital arrangement, underscored by Archbishop Cranmer's stirring prophetic speeches. He looks forward to the little Elizabeth's eventual reign and her accomplishments, the promises on this land of a 'thousand thousand blessings, / Which time shall bring to ripeness' (5.4.19–20). Cranmer also foresees the accession of James who will be 'As great in admiration as herself' (42); indeed, he shall flourish 'And like a mountain cedar reach his branches / To all the plains about him' (53–4). Did not the recent wedding of another Elizabeth and Frederick validate Cranmer's prophecy? Lennox and others might rightly conclude such in the exciting and festive days of early 1613.

This same play with its glorious and hopeful ending neverthe-less contains that complicating business of divorce. In that sense, it unwittingly looks forward to the events of the latter half of 1613. The issues of conscience, marriage, and divorce had already begun to grip the divorce proceedings that began shortly prior to the performance of *Henry VIII*. Before she could marry Robert Carr in 1613, Frances Howard had to dispose of her husband, Robert Devereux, third Earl of Essex, whom she had married in early January 1606. At the time of the wedding, she was thirteen years old and he almost fifteen. Thus, their ages barely made their wedding legal. Clearly, this marriage came about because of social and political ambitions, principally from Frances' father, Thomas Howard, Earl of Suffolk and Lord Chamberlain, and her notorious great-uncle Henry Howard, Earl of Northampton. The Howards had come into increased favour under King James, who tolerated their not so secret Catholicism. They sought to solidify their political power in a group that countered the influence of the earls of Southampton and Pembroke, and probably Lennox, for example. James had earlier been fascinated with Essex's father, also named Robert, who had been Queen Elizabeth's last favourite. His hare-brained, abortive uprising on 8 February 1601, attempting allegedly to rid Elizabeth of her bad advisers, led, however, to his arrest, trial, and execution. The son seemed never to share his father's magnetic personality, but countless writers and others kept alive a myth about the heroic second Earl of Essex. Shakespeare and Daniel, among others, certainly gave fictional voice to his exploits. James did restore titles to the younger Essex and made him a page in the service of Prince Henry.

Neither Frances nor Robert, however, gave any evidence of their desire for this arranged marriage, nor did they provide any insight into their possible preparation for marriage. But get married they did, amid much pomp and circumstance, on 5 January 1606, with James's support and best wishes. Dr James Montagu, Bishop of Bath and Wells, presided in the Chapel Royal, and James himself gave the bride away. The festivities included Ben Jonson's masque *Hymenaei*, which took place on the wedding night, and the *Barriers*, which occurred on 6 January, and in which Lennox participated, serving the cause of Truth. But as the festivities ended, the husband and wife went their separate ways; she returned to her parents, and he eventually went on a continental tour of two years' duration, not to return until 1609. Because of their youth, no one expected sexual consummation of the couple. Frances presumably continued her education; and she emerged at court in early 1609, when she danced in Jonson's *The Masque of Queens*, sponsored by Queen Anne, on 2 February. She subsequently danced the role of 'Lea' in Samuel Daniel's masque *Tethys' Festival*, presented as part of the celebration of Prince Henry's installation as Prince of Wales on 5 June 1610.[1]

Flushed with his European experiences, Essex returned in early 1609, ready to claim his bride and begin married life. Frances did not make this easy; in fact, she produced all kinds of obstacles, even potions, and considerable obstinacy. Essex's determination to take her to his country estate at Chartley only exacerbated the problems. Frances preferred to remain at court and enjoy the excitement there. She thought of Chartley as a prison. Apparently, they never consummated their marriage; at least they so testified later. Opinion and Truth, which squared off in Jonson's *Barriers*, now emerged in their lives, and truth took a drubbing, while many people had opinions about them. By early 1613, apparently both Frances and Robert desired a divorce, thus ending the charade and pain of their supposed marriage. Not only had Frances developed an active and deep aversion to her husband but also she had begun a love affair with Robert Carr, Viscount Rochester, creating a vexed love triangle – one of several relationship triangles that emerged.

Carr, a Scot, had come south with King James in 1603, serving in a minor capacity as royal page. But at the Accession Day Tilt in 1607 at Whitehall, Carr fully captured the king's attention. Appearing under the aegis of Sir James Hay, another transplanted Scot, Carr entered the tilt. Despite his skill as a horseman, Carr fell from his horse and broke his leg. James immediately took notice of this attractive young man and became solicitous of his welfare, insisting that the king's own physicians take care of him. The king visited Carr regularly and even began to try to teach him Latin. This eventually led Thomas Howard to write to John Harrington in 1611, saying, 'If any mischance be to be wished, tis breaking a leg in the Kings presence, for this fellow [Carr] owes all his favour to that bout; I think he hath better reason to speak well of his own horse, than the Kings Roan jennet'.[2] In addition, Howard describes Carr as 'straight-limbed, well-favoured, strong-shouldered, and smooth-faced, with some sort of cunning and show of modesty; tho, God wot, he well knoweth when to shew his impudence'.[3] Just the sort of young man to attract the king's attention and favour.[4]

As a sign of Carr's emerging prominence, John Chamberlain wrote to his friend Dudley Carleton on 30 December 1607: 'Sir Robert Carre, a younge Scot and new favorite is lately sworne gentleman of the bedchamber.'[5] Two things stand out about Chamberlain's simple observation: how quickly Carr had become a 'favourite' and what an important position he had gained, Gentleman of the Bedchamber. Early in James's English reign the King's Bedchamber essentially supplanted the Privy Council as the political centre of the government. With one exception, Philip Herbert, Earl of Montgomery, all the Gentlemen of the Bedchamber were Scots, starting with Lennox; and they basically controlled access to the king, having the most intimate contact with the king's person.[6] Befitting a 'favourite', King James wanted Carr physically near him as he sought to shape Carr's future. In March 1608, Henryck Van Hulfen received a payment of £300 'for a tablet of gold set with diamonds, and the King's picture, given by the King to Rob. Carr, Gentleman of the Bedchamber'.[7] In a scant year Robert Carr had been lifted off the tiltyard and placed in the upper reaches of the king's affection: the king had sent him his picture, surely a love token.

In 1609, James gave Carr Sir Walter Ralegh's estates at Sherborne, a gift that rankled the Ralegh family grievously. 'Royal gifts to the new favourite began early and continued throughout Carr's career. … The king also gave Carr major grants of cash and … lands which provided one of the only long-term sources of crown income.'[8] James in March 1611 created Carr Viscount of Rochester, which carried with it a seat in the English House of Lords; he thus became the first Scot to sit in the English Parliament. Carr became a Knight of the Garter in April of that same year, and in 1612 he gained a seat on the Privy Council. James also made him Lord Treasurer of Scotland in 1613, and he served as a kind of personal secretary to the king. This led the Venetian Ambassador, Antonio Foscarini, to observe: Carr 'holds the privy seal, with whom the king decides everything and in whom His Majesty confides above all others.'[9] The death of Robert Cecil, James's chief political and government adviser, in May 1612 enlarged Carr's prospects by removing a major obstacle: Cecil's disfavour, which Queen Anne and Prince Henry shared intensely. Carr thus began to fan out across the political landscape, gathering titles, offices, and considerable power, all the product of the king's generosity. No one could possibly doubt where he stood in James's favour.

Lennox certainly understood Carr's status, and so did the Howards. Therefore, not surprisingly Frances Howard's affections began to move in Carr's direction, no doubt encouraged especially by her great-uncle Northampton. A potential alliance or even marriage with Carr would strengthen the Howards' political position. With the family's knowledge if not support Frances made overtures toward Carr and reciprocated his attention. A letter from John Holles places Lennox in at least one scene of an encounter between

Frances and Carr. Apparently she had written to Carr asking him to meet her at Chesterford Park. 'When he had arrived he had found her sitting with the Duke of Lennox. Seconded by Lennox, Frances had then urged him to marry her, saying that there was nothing to stop them.'[10] According to Holles, Carr was not ready for this possibility: '"Your Lordship replied that you had yet made no fortune, that you were at the King's bestowing. … nevertheless, she pressing you still, and my Lord of Lennox in her behalf, your Lordship said you would try the King".' Clearly Frances Howard wanted to dissolve her marriage with Essex. That process would not be simple, as the events of 1613 bear out.

The thorny problem of divorce derived from moral and legal constraints, as Shakespeare and Fletcher understood and represented in *Henry VIII*. The developing illicit relationship of Frances Howard and Robert Carr encountered another difficulty in the person of Thomas Overbury, a handsome and highly intelligent young man and also a talented poet, prose writer, and government operative. Overbury's connection with Carr produced yet another problematic relationship triangle (Howard–Carr–Overbury). Overbury had met Carr during his travels to Scotland in 1601, and they became friends. Meanwhile, Overbury secured a position in Cecil's service, having already been educated at the Middle Temple and Queen's College, Oxford. Cecil sent him abroad for seasoning, and he returned to court service in 1606; soon thereafter he renewed and developed his friendship with Carr.[11] This intensifying relationship served both men: Overbury had the intelligence and savvy that Carr desired, and Carr had the charm and status that Overbury longed for.

Overbury began to supply the brainpower that Carr needed in order to carry out his important political duties and to develop his political ambitions. 'Overbury's intimacy with Carr made him a broker of access to and influence with the favourite, just as Carr was the broker of access to and influence with the king.'[12] Some kind of intense personal relationship developed, which provoked a sense of threat to the Howards and to King James. After all, in assisting Carr, Overbury had begun to have access to all important state documents and secrets. But he saw Frances Howard as a hindrance to his involvement with Carr, and thus he tried to defame her and discourage Carr from continuing his affair, let alone the possibility of marrying her. Some saw Overbury as the 'favourite's favourite'. This cosy, if tortured, relationship James came increasingly to dislike, in part because it potentially diluted Carr's devotion to him. The king decided to act in order to untangle the triangle of Carr–Overbury–James.

Partly for political reasons, partly out of personal desire, James wanted to get rid of Overbury's influence and perhaps also his increasing knowledge. On 21 April 1613, having recently bade farewell to his daughter and son-in-law, the king sent Overbury to the Tower, from which he would not emerge alive. Writing to Dudley Carleton on 29 April, John Chamberlain reports: 'The King hath long had a desire to remove him from about the Lord of Rochester, as thincking yt a dishonor to him that the world shold have an opinion that Rochester ruled him and Overburie ruled Rochester wheras he wold make yt appeare that neither Overburie nor Rochester had such a stroke with him.'[13] James had sent Lord Ellesmere, the Lord Chancellor, and the Earl of Pembroke to Overbury to make him an offer of an ambassadorial position, under the guise, as Chamberlain notes, of the king's good will 'wherby he had an intent to make use of his goode parts, and to traine him for his further service and therefore they offered him his choice to be employed either by the archduke, or into Fraunce or into Moscovie'. Overbury made his excuses, such as not knowing the languages, and refused, giving the lords 'a peremptorie aunswer that he could not yield to go, and that he hoped that the King neither in law nor justice could compel him to leave his countrie'. His response incensed James, and led to his imprisonment in the Tower from which Overbury expected a quick release. April became a cruel month.[14]

Chamberlain wrote to Ralph Winwood on 6 May: 'Some say my Lord of Rochester tooke Sir Thomas Overberies committing to hart.'[15] Certainly Carr gave Overbury repeated assurances about working for his release; on the other hand, Overbury's imprisonment served Carr's purposes, ridding him of an insistent impediment to his desire and designs for Frances Howard. In fact, Carr had been dependent on Overbury's letter-writing skills in his pursuit of Frances, whom he wooed in part through Overbury's voice. This point Overbury makes to Carr: 'when you fell in Love with that Woman, as soon as you had wonne her *by my Letters*, … then used your own for common Passages'.[16] Another report indicates that Overbury also served as deliverer of these letters.[17] Like James, Overbury did not want a triangular relationship; he jealously guarded his connection to Carr. Increasing desperation characterised the letters that Overbury wrote to Carr, pleading for deliverance from the Tower.

Some of the letters also contain threats, as when Overbury writes: 'All I intreat of you is, that you will free me from this place, and that we may part friends. Drive me not to extremities, lest I should say something that you and I both repent.'[18] He characterises himself as one '*to whome you owe more than to any Soule living, both for your Fortune, Understanding, and Reputation*' (160). Overbury repeatedly drops large hints at something slightly scandalous and something certainly secret between them. Indeed, Carr apparently forgets 'him betwixt whom was *nine yeares Love*, and such Secrets of all kinds have passed' (161). Overbury also informed Carr that he had prepared a prose narrative of their relationship, which he has 'sealed it *up under eight Seales*, and sent it by a Friend of myne whom I dare trust' (163). Carr had much reason to be frightened by such a document for what it might reveal. Therefore, he made few efforts to assure Overbury's release. Overbury's failing health and eventual death on 14 September 1613 solved Carr's dilemma, so long as he could round up their letters and find Overbury's narrative.

Returning to London in October, Chamberlain wrote to Dudley Carleton on the 14th: 'Sir Thomas Overburie died and is buried in the Towre. The manner of his death is not knowne for that there was no body with him not so much as his keeper, but the fowlenes of his corps gave suspicion and leaves aspersion that he shold die of the poxe or somewhat worse.'[19] The 'somewhat worse' would eventually become known. For the moment, this bright young man had died an ignominious death and received an anonymous burial. His friends, Chamberlain insists, 'speake but indifferently of him'. At least three people breathed a sigh of relief at Overbury's death: Frances Howard, Carr, and the king, who thereby formed another triangle. Each had a slightly different reason for relief. For others, indifference governed their responses to Overbury's death.

While languishing several months in the Tower, Overbury apparently never fully understood why Carr and other friends did not enable his freedom. He did not comprehend the several agendas arrayed against him. Clearly the king and Carr found it convenient for Overbury to remain in prison, if only for an extended period of time. But the Howards and Frances Howard in particular also had their reasons for keeping Overbury there. Thomas Howard and

Henry Howard collaborated on first removing the Lieutenant of the Tower and replacing him with Sir Gervase Elwes, who would do their bidding. Then they secured the services of Richard Weston, who would become the 'keeper' of Overbury; he also would follow their orders. The Howards wanted to drive a permanent wedge between Carr and Overbury and in the process draw Carr closer to them and further solidify their considerable political power. Despite their efforts, the Tower remained as it had always been a 'permeable' prison with lots of outside traffic of friends and relatives who visited the prisoners. Therefore, Overbury was able to send letters out and receive certain items, including medicines that would make him sick, thereby, he thought, presumably creating sympathy for his plight.

Into this environment stepped Frances Howard, who wanted to get rid of Overbury permanently: she wanted exclusive access to Carr. When the divorce proceedings hit a snag, she apparently designed a plan of systematically poisoning Overbury – the 'somewhat more' of Chamberlain's letter. Frances was no stranger to the dealings of, for example, Anne Turner and Simon Forman, well-known persons capable of producing the desired potions. Indeed, Frances may have used some on her husband Essex. She confronted Overbury's situation with relentless determination and evil intent, and she succeeded, thanks to much help inside the Tower. Overbury would seem to recover occasionally, only to lapse back into an even worse state. The whole process took time, but it worked. What had seemed relatively tame intentions of Carr and the Howards gained a determined purpose in Frances Howard, who presumably undertook this deadly project without the knowledge of others. In fact, in mid-August, Overbury had pledged his allegiance to Suffolk, Frances' father, and agreed to further Carr's friendship with the Howards. On the basis of this action, Overbury expected immediate release.[20]

Not until 1615 did the whole conspiracy become known. Small wonder that Overbury's death never received full medical and legal inquiry in September 1613, despite a letter from Northampton to Gervase Elwes, instructing him on what to do with Overbury's body. On the back of this letter Elwes wrote: 'Notwithstanding Sir Thomas Overbury dying about five in the Morning, I kept his Body unburied until three or four of the Clock in the Afternoon. The next Day Sir John Lidcote [Overbury's brother-in-law] came thither;

I could not get him to bestow a Coffin or a Winding-Sheet upon him. The Coffin I bestowed; but who did winde him, I know not. For indeed the Body was very noysome; so that notwithstanding my Lord's Direction, by reason of the Danger of keeping the Body, I kept it over long, as we all felt.'[21] Elwes had in fact refused to deliver the body to Lidcote for a family burial, following Northampton's instructions to him. The Earl had also sent an emissary to the Tower to view the body; this person sent back a gruesome and graphic report. 'Despite the fact that so little time had elapsed, the body already smelt appallingly obnoxious, and was decomposing abnormally quickly.'[22] A brief coroner's inquest ruled that Overbury had died of natural causes. Thus, a quick burial in St Peter ad Vincula, the chapel attached to the Tower, seemed to deflect the issue – out of sight, out of mind. As the Tower received Overbury's body for burial, so the divorce proceedings came to the desired conclusion for Frances Howard and Robert Carr, clearing the way for their marriage.

But the course of true divorce never did run smoothly. On 29 April, Chamberlain wrote to Dudley Carleton about the possibility of divorce: Essex 'was content (whether true or fained) to confesse insufficience in himself, but there happened an accident of late that hath altered the case'.[23] Chamberlain has put his finger on one of the principal issues: namely Essex's acknowledgement of failure to consummate his marriage to Frances Howard. At the same time a woman accused Frances of using potions to try to harm her husband; this charge complicated the early negotiations. Nevertheless, a preliminary meeting took place in May 1613 between Suffolk and Northampton, representing Frances, and the Earl of Southampton and Lord Knollys, representing Essex. Clearly at this point both husband and wife desired divorce, and King James had come around to this view as well. Therefore, the king appointed a commission in May to hear the case. This commission consisted of: George Abbot, Archbishop of Canterbury; John King, Bishop of London; Lancelot Andrewes, Bishop of Ely; Richard Neile, Bishop of Coventry and Lichfield; six civilians and lawyers: Sir Julius Caesar, Chancellor of the Exchequer; Thomas Parry, Chancellor of the Duchy of Lancaster; Sir Daniel Dunne, Dean of the Court of the Arches; Dr Thomas Edwards, Chancellor of the Bishop of London; Sir John Bennet, Judge of the Prerogative Court of Canterbury; and Dr Francis James. Abbot served as chair of the group, which began hearing the case on 17 May. From the outset the archbishop took a dim view of the whole business and tried bootlessly several times to get the king to remove him.

The commission confirmed that the couple had married legitimately and that they had lived together as man and wife for three years. The 'libel', the official charge, claimed that Frances Howard 'desirous to be made a mother, from time to time, again and again yielded herself to his power, and as much as lay in her offered herself and her body to be known'.[24] But, apparently, Essex was incapable of having sex with his wife, although he insisted that he had no such problem with other women. Chamberlain, writing to Carleton, on 10 June, remains hopeful that the proceeding will end soon. He adds: 'all the difficultie is that though he be willing to confesse his insufficiencie towards her, yet he will be left at libertie to marrie any other, and stands upon yt that he is *maleficiatus* only *ad illam*'.[25] According to the records of the 'trial', Essex had confessed 'that although he did his best endeavour, yet he never could; nor at this time can, have copulation with the said lady Frances, no not once'.[26] Some had suggested at the beginning of the hearing that Essex's impotence derived from witchcraft; but Abbot insisted that no such cause could be found in scripture or in church teachings, a position to which James, the author of *Demonologie*, took great exception.

Wanting to secure his manly reputation and the prospect of remarrying, Essex had to claim impotence only with Frances, and he in fact began to shift the blame to her. Numerous witnesses appeared before the Commission and confirmed the efforts of the couple to consummate the marriage. Frances insisted that she remained a virgin, and the court decided to test this claim by having a group of women, five matrons and two midwives, physically examine her. They confirmed her assertion and found her 'fitted with abilities to have carnal copulation, and apt to have children'.[27] Chamberlain writes to Carleton on 23 June: 'the Lady hath ben visited and searcht by some auncient Ladies and midwifes expert in those matters, who both by inspection and otherwise find her upon theyre oath a pure virgin'.[28] No such physical examination of Essex took place, thereby allowing him to retain some semblance of dignity. But one report indicates that there had been some sentiment for such an examination: 'The Common People were offended with the Canons, and wish'd, that *Essex* might have as many Women to aspect him for his sufficiency, that he might have Justified himself upon others, or have Physicians (by Art) to certifie his Natural impediment.'[29] Frances meanwhile swore an oath that her husband was impotent.

Then the divorce proceedings stalled, being postponed on 5 July until the next law term. A divided, apparently deadlocked, commission could not come to an agreement, much to James's chagrin. He bristled at Abbot's intransigence, even as the Archbishop asked again to be removed from the process. John Chamberlain had a chance encounter with Lancelot Andrewes, Bishop of Ely, which he records in a letter to Carleton, dated 1 August: 'At my last beeing with the bishop of Ely ... I found which way he bent, for he made no daintie [scruple] to tell me his opinon, which I could wish were otherwise yf there be no more reason in yt then I see or conceave.'[30] The Earl of Southampton wrote to Sir Ralph Winwood in early August about the divorce, noting the king's determination to get the result he wanted and observing that some of the bishops had apparently changed their minds in favour: 'For the Businesse it self, I shall be glad, if it may lawfully ... go forward; though of late I have been fearful of the Consequence.'[31] Although Andrewes favoured granting the divorce, to Chamberlain's dismay, James did not yet have sufficient votes. So, he did the kingly thing: he appointed two more bishops, the Bishop of Winchester, Thomas Bilson, and the Bishop of Rochester, John Buckeridge, confident that they would vote the correct way. Bilson thus joined two other fellow translators of the King James Bible, Abbott and Andrewes, on the commission. The new appointees voted 'correctly', so that on 25 September, by a vote of seven to five, Frances Howard and the Earl of Essex gained their divorce. Chamberlain reports to Carleton on 14 October the king's instructions to the commission: 'the morning that the matter was to be decided, the King sent expresse commaundment, that in opining they shold not argue nor use any reasons, but only geve theyre assent or dissent'.[32] James had grown weary of the delay and wanted a clear-cut decision; apparently he feared that any further discussion might persuade someone else to oppose the divorce. Less than two weeks after Overbury's death, Frances Howard had the divorce, and the path to a wedding opened up: death–divorce–wedding. Throughout this process Robert Carr had been the emotional centre, triggering the vying among Frances Howard, Thomas Overbury, and King James for his favour and love.

As Frances had gained something she wanted, so did the Duke of Lennox. He had longed for an English title to complement his Scottish one. On 6 May 1613, Chamberlain wrote to Ralph Winwood: 'The Duke of Lennox had a pretence to be made duke or erle of Richmond and so by consequence an English peere of parlement, and to that purpose had procured divers noble mens hands to present to the King in his behalfe, but finding more difficultie in the prosecution of yt then he expected hath geven yt over for the time.'[33] Then on 6 October, Lennox received the desired prize, as Chamberlain acknowledged in a letter to Dudley Carleton, 11 November: 'The Duke of Lennox hath his patent to be baron of Sutterington and earle of Richmond but there needed no creation beeing invested with a greater dignitie before' (485). Quietly Lennox received the desired English title and thereby became a member of the English House of Lords, a singular achievement for this transplanted Scot-Frenchman.

In that same letter to Carleton, Chamberlain notes the installation of Carr as Earl of Somerset, which took place on 4 November. He writes: 'Upon Thursday last the Vicount Rochester was created baron of Branspeth in Westmerland and earle of Somerset. The action was don with much solemnitie, sixe erles assisting him' (485). The earls of Montgomery, Pembroke, Southampton, and Worcester accompanied Carr, wearing their robes and capes, preceded by silent drums and trumpets into the Banqueting House in Whitehall Palace. 'The Vicount Rochester in his surcoate and hode of crymosin velvet, in an ordinary hatt, with his rapier, between the Earle of Northampton and the Earle of Nottingham, in their roabes of estate and coronets; and by them presented to the King (who satt in state with the Queene and Prince) with due reverence.'[34] This was 'a political event, designed to express the unity of crown and court, come together for the elevation of Robert Carr into a new and more glorious station. The queen, long Carr's enemy, was prevailed upon to join her husband under the cloth of estate … thus by her presence sanctioning Carr's promotion.'[35]

The ceremony closed as the Garter delivered the patent to the Lord Chamberlain, who gave it to the king, who then gave it to Sir Thomas Lake to read. 'When the created Earle had rendered thanks, and the King had used a short speache to him, the trumpets sounded and the drummes strake, and so [they] returned to the Councellchamber, where they all dined in their roabes, with their cappes of estate, he sitting at the table's ende uppermost.'[36] With other noblemen also present, the event depicted union among former warring parties, as Carr processed supported by the Howards – Northampton and Nottingham. Even Queen Anne lent her tacit support. Carr was approaching the apogee of his power, to be solidified by the wedding at the end of 1613.

At first, the wedding was to be a somewhat simple affair, as Chamberlain reports on 11 November to Dudley Carleton: 'The mariage was thought shold be celebrated at Audley-end [home of Frances' father] the next weeke, and great preparation there was to receve the King, but I heare that the Queene beeing won and having promised to be present, yt is put of till Christmas and then to be performed at White-hall.'[37] The change in plans, thanks in no small part to the change in Anne's attitude, led James to assume the cost of the whole endeavour, an expense that he could ill afford. Giovanni Battista Gabaleone, the somewhat newly arrived Ambassador from the Duchy of Savoy, reported on the preparations in early December: 'At court they are working day and night on shows for the Earl of Somerset's wedding; the dancing festivals will be held in the royal hall as they were for the Prince Palatine, and there will be masques of great moment. It is estimated that his Majesty stands to spend more than a hundred thousand scudi on his part in these nuptials.'[38]

On St Stephen's day, 26 December, the Duke of Lennox and many other noblemen and court officials gathered with the king and queen at the Chapel Royal in Whitehall for the marriage of James's favourite and the newly divorced Frances Howard (see Figure 10). Her great-uncle the Earl of Northampton led her into the chapel. 'She was maried in her haire', Chamberlain reports, a sign of her virginity.[39] The Dean of Westminster, George Montaigne, preached and 'bestowed a great deale of commendation on the younge couple', Chamberlain says. But the Dean of the Chapel Royal, James Montagu, Bishop of Bath and Wells, led the service and officially joined the couple in marriage. Chamberlain cannot resist observing that Montagu had performed Frances' wedding to Essex in 1606; this 'fell out somwhat straungely that the same man, shold marie the same person, in the same place, upon the self-same day (after sixe or seven yeares I know not whether) the former partie yet living'. Few could pass up the irony.

Chamberlain notes: 'The King and Quene were both present and tasted wafers and ypocras as at ordinarie weddings' (495–6).

10 Engraving of Robert Carr, Earl of Somerset, and his wife
Frances Howard from Michael Sparke,
The Narrative History of King James (1651)

Archbishop Abbot attended, but the Bishop of London did not. Chamberlain records a partial but stunning list of gifts that the new couple received. The Earl of Northampton, for example, gave 'plate to the value of fifteen hundred pound, besides a sword to the bridegroome, the hilts and all the furniture of gold curiously wrought and enammeled' (497). Ten days of festivities followed, stretching to 6 January 1614, rivalling anything seen at court since the February wedding, and not to be equalled again in the Jacobean period. It takes little imagination to understand the significance of this wedding, politically and culturally.

After the wedding ceremony a little later in the evening, the court gathered in the Banqueting Hall within Whitehall Palace; there they saw Thomas Campion's masque, generally known as *The Somerset Masque* or *Masque of Squires*. Campion had had pride of place at Princess Elizabeth's wedding with the presentation of his *Lords' Masque* on the evening of the wedding, and he had provided a progress entertainment in April for Queen Anne. Clearly, 1613 was a great year for this poet, musician, playwright, and physician. For this masque Campion could not rely on the artistry of Inigo Jones, who had left for Italy in February and did not return to England for two years. Instead, Campion used the services of the Florentine architect Constantine de Servi, who had received an annual pension from Prince Henry. Campion makes clear in his text, however, his dissatisfaction with de Servi's designs. As with his masque for the earlier royal wedding, Campion emphasises the theme of transformation. One can certainly note the seeming 'transformation' of Queen Anne, who had surrendered, at least in public, her antipathy to Robert Carr, having appeared at his investiture as Earl of Somerset and having allowed the wedding to take place in Whitehall. Accordingly, Campion makes her a central figure in the masque, displacing, as it were, the usual prominence of King James.[40]

In an unusual move, Campion constructed two diverse worlds in the masque: an allegorical world, allied with the court, and the more realistic world of London, explicitly linking Whitehall and Guildhall. The entertainment stands between these often competing worlds. In terms of design, Campion created '*an Arch Tryumphall, passing beautifull, which enclosed the whole Workes*'.[41] In such an arch, Campion may be recalling the stunning triumphal arches that dominated London on the occasion of James's royal entry into the city on 15 March 1604, and whose engravings in Stephen Harrison's *Arches of Triumph* had received a new edition in 1613. The first movement of the narrative involves knights who had attempted to make their journey to London for this wedding. Four

Squires emerge from the setting of woods and a sea scene, and they express their grief for the knights who have been changed into pillars of gold. They have been trapped in a literal and figurative storm by 'Deformed *Errour*, that enchaunting fiend, / And wing-tongu'd *Rumor*' (269). The Second Squire's description of the storm echoes the storm in *The Tempest*, a production of which the court would have seen in early 1613. These knights, changed into pillars of gold, are 'Faire to our eyes, but wofull to beholde' (270).

Their imprisonment has come about because of the work of Error and Rumor, who must surely reflect, however covertly, on the recent court discussions about Carr and Frances Howard. In Campion's view these figures lead to destruction, as the following antimasque clearly shows. In this section numerous figures of confusion and destruction appear, such as Error, Rumor, Curiosity, Credulity, the four Winds, and the four parts of the earth, who enter '*in a confused measure*' (271). Campion carefully delineates how these figures should be depicted, as he taps into well-established traditions of iconographical representation. Thus, Rumor, for example, appears '*in a skin coate full of winged Tongues, and over it an antick robe; on his head a Cap like a tongue, with a large paire of wings to it*' (271). After a dance of strange confusion, Eternity, the three Destinies, and Harmony with nine musicians appear and bring orderliness and beautiful music, singing, 'Vanish, vanish hence, confusion'.

Eternity sings and presents a 'Sacred Tree, / The Tree of Grace and Bountie, / Set it in Bel-Annas eye, / For she, she, only she / Can all Knotted spels unty' (272). As the song ends, the Destinies place the Tree of Gold before Queen Anne as the Chorus sings: 'Since Knightly valour rescues Dames distressed / By Vertuous Dames let charm'd Knights be released'. Campion turns on its head the usual narrative expectation of romance, and he shifts power to the queen. One of the Squires says to her: '(Great Queene), vouchsafe us a divine touch't bough' (273). The stage directions read: '*the Queene puld a branch from the Tree and gave it to a Nobleman, who delivered it to one of the Squires*'. According to one source, that 'nobleman' was the Earl of Pembroke.[42] Singled out in this extraordinary way, Anne responded correctly, underscoring rec-onciliation; and transformation occurred, a clear example of her power. The maskers, previously charmed, came forward to dance, included among them the Duke of Lennox, the earls of Pembroke and Montgomery, and three of Frances' brothers.

Just as suddenly the scene changed to London and the Thames, all *'very arteficially* [artfully] *presented in their place'* (273). As one of the Squires lifts the bough, the Chorus sings, 'Vertue and Grace, in spight of Charmes, / Have now redeem'd our men at Armes' (274). Therefore, the knights can participate in London's life, including this wedding. The masque now moves to refer to the wedding explicitly, singing of love's delight. In this scene, four barges appear as on the Thames; and the 'skippers' in them sing, followed by dancing. The Squires, who had begun the masque, return at the end to extend their wishes and blessings to the newly married couple, 'The honour'd Bride-groome and the honourd Bride' (276). The masque closes, reminiscent of the end of *A Midsummer Night's Dream*, sending all off to sleep, 'And so godnight to all, godnight to all'. London and court sing with one voice of rejoicing, and the queen enables transformation, whatever her private thoughts might have been about this marriage. Anne transcends narrow political and personal constraints and instead participates actively in a lively fictional court drama, helping ratify this marriage as the celebratory mode seeks to wipe out resistance and rumour.

Catching their breath, Lennox and others of the court got ready for Ben Jonson's *A Challenge at Tilt, At a Marriage*, the first part of which took place on 27 December, followed by the tilt on 1 January. Jonson had earlier written *Hymenaei* for the 1606 wedding of Frances Howard and the Earl of Essex. He had, however, been travelling throughout Europe since spring 1612, serving as mentor to Wat Ralegh, son of Sir Walter, and had only returned to London in summer 1613. He had thus missed all the court excitement of the earlier part of the year and had in a sense been outflanked by Thomas Campion. But now he got his chance.

The *Challenge* involved the appearance of two Cupids, each vying for supremacy, one representing the bride and the other the bridegroom. Their conversation, unlike that of Campion's masque, emphasises the sexual nature of the couple's union. The Second Cupid, for example, asks: 'Was it not I that yesternight waited on the bride into the nuptial chamber, and against [forward] the bridegroom came, made her the throne of love?'[43] The First Cupid responds: 'And did not I bring on the blushing bridegroom to taste those joys? ... Did I not shoot myself into him like a flame, and made his desires and his graces equal?' (200). Cupid adds: 'His very undressing, was it not love's arming?' (Much of this seems to look askance at Essex's presumed lack of sexual prowess.) First Cupid lays down the challenge: a group of knights 'by their virtue shall maintain me to be the right Cupid, and the true issue of valor and beauty' – hence the Tilt on 1 January. Chamberlain reports: 'The bases, trappings and all other furniture of the one partie was murrey and white which were the brides colours, the other green and yellow for the bridegroome. There were two handsom chariots or pageants that brought in two Cupids, whose contention was whether were the truer his or hers, each maintained by theyre champions, but the current and prise you must thincke ran on her side.'[44] The Italian Gabaleone reports: 'there was a tilt run on New Year's Day (their style), face to face, with very rich clothing and liveries, and triumphal chariots that were a most lovely sight and a great expense to the lords'.[45] Chamberlain cannot recall the names of all the challengers; but he does remember Lennox, and the earls of Pembroke, Montgomery, Dorset, and Rutland. Ten knights favoured First Cupid and ten Second Cupid. Finally, the trumpets sound and the tilting began.

After the tilting, each side claimed victory, only to be interrupted by the appearance of Hymen, who says that they both must yield: 'this is neither contention for you nor time fit to contend. There is another kind of tilting would become love better than this; to meet lips for lances, and crack kisses instead of staves' (204). Hymen insists on the equality of both Cupids and redefines love's contention, asking who loves most. True love comes about when the lover transforms himself or herself into the person of his or her beloved; they thereby construct a concord of worthy love. Hymen bids the knights depart as 'honorable friends and servants of love'.

On 29 December, the King's Men performed Jonson's *The Irish Masque at Court*; at the king's request they performed it again on 3 January.[46] Chamberlain writes to Carleton: 'The loftie maskers were so well liked at court the last weeke that they were appointed to performe yt again on Monday' (1: 498). This strange entertainment, complete with rather bizarre Irish dialect, comes across as comical. The well-nigh incomprehensibility of their language must have been part of the fun. Perhaps Jonson intends to undo Campion's seriousness. Like the knights in Campion's masque, four Irishmen have landed on England's shores but without proper garments fit for a wedding. Amusingly, they seem to have trouble even recognising King James. Thus, Dermock asks, 'Phair ish te king?'; and Donnell asks, 'Phich ish te king?' (207). Such confusion, borderline heretical, apparently caused much amusement, even for James. A grand sort of dislocation, defamiliarisation goes on here, as Jonson pokes fun at the typical masque. Given the centrality of the king's physical location for such performances, how could one not recognise him? While Ireland had recently undergone considerable turmoil under the oppressive English rule, these Irishmen in the masque present no coherent political message. They have merely come for a wedding.

They have been able to gather news of this event even in Ireland, as Dennis acknowledges: 'tere vash a great newsh in Ireland of a great bridal of one o' ty lords here, an't be' (208). The Irishmen have brought others with them to dance in the wedding celebration. They also insist that Ireland contains 'many o' great goot subshects' who love the king heartily. They then dance to the bagpipe 'and other rude music' and give way to a group of gentlemen who dance 'in their Irish mantles', the gentlemen being presumably the likes of the Duke of Lennox and other courtiers (210). A Gentleman of Ireland, appearing with a Bard, addresses the audience, bidding the rough Irishmen farewell. He says in perfect English: 'Advance, immortal bard, come up and view / The gladding face of that great king in whom / So many prophecies of thine are knit' (211). The Gentleman singles out James's virtues: 'This is that James of which long since thou sung'st / Should end our country's most unnatural broils' (211). This king has brought peace and harmony, fulfilling the prophecies. The performers, the King's Men, would surely recall *Henry VIII* that they had performed a few months earlier, which ended with just such prophecies. The masque closes with two songs by the Bard, who notes how quickly 'a spring / Works in the presence of a king' (212). The final song derives its imagery from winter's season; yet, 'all get vigor, youth and sprite, / That are but looked on by his light'. Nature and the king's power coalesce to provide hope and renewal even in this unusual masque. The Bard sings: 'So breaks the sun earth's rugged chains / Wherein rude winter bound her veins.' James had commissioned Jonson to write this masque, so we cannot be surprised at its focus on the king. The choice of Irish characters, however, comes unexpectedly.[47]

Jonson also wrote a poem addressed to Somerset on his wedding day. This twenty-six-line, rhyming couplet poem begins enthusiastically in praise of the day and the true friends who have gathered for the wedding: 'their love not bought'.[48] Jonson places himself among such people as he wishes for Somerset, 'virtuous Somerset', all joy. Jonson makes a passing reference to Thomas Overbury and his poem 'The Wife', not published until the next year: 'May she whom thou for spouse today dost take / Out-be that wife in worth thy friend did make.' The poet also takes note of Frances' former husband: 'And thou to her, that husband, may exalt / Hymen's amends, to make it worth his fault' – an apparent reference to Essex's alleged impotence. Then follow eight lines, linked by the word 'So': 'So be there never discontent or sorrow'; 'So be your concord still as deep'; 'So may those marriage-pledges comforts prove'; 'So in their number may [you] never see / Mortality, till you [im]mortal be'. Jonson concludes: 'Th[a]t all that view you then and late may say, / Sure, this glad pair were married but this day!' Later revelations, of course, tarnish the idealism of this poem; but for the moment Jonson fulfils his role as celebrant of this glorious occasion, full as it seems to be of hope.

Just as Campion's masque shifted its scene to London, so does the entertainment for Frances Howard and Robert Carr. King James on 31 December requested that the Lord Mayor of London, Thomas Middleton, entertain the newly married couple. On this same day, Middleton wrote to the Privy Council: 'For the avoiding of abuses in tippling houses to the maintenance of drunkenness and vice he had lately taken some courses … and done his best to remedy these enormities.'[49] Whitehall sends a message to Guildhall; Guildhall sends one to Whitehall. The mayor may have expected some commendation for his action, but he got instead a request from the king. When the mayor objected that he could not accommodate such a gathering, the king urged him to think again. As John Chamberlain puts the issue succinctly: 'he making an excuse that his house was too litle to receve them, yt was not accepted'.[50] Therefore, the mayor arranged for the city to present entertainment at the Merchant Taylors' Hall, apparently chosen for its size, beauty, and previous theatrical performances, and perhaps also because the king had officially visited this guild in 1607. With only four days' warning, the city had to come up with something and thus hired Thomas Middleton, the playwright, to write a masque, which was performed on 4 January 1614. Middleton had, of course, already written the pageant for the opening of the New River on 29 September and the following month, on 29 October, the splendid Lord Mayor's Show; therefore, he would have been well known to the city authorities. City records reveal a payment to Middleton for his masque, generally known as the *Masque of Cupids*, of which no text survives.

The court thus went to the city. Roger Coke explains: 'But *Whitehall* was too narrow to contain the Triumphs for this Marriage, they must be extended into the City.'[51] London becomes the outlet for court entertainment. Chamberlain reports the spectacular procession: 'they went yesternight about six a clocke, thorough Cheapside all by torchlight, accompanied by the father and mother of the bride, and all the Lords and Ladies about the court. The men were well mounted and richly arrayed making a goodly shew, the women all in coaches.'[52] Sir Ralph Winwood had given four horses to the married couple to escort the bride's new coach. With the Duke of Lennox leading the way, the procession created quite a stir, moving smartly through Cheapside, the same area of Middleton's *Chaste Maid in Cheapside*, to the Merchant Taylors' Hall as citizens marvelled. Out of the dark and chill of this January night, the elegant procession, its lights puncturing the darkness and creating a joyful glow, became part of the entertainment. The dazzling lights recall the ones that moved along the Thames for Beaumont's February wedding masque as it moved from Southwark along the river to Whitehall. The Italian envoy Gabaleone confirms many of the details of this event: 'The wedded couple left their lodging at five in the afternoon accompanied by a hundred knights, all lords, earls and barons, dressed most superbly, on horseback, ranked two by two. ... Every knight had a single groom with a torch in his hand walking at his side.'[53] This procession moved through 'the whole length of the city. There the people had gathered, making a wonderful sight because of the great quantity of lights they had with them at windows and in the streets' (82). Chamberlain concludes his report: 'I understand that after supper they had a play and a maske after that a banket'. Another report indicates that the 'Aldermen of London, in their scarlet robes, entertained them with hearty welcome, and feasted them with all magnificence'.[54] The noble guests did not return to Whitehall until three o'clock the next morning. But the celebration of this wedding had not yet ended.

On 6 January, the court witnessed the performance of *Masque of Flowers*, financed by Francis Bacon, who, with Carr's support, had become Attorney-General in 1613. Small wonder that he felt obligated to provide entertainment for the newly married couple.

Chamberlain reports: 'Sir Fra: Bacon prepares a maske to honor this mariage which will stand him in above 2000li, and though he have ben offered some helpe by the house [i.e., Gray's Inn], and specially by Master Sollicitor Sr.Hen: Yelverton, who wold have sent him 500 li yet he wold not accept yt.'[55] Bacon had tried to round up the help of the various Inns of Court, who had assisted in Princess Elizabeth's wedding; but only the Gray's Inn group could participate here at the beginning of the year. And, of course, Bacon had been involved with Beaumont's masque for the February wedding; indeed, Beaumont had dedicated his text to Bacon.

An unidentified trio, 'I.G., W.D., and T.B.'. dedicate the *Masque of Flowers* to Bacon in behalf of the Gentlemen of Gray's Inn. They offer the text to those who were present because the entertainment received such approbation, and 'represented to those that were absent, by committing the same to the press'.[56] The writers add: 'The dedication of it could not be doubtful, you having been the principal, and in effect the only person, that did both encourage and warrant the gentlemen.' They applaud Bacon's support of the men of Gray's Inn; and they marvel that 'in time of a vacation, and in the space of three weeks', they could prepare this masque (160). Like the authorities in London, the Gray's Inn people had precious little time to prepare. But on Twelfth Night, Lennox, the royal family, and others gathered in the Banqueting House in Whitehall for the show, an exclamation point on several days of wedding celebration.

Like Campion and others, the author(s) of this masque chose to emphasise 'transformation'; in this case, changing flowers into men, who had previously been transformed from men to flowers. The planners present a perspective of a city from which emerges Winter, *'attired like an old man, in a short gown of silk shag'* (161), who relishes his season. But Primavera, Spring, enters and counters this view, covered as she is in flowers. After their brief debate, Gallus enters, *'in post, attired like a post'* (162). He comes as Sun's messenger, and he brings with him a letter addressed to both Winter and Spring. In a sense the epistle dedicatory that prefaces the text transforms into an epistle within the text in a move unprecedented in any Jacobean masque. Winter reads aloud Sun's letter, which orders Winter to present winter sports and Spring, 'sports of a more delicate nature' (163). Sun orders Winter to acknowledge the challenge between Silenus and Kawasha, the former arguing in behalf of wine and the latter, for tobacco. And Sun, by analogy King James, orders Primavera to return the flowers to men 'and present a dance at this marriage'. This letter also contains a 'Postscript', which suggests that letters have been directed to Summer and the Harvest for action at some later point. The remainder of the masque fulfils the requirements of this exceptional letter.

An antimasque appears, with Silenus, mounted '*upon an artificial Ass*', and Kawasha, dressed like an Indian (164). They bring with them a motley crew of followers, who engage in song, dance, and debate about the relative virtues of wine and tobacco. Silenus notes the contrast of Kawasha's group with former heroic figures: 'The Worthies they were nine, 'tis true, / And lately Arthur's knights I knew, / But now are come up worthies new, / The roaring boys, Kawasha's crew' (166). Kawasha insists that while Silenus 'taps the barrel, … / Tobacco taps the brain.' Surely the author knew of James's anti-smoking tract, *Counterblast to Tobacco* (1604). The antimasque ends with more song and dance, only to be followed by yet another antimasque of dance.

The main masque appears as the curtain opens to reveal a magnificent garden, complete with fountain, a globe, and a golden statue of Neptune. At the end of the garden appeared a mount, '*raised by degrees, resembling banks of earth covered with grass*' (167). '*Upon a grassy seat under the arbour sat the Garden-gods, in number twelve, appareled in long robes of green rich taffeta*' (168). In their midst sat Primavera; the whole group moved toward the King and began to sing about the charm that had changed men into flowers. But now, 'Hearken, ye fresh and springing flowers, / The Sun shines full upon your earth; / … Descend you from your hill' (168). A second song refers specifically to the transformation of the flowers into men: 'Your leaves are turn'd into fine hair, / Your stalks to bodies straight and fair' (169). A group of masquers, presumably courtiers, has received gifts from the newlyweds: on every masquer's left arm '*a white scarf fairly embroidered sent them by the bride, and on their hands a rich pair of embroidered gloves sent them by the bridegroom*' (169). A third song refers to the ladies who have joined the dance; and a fourth song comments on the King: 'This isle was Britain in times past, / But then was Britain rude and waste; / But now is Britain fit to be / A seat for a fifth monarchy' (170). The final song addresses 'the lovely couple': 'Receive our flowers with gracious hand / As a small wreath to your garland' (171). A note at the end of the text indicates that James asked for the first antimasque again; then the masquers removed their masks and approached the royal family, king, queen, and prince, and kissed their hands. Not only have flowers been transformed into men, but also the once unruly kingdom has been changed into a glorious garden, suitable for the likes of Frances Howard and Robert Carr. Gabaleone reports: 'the whole festivity went off to the great delight of their Majesties'.[57]

This glorious garden of a wedding John Donne also celebrated in poetry. Like Bacon, he understood the patronage system and had hopes that Carr might eventually help him in his frenzied search for a court appointment. In his *Epithalamion* Donne captures the festivities that have surrounded the wedding, as in Section VII of the poem, called 'Feasts and Revells'. Donne writes: 'For every part to dance and revell goes. / They tread the ayre, and fal not where they rose. / Though six houres since, the Sunne to bed did part, / The masks and banquets will not yet impart / A sunset to these weary eyes.'[58] Although not present for the festivities, Donne can imagine them or has heard a report of them. He had also written such a poem for Princess Elizabeth's wedding earlier in the year.

The poem actually begins with an 'Ecclogue', which presents 'Allophanes', who encounters 'Idios', the poet out in the countryside. Allophanes contrasts the grim weather conditions of the late December day with the lively and warm conditions of the court and wonders why Idios would choose to be in the country. As Allophanes notes: 'At Court the spring already advanced is' (178), an idea that the *Masque of Flowers* has articulated. He also discusses the bride's bright eyes that 'kindle other Ladies eyes', an image that threads its way through the poem (179). But Idios has a rather different perspective, insisting that the court is not merely a 'location' and that he can simultaneously be in the court and in the country. Idios concludes: 'So is the Country of Courts, where sweet peace doth, / As their one common soule, give life to both, / I am not then from Court' (179), a view greeted sceptically by Allophanes, who nevertheless begins to lay out an argument for the power of kings. Idios thinks that he has had nothing to contribute to all the festivity and has therefore withdrawn from the great feast. He does, however, offer his 'song', the epithalamion, saying: 'But since [until] I am dead, and buried, I could frame / No Epitaph, which might advance my fame / So much as this poor song' (181).

The song that follows traces the loving couple through the day of their wedding, beginning with the season of the year's death, which nevertheless cannot die in the face of such brightness and the fire of love: 'The fire of these inflaming eyes, or of this loving heart'. The poet also comments on the couple's 'equality', that is, that each takes on characteristics of the other's gender: 'The bridegroome is a maid, and not a man. / … then the bride / Becomes a man' (182). Art cannot divide them since 'both have both th'enflaming eyes, and both the loving heart' (182). The next two stanzas focus on the awakening first of the groom and then the bride, and then in stanza V the bride's 'apparelling'. The poet offers his benediction on this 'blest payre of Swans', hoping that they may 'Raise heires, and may here, to the worlds end, live / Heires from this King, to take thankes, you, to give' (184). Donne includes the obligatory stanzas about the couple's going to bed on their wedding night; and he may stretch the point a bit when he writes: 'Their soules, though long acquainted they had beene, / These clothes, their bodies, never yet had seene' (185). He provides his 'good-night': 'May these love-lamps we here enshrine, / In warmth, light, lasting, equall the divine' (185). Idios offers this song as his 'perfect sacrifice', which he would burn. But Allophanes prohibits such destruction, promising to take the paper on which Idios has written 'Backe to the Court, and I will lay it upon / Such Altars, as prize your devotion' (186).

The fire of imagination burns brightly in Donne's poem, this offering that comes like incense to the court's altars. The circular structure of the larger poem begins and ends with Allophanes and Idios in conversation. But the 'main masque', as it were, focuses on the wedding and the subsequent entertainment, a festive event where the sun drives away the December darkness. Writing doubtless for many others, the poet insists that he can be present even though absent, of the day but not in the day; indeed, the poem enables its readers to participate. The court thereby reaches all the land, whether London or far more remote locations, long after the days of celebration have ended. Donne's 'perfect sacrifice' enflames memory and desire.

But the poet conveniently – and understandably – overlooks the messy divorce and intrigue that eventually led to this wedding. In retrospect, the darkness of Overbury's death (later revealed to be murder) hangs over the celebration. The tangled web of relationships inherent in the Howard–Carr marriage at moments seems to echo some of the tragedies, performed or published in 1613. Political ambition and personal desire dominate, compromising the ideals of a wedding. The happy notes of this late 1613 wedding and its masques and other festivities nevertheless include a strident and ominous contrapuntal sound, not yet fully heard. The bright and shiny Jacobean court and city may resemble a play, but it only looks like a comedy, one more satiric than romantic.

Notes

1 For a reliable account of Frances Howard and her marriages and other machinations, see David Lindley, *The Trials of Frances Howard: Fact and Fiction at the Court of King James* (London: Routledge, 1993). I am much indebted to Lindley's presentation of evidence and analysis.

2 John Harrington, *Nugae Antiquae* (London, 1779), 2: 276.

3 Harrington, *Nugae Antiquae*, 2: 275.

4 For a discussion of James's devotion to male favourites, see my *King James and Letters of Homoerotic Desire* (Iowa City: University of Iowa Press, 1999). The section on Carr appears on pp. 65–97.

5 *The Letters of John Chamberlain*, ed. Norman E. McClure, 2 vols (Philadelphia: American Philosophical Society, 1939), 1: 249.

6 For a convincing analysis of this arrangement, see Neil Cuddy, 'The Revival of the Entourage: The Bedchamber of James I, 1603–1625', in *The English Court: From the Wars of the Roses to the Civil War*, ed. David Starkey (London: Longman, 1987), pp. 173–225.

7 *Calendar of State Papers Domestic* (London, 1858), 7: 417.

8 Alastair Bellany, *The Politics of Court Scandal in Early Modern England: News Culture and the Overbury Affair, 1603–1660* (Cambridge: Cambridge University Press, 2002), p. 33. Bellany analyses the relationships among King James, Carr, and Overbury, pp. 25–56. Bellany pays considerable attention to the vexing issue of understanding the extent and purpose of Carr's political activities; see especially pp. 36–40.

9 *Calendar of State Papers Venetian, 1613–1615* (London: HMSO, 1907), 13: 219.

10 Reported in Anne Somerset, *Unnatural Murder: Poison at the Court of James I* (London: Weidenfeld & Nicolson, 1997), p. 103. This book offers a compelling account of the whole business of Carr and Frances Howard and the murder of Overbury.

11 For an extended discussion of Overbury, see William McElwee, *The Murder of Thomas Overbury* (London: Faber & Faber, 1952).

12 Bellany, *Politics of Court Scandal*, p. 42.

13 *Letters of John Chamberlain*, 1: 443.

14 See Bellany's discussion of 'The Fall of Thomas Overbury', pp. 50–6, in *Politics of Court Scandal*.

15 *Letters of John Chamberlain*, 1:448.

16 Quoted in Philip Gibbs, *King's Favourite: The Love Story of Robert Carr and Lady Essex* (London: Hutchinson, 1909), p. 162.

17 See Michael Sparke, *The Narrative History of King James* (London, 1651), p. 19.

18 Gibbs, *King's Favourite* p. 160. All quotations will come from this edition.

19 *Letters of John Chamberlain*, 1: 478.

20 See Bellany's discussion of this pact, *Politics of Court Scandal*, pp. 54–5.

21 Quoted in Ralph Winwood, *Memorials of Affairs of State in the Reigns of Q. Elizabeth and K. James I*, ed. Edmund Sawyer (London, 1715), 3: 481.

22 Somerset, *Unnatural Murder*, p. 195. Somerset bases her information on a manuscript in the Cambridge University Library.

23 *Letters of John Chamberlain*, 1: 444.

24 Quoted in Lindley, *The Trials of Frances Howard*, p. 81.

25 *Letters of John Chamberlain*, 1: 456.

26 Quoted in Lindley, *The Trials of Frances Howard*, p. 81.

27 Lindley, *The Trials of Frances Howard*, p. 82.

28 *Letters of John Chamberlain*, 1:461.

29 Thomas Frankland, *The Annals of King James* (London, 1681), p. 3.

30 *Letters of John Chamberlain*, 1:469.

31 In Winwood, *Memorials of Affairs of State*, 3: 475.

32 *Letters of John Chamberlain*, 1:478.

33 *Letters of John Chamberlain*, 1: 449.

34 From Camden's MS, quoted in John Nichols, *The Progresses, Processions, and Magnificent Festivities of King James the First* (London 1828), 2: 702.

35 Bellany, *Politics of Court Scandal*, p. 56.

36 Nichols, *Progresses of King James*, 2: 702.

37 *Letters of John Chamberlain*, 1: 485.

38 Gabaleone's reports can be found in John Orrell, 'The London Court Stage in the Savoy Correspondence, 1613–1675', *Theatre Research International* 4 (1979): 80; 79–94.

39 *Letters of John Chamberlain*, 1:495.

40 For discussion of the masque, see Jerzy Limon, *The Masque of Stuart Culture* (Newark: University of Delaware Press, 1990), pp. 170–97; Kevin Curran, *Marriage, Performance, and Politics at the Jacobean Court* (Farnham: Ashgate, 2009), pp. 129–41. Curran's astute analysis of all the entertainments for this wedding appears on pp. 129–60. See also the analysis of Martin Butler, *The Stuart Court Masque and*

Political Culture (Cambridge: Cambridge University Press, 2008), pp. 214–19. Butler writes: 'The masque confronted the marriage's problems and attempted to manage them symbolically' (p. 217). James Knowles discusses all of the entertainments for the wedding in his *Politics and Political Culture in the Court Masque* (New York: Palgrave Macmillan, 2015), pp. 53–92. Knowles, like Butler, focuses on the political implications of the masques.

41 All quotations come from *The Works of Thomas Campion*, ed. Walter Davis (New York: Doubleday, 1967), p. 268.

42 Cited by Curran, *Marriage, Performance, and Politics*, p. 133.

43 *Ben Jonson: The Complete Masques*, ed. Stephen Orgel (New Haven: Yale University Press, 1969), p. 199. All quotations from the Jonson entertainments here will come from this edition. Knowles, *Politics and Political Culture*, examines this Tilt, pp. 74–7. He suggests that this Tilt 'restages the *Barriers at a Marriage* performed for Essex and Frances Howard in 1606, making the second marriage a continuation of the King's union policies' (74).

44 *Letters of John Chamberlain*, 1: 498.

45 Orrell, 'The London Court Stage', 81.

46 For discussion of this curious masque, see Martin Butler, *Stuart Court Masque*, pp. 121–3. Butler writes: 'The masque is best understood less as wanton falsification of colonial realities than as an image of what James's government thought it was achieving' (p. 122). Knowles, *Politics and Political Culture*, has an extended analysis of this masque, pp. 78–92. Knowles argues that this masque 'registers a darker political climate', prompted by the 'disquiet' over the marriage and the 'advancement of the Howards' (84). He adds: 'The masque embodies and seeks to negotiate many of the strains surrounding Carr, his marriage, and the factional shifts that occurred due to the nuptials' (89).

47 For a political critique of this masque, see David Lindley, 'Embarrassing Ben: The Masques for Frances Howard', *English Literary Renaissance* 16 (1986): 343–59. Lindley emphasises the smugness of the masque in its attitude toward the Irish. Lindley writes: 'The message of the masque is therefore directed *at* the benighted and comic Irish from the point of view of secure and self-satisfied English and Scottish masquers' (p. 357).

48 *Ben Jonson*, ed. Ian Donaldson (New York: Oxford University Press, 1985), p. 449.

49 *Analytical Index to the … Remembrancia*, eds W. H. Overall and H. C. Overall (London, 1878), p. 541.

50 *Letters of John Chamberlain*, 1: 499.

51 Roger Coke, *A Detection of the Court and State of England* (London, 1696), 2: 69.

52　*Letters of John Chamberlain*, 1: 499.

53　Orrell, 'The London Court Stage', 81–2.

54　Quoted in *The Collected Works of Thomas Middleton*, gen. eds Gary Taylor and John Lavagnino (Oxford: Oxford University Press, 2007), p. 1030. See there the discussion of this lost masque, pp. 1027–33. The editors attribute two songs about Cupid that presumably were used in the masque. One wonders if Middleton has cast his eye back on Jonson's *Challenge at Tilt*.

55　*Letters of John Chamberlain*, 1: 493.

56　*The Masque of Flowers*, ed. E. A. J. Honigmann in *A Book of Masques*, eds T. J. B. Spencer and Stanley Wells (Cambridge: Cambridge University Press, 1967), p. 159. All quotations will come from this edition. Butler, *Stuart Court Masque*, observes: 'The Masque of Flowers was the only masque to invoke a specifically British theme' (p. 216).

57　Orrell, 'The London Court Stage', 82.

58　*The Complete Poetry of John Donne*, ed. John T. Shawcross (New York: Doubleday, 1967), p. 184. All quotations come from this edition.

Epilogue

As the dust settled over the Howard–Carr wedding, the Duke of Lennox returned to his lodgings in the Holbein Gate at Whitehall and to his routines. The nearby Cockpit Lodgings in the palace meanwhile gained new occupants, namely, the Earl of Somerset and his bride, Frances Howard. Their new housing certainly reflected the king's regard for the earl and the desire to have him nearby. In fact, Somerset was probably at the height of his political power in early 1614. He and his wife took over the palace space formerly occupied by Princess Elizabeth.

She, of course, after her wedding in 1613, had moved to the Continent and had settled into a pleasant life with her husband in Heidelberg. On 2 January 1614, Elizabeth gave birth to the first of fourteen children: a son, named Frederick Henry, a name that obviously combines the identity of the two most important men in her life, her husband and her late brother. Citizens of all stripes greeted this birth in the Palatine and in England and Scotland with universal rejoicing, once the word crossed the English Channel. The citizens of Perth, for example, in a report of 18 January, generated many bonfires and much ringing of church bells.[1] King James and the court celebrated, in part because this birth solidified the order of succession to the English crown. In a letter, dated 10 February, Elizabeth wrote to her friend the Duchess de la Tremoille, giving thanks to God for the son which she has been given; she hopes that one day he will give contentment to all: '*le fils que sa bonté m' a donné, puisse un jour, par sa grace, donner le contentement que je desire a tous ses parents*'.[2] Later, in the following year, Elizabeth reported to her father: 'The Elector and my little black baby are very well, thank God'[3] – 'black baby' apparently being her affectionate term for Frederick Henry.

On 6 March, the son's baptism took place. King James, a godparent, appointed the Prince of Anhalt to serve as his representative; many other notables participated as well. 'The Princess Catherine, second sister to the Elector, carried the infant, and the Prince of Anhalt, as representative of King James, occupied the first place of honour, and presented him at the font.'[4] There Frederick Henry received his name amid much music and a sermon. He also gained a stunning array of gifts, including the 'basin and ewer' from King James, weighing 600 ounces and valued at £2,000. Plays, hunting, and other forms of entertainment governed the Heidelberg court for the week following. This healthy child, who survived an early bout with the measles, nevertheless died in 1629 as the result of a drowning accident. This experience Princess Elizabeth found especially painful, given the loss of Prince Henry in 1612 – a memory still raw for the princess.

In England, James's thoughts focused on the possibility of convening the Houses of Parliament. Understandably wary after the abysmal failure of the 'Great Contract' of the 1610 Parliament, James received conflicting advice, largely pitted along the fault line of the Howard versus anti-Howard factions. Henry Howard, Earl of Northampton, thought that such a session would be disastrous, while Francis Bacon and Henry Neville, among others, argued that it would be worth the risk, given the king's desperate need for funds. James finally decided to bring Parliament into session; thus, on 5 April, he made his way from Whitehall Palace to Westminster's parliament house.

Don Diego Saramiento de Acuña, Count Gondomar, recently arrived Spanish Ambassador, had been invited by James to attend the sessions. He left behind a vivid account of at least the early parts of the two-month-long session. Gondomar described the elegant royal procession thus: 'the King left the palace at noon with a large retinue on horseback. The trumpets preceded all, and after them came the King's guard on horseback, fifty persons strong; and after them came the supreme magistrates of the kingdom.'[5] Prince Charles followed, dressed 'with a large cape of crimson velvet trimmed with ermine; his breeches and vest were made of white satin'. The Earl of Shrewsbury came after him, carrying the cap of estate; then came the Duke of Lennox, who 'rode on his left side carrying the sceptre, as Earl of Richmond'. Others followed, such as Charles Howard, Earl of Nottingham and Lord Admiral, 'appointed

High Steward by the King for this occasion' (5). Next to him rode his kinsman Thomas Howard, Earl of Suffolk, Chamberlain to the King. James wore a 'gold crown with pearls, diamonds, and rubies, trimmed with ermine, and a very large crimson cape made of velvet trimmed with ermine'. His shoes, stockings, vest, and breeches were all white; he held in his hand a sword, 'unshielded and pointing upwards'. The Earl of Somerset rode alone behind the king, acting as Master of the King's Horse, followed by the remaining members of the Privy Council. This dazzling array of colour and statement of prestige clearly intended to impress all spectators and to construct an image of royal power. Although James was in effect going to Parliament to ask for money, he clearly wanted to give a different kind of impression: not so much a supplicant as a powerful ruler.

Because of recent parliamentary elections, a disproportionate number of members of the Commons were new; this increased the difficulties of successfully completing legislation. Just a few days before Parliament opened, James appointed Sir Ralph Winwood as Secretary, whose job included representing the king to Parliament. Alas, he was totally inexperienced in parliamentary matters. Ineptitude, incompetence, and ignorance governed much that went on in what became forever thereafter known as the 'Addled Parliament'. Battles over royal and parliamentary prerogatives broke out regularly. Entrenched forces wanted to grant the king nothing. Much of the conflict centred on 'impositions', those Crown-levied customs duties, payments over and beyond the normal schedule of rates authorised by Parliament. James rightly argued that all of his advisers on this issue had served Queen Elizabeth and therefore understood these levies to be lawful. In order to make his case on this and many other matters, James addressed Parliament three times: 5 April, 9 April, and 4 May, the last two speeches mainly reiterating his earlier points and probably a sign of increasing desperation.

After his spectacular arrival on 5 April, the King entered Parliament where members stood bareheaded. 'The King, having ordered them to quiet down, after a long period of silence began his speech, saying that in it he would deal with three subjects: soul, person, and Exchequer.'[6] The matter of 'soul' focused on religion and the fight against Catholics, as James urged that laws be rigorously enforced against those who favoured the Pope. He pointed out that he had married Princess Elizabeth to Frederick 'because he was of the same religion' (7). With a rhetorical move that he had used at the beginning, James 'stopped briefly' before continuing. He argued 'that the execution of the laws was a good thing', although he did not advocate more stringent laws.

In addressing the issue of 'person', James meant the matter of royal succession, not unlike the way that he had discussed this in his first speech to Parliament on 19 March 1604. He also made the bracing claim that God had taken away Prince Henry as punishment to the king or to the king as the embodiment of the people and their faults and sins (8). But now the king has a grandson (Frederick Henry). Therefore, 'it would be very convenient that the Prince, his legitimate grandson, son of his legitimate daughter, legitimate wife to the Palatine, were declared worthy successor to the kingdom'. James likened the process and the expansion of kingdoms to the action of King Henry VII, who had married his 'eldest daughter [Margaret] to the King of Scotland – the present King's grandfather – and his second daughter [Mary] to the King of France'. Fortunately, in James's view, God's great mercy was also manifest in 'not sending children to the two Marys', Mary Tudor married to the King of Spain, and his mother while married to the King of France. Therefore, James 'hoped that all would appreciate his good judgment in marrying his daughter to the Palatine, since he had looked after the general welfare rather than his own' (8). James has thus secured the kingdom's future, a point of some worry with Henry dead and Charles subject to frail health.

The last point touched on money, but carefully. James claimed that Princess Elizabeth's wedding had put him in debt, conveniently ignoring the unmanageable debt that he had been accumulating since 1603. James 'had to ask for their [Parliament's] help; he did not want to press them in this matter, but only to ask for the aid they could give him without discomfort' (9). He saw it as the country's obligation to support the royal family financially as subjects have traditionally supported their king. James gingerly avoided at this point the troublesome matter of 'impositions'. That would come later. In another contemporary source, James expressed the hope that this parliament 'shall be called the parliament of love'.[7] To use Chaucer's title for a poem, the parliament might more accurately be known as the 'Parliament of Fowls' (even, 'Fouls' or perhaps 'Fools').

John Chamberlain in a series of letters to Dudley Carleton tracked the goings-on of the Parliament. For example, Chamberlain wrote to Carleton on 12 May: 'The house is full of busines and many yrons are in the fire, but yet we see no great matter dispatcht, for hitherto they have ben much troubled with disputes about elections and privileges.'[8] Much noise and stirring about but no action. The irons in the fire produced much heat but no illumination. On 19 May, Chamberlain wrote to Carleton: 'The parlement is now altogether occupied in crieng downe impositions, and searching recordes for that purpose but with what successe we shall see hereafter.'[9] The shenanigans included John Hoskins's intemperate outburst against all foreigners in which he made a dark reference to the 'Sicilian Vespers', the event in 1282 in which at the signal of bells calling Sicilian worshipers to vespers, they rose up and massacred all the French on the island. King James understood this as a threat to him and his Scottish entourage; thus, he sent Hoskins off to prison where the parliamentarian might rethink his speech. But Parliament could not even get around to acknowledging Frederick Henry as a legitimate successor to the crown. Such inaction led to James's dissolution of Parliament on 7 June and to this assessment from an anonymous diarist: 'so it was concluded to be no parliament, no act being passed'.[10] No Parliament of love – an Addled Parliament instead.

This Parliament seemed to put a final punctuation mark on the long arc of 1613, which truly began with Prince Henry's death, preceded by the strange interlude of Mary, Queen of Scots's reburial, her 'translation'. Dramatic productions provided solace to a grief-stricken court, as did the excited preparations for Princess Elizabeth's wedding, which helped transform the country's grief into joy. Her marriage to Prince Frederick and all the attending celebrations outshone any cultural event in the Jacobean court – perhaps in the country – up to the time of James's death in 1625. This marriage created a 'German connection' that affected and determined Britain's future history, including the houses of Hanover and Windsor and their monarchs with direct connections back to Princess Elizabeth and her progeny.

The burning of the Globe Theatre in June 1613 caused cultural distress and loss, but even it rose phoenix-like in 1614, to remain a fixture on London's south bank until the Puritans pulled it down in the 1640s. Its endurance and that of other theatres, including the Hope built in 1614, and the active and numerous dramatic companies provide ample evidence of a vibrant cultural force. Publication of plays and theatre performances in 1613 (at court and in the public theatres) underscore the growing cultural power of London's theatrical landscape, from which Shakespeare was beginning to exit, but leaving behind an exceptionally rich heritage.[11]

London's industrious printers produced an avalanche of books in 1613, containing a stunning range of materials, from sermons to books on husbandry, music, poetry, and drama. These books link the public and private spheres of England's culture, as they bridge the distance between Whitehall and the City of London. Here the public and private spheres intersect and resonate. Public publication leads to private reading and rumination, enabling and expanding a vast and rich cultural enterprise. Courtier and worker could jostle side by side at London's book stalls whose wares complement and sometimes complete the cultural process.

The wedding of Frances Howard and Robert Carr at year's end also prompted excitement and widely divergent theatrical entertainments, which could obscure the messy divorce that preceded the wedding. With the Duke of Lennox in the lead, a glorious procession made its way through London's dark streets with their torches and carriages to arrive at the Merchant Taylors' Hall for additional entertainment at the City's cost, in honour of this wedding. Interspersed in this celebration came news that prompted even more rejoicing: the birth in Germany of Frederick Henry, Elizabeth's first child and the first royal grandchild in decades. The dark side of the Carr–Howard marriage had not yet come to light: namely, the murder of Thomas Overbury in the Tower in September 1613. In time, revelations will spell the end to their favoured court status as each stood trial in 1616 where the court established their guilt, overt and ancillary.

The next decade cast a rather dark shadow across the Jacobean court with only momentary celebratory breakthroughs, such as Prince Charles's official investiture as Prince of Wales in 1616 (which Queen Anne chose not to attend). King James, accompanied by Lennox, made a long-deferred, nostalgic trip to Scotland in 1617, absent Anne, who remained behind. None of these events triggered the cultural excitement that had been obvious in 1613. Anne died mainly alone at Hampton Court on 2 March 1619, after increasing melancholy and remoteness from the court. Antonio Donato, Venetian Ambassador, commented on her death: she 'released herself from a prison of perpetual death'.[12] Her funeral did not take place until ten weeks later as James scurried about looking for money for the burial. Elizabeth and Frederick unwisely accepted the invitation to become King and Queen of Bohemia, which they did in autumn 1619. Within a year they had been driven out of Prague by Catholic forces aligned with the Spanish–Hapsburg powers. Then the Bavarians defeated the Bohemians at the Battle of White Mountain in November 1620. In the ensuing disaster, Frederick and Elizabeth escaped with their lives and looked back on Prague in flames, its smoke erasing forever their dreams of being a king and queen. Instead, they basically became European nomads because the Spanish had captured Frederick's own principality in Germany. They finally settled in the Hague, unable because of James's intransigence to return to England. The Duke of Lennox finally in 1623 received the much-coveted English title of Duke of Richmond, but died within six months of obtaining it. His death and funeral occasioned an outpouring of grief, especially from the king. James himself died on 27 March 1625, twenty-two years almost to the day since he ascended to the English throne. Except for the first thirteen months of his fifty-nine years, James had been a king – from cradle to grave.

On 24 March 1614, the Duke of Lennox gathered along with eleven other combatants in the Tiltyard at Whitehall for the annual Accession Day Tilt. (For the first time in recent years neither Prince Henry nor Princess Elizabeth was present for the event.) This tournament simultaneously continued and completed the narrative arc of 1613. It included several familiar combatants, such as the earls of Pembroke, Montgomery, Dorset, and Lord James Hay – all seasoned veterans of such tournaments. Each person carried with him a shield with *impresa* and motto (only evidence of the mottoes survives). Henry Wotton had complained about the incomprehensibility of the *imprese* and mottoes in the 1613 tilt. The limited information for 1614 makes such a complaint again likely. The Earl of Montgomery with the motto '*Rex Rex*' seems to be hedging his bets; perhaps his shield had some kind of image that reflected on King James.[13] Lord Hay's shield contained the ambitious motto '*Superat et ardet*', meaning that he triumphs and burns for victory. The Earl of Dorset underscores his reliance on the spirit with his motto: '*Substantia pendet ab umbra*'. Doubtless evidence about costuming would aid in understanding the point of the tilters' mottoes.

Descending from his rooms in the Holbein Gatehouse, Lennox entered the nearby tournament field, carrying with him his shield with its *impresa* and motto. Lennox had chosen '*Plus restat*' as his motto, meaning, 'he stands more firm', or 'he stands stronger'. Perhaps his shield contained a drawing of a fortress; perhaps he wore a warrior costume – anything to convey strength and resolution. King James would have agreed with Lennox's motto, recognising in him a faithful confidant of some thirty years who remained trustworthy, ever standing strong and firm in the king's behalf. On this dazzling day in early 1614, James could think back to the young Ludovic Stuart, who arrived in Scotland in 1583 as the phoenix, replacing his now deceased father. As James thought of their solid relationship, he might have recalled the words from Shakespeare's *The Phoenix and the Turtle* as characterising and defining their love: 'So they loved, as love in twain / Had the essence but in one; / Two distincts, division none: / Number there in love was slain.' No division here; their love has slain division. In the Whitehall Tiltyard, Lennox embodied the praise from George Chapman in a dedicatory sonnet in his translation of *The Iliad* (1609): 'Amongst th' Heroes of the Worlds prime years, / Stand here, great Duke, and see them shine about you / … looke without you, / For subjects fit to use your place, and grace'. *Plus restat* indeed.

The cultural excitement of a royal wedding and an aristocratic one, the cultural investment in a royal funeral, the resonance and solace of unparalleled drama performances and publication, the unstinting productivity of writers and printers all combined to make 1613 an exceptionally important year, as the circulation of cultural power moved ceaselessly along the axis from the Holbein Gatehouse to Blackfriars, from Whitehall to Guildhall in Shakespeare's London. The impact of events changed lives and altered the course of English history. The year closed as a mingled yarn of tears and rejoicing, of fire and phoenix, of challenge and fulfilment, of day stars and setting sun, all constructing unsurpassed richness.

Notes

1 Information taken from the account in Mary Anne Everett Green, *Elizabeth Electress Palatine and Queen of Bohemia*, revised by S. C. Lomas (London: Methuen, 1909), p. 93.

2 *The Letters of Elizabeth, Queen of Bohemia*, ed. L. M. Baker (London: Bodley Head, 1953), p. 35.

3 *The Letters of Elizabeth*, p. 46. Frederick also wrote to Sir Thomas Edmondes, Ambassador to France, announcing the birth of their son, referred to as '*un jeune fils*', and praises '*la grace Diuine*', and hopes that God will continue to bless the child: British Library, Stowe MS 174, f. 205, dated 23 January 1614.

4 Green, *Elizabeth*, p. 94. See also the account in John Nichols, *The Progresses, Processions, and Magnificent Festivities of King James the First* (London, 1828), 2: 756–8.

5 Quotations come from the marvellous compilation: Maija Jansson, *Proceedings in Parliament 1614 (House of Commons)* (Philadelphia: American Philosophical Society, 1998), p. 4. For a summary of this Parliament, see David Harris Willson, *King James VI & I* (New York: Oxford University Press, 1956), pp. 344–8; and Alan Stewart, *The Cradle King* (New York: St Martin's Press, 2003), pp. 251–6.

6 Jansson, *Proceedings in Parliament*, p. 7. All quotations from James's speech come from this source.

7 Carte 77, Bodleian Library, reproduced in Jansson, *Proceedings in Parliament*, p. 19.

8 *The Letters of John Chamberlain*, ed. Norman Egbert McClure (Philadelphia: American Philosophical Society, 1939), 1: 528

9 *Letters of John Chamberlain*, 1: 531.

10 Found in Jansson's *Proceedings in Parliament*, p. 443. The original diary exists in the Spencer Research Library, University of Kansas, MS E237.

11 Andrew Gurr has pointed out that Shakespeare apparently did not participate in the financing and rebuilding of the Globe in 1614: 'Venues on the Verges: London's Theater Government between 1594 and 1614', *Shakespeare Quarterly* 61 (2010): 468–89.

12 *Calendar of State Papers Venetian, 1617–1619* (London: HMSO, 1908), 15: 494.

13 Information about the mottoes comes from John Nichols, *Progresses of King James*, 2: 759.

Index